ALL THE 3S OF THE BIBLE

HERBERT LOCKYER

WHITAKER
HOUSE

ALL THE 3S OF THE BIBLE

Previously published by Baker Book House under the title
Triple Truths of Scripture, 3 volumes

ISBN: 978-1-60374-637-3
Printed in the United States of America
© 1973, 2012 by Ardis A. Lockyer

Whitaker House
1030 Hunt Valley Circle
New Kensington, PA 15068
www.whitakerhouse.com

Library of Congress Cataloging-in-Publication Data

Lockyer, Herbert.
All the 3s of the Bible / Herbert Lockyer.
p. cm.
Summary: "Bible teacher Dr. Herbert Lockyer's exhaustive study of the number three through Scripture is a resource for pastors, Bible study and youth group leaders, Sunday school instructors, and any believer who desires to delve deeper into Scripture"—Provided by publisher.
Rev. ed. of: Triple truths of Scripture.
Includes bibliographical references.
ISBN 978-1-60374-637-3 (trade pbk. : alk. paper) 1. Bible—Introductions. 2. Trinities. I. Lockyer, Herbert. Triple truths of Scripture. II. Title.
BS475.3.L63 2012
220.6—dc23
                            2012033618

1 2 3 4 5 6 7 8 9 10 **Ⱳ** 18 17 16 15 14 13 12

To my good friends and neighbors,

Walter and Nora Duke

CONTENTS

INTRODUCTION

The main purpose of an introduction is to *introduce—to* introduce the subject matter, and to introduce the writer of it to the reader. The introduction or preface must also bear some proportion to the length of the work itself. John Milton's masterly poem *Paradise Lost* is introduced by twenty-five lines of stately verse. If we are familiar with the front door, then we are likely to know the rooms of the house. Whether it is a book or a sermon, the preludes should not be overloaded. An old woman who listened to John Howe, a Puritan preacher, who was very partial to long introductions, said, "He was so long in laying the cloth that I began to despair of getting any dinner."

The mission of the work before you is to prove the truth of the Latin proverb, that "all good things go in threes," and, as a medieval saying states, that "three is the most perfect number." On the other hand, the number *three* also suggests imperfection. A French proverb says, "A secret between two is a secret of God; a secret between three is a secret of everybody's," or, as an Italian proverb expresses, "Three know it; all know it." Furthermore, as we shall see, the world, the flesh, and the devil are spoken of in the Bible as a most unholy trinity.

Writers from early times have expended great ingenuity in extracting mystical and symbolical significance from the number *three*. Apart from fanciful interpretations, however, there are several legitimate illustrations of the symbolism of three. Dr. E. Bullinger, in his *Number in Scripture,* points out that, in this number, we have quite a new set of phenomena.

We come to the first geometrical figure. Two straight lines cannot possibly enclose any space, or form a plane figure; neither can two plane surfaces form a solid. Three lines are necessary to form a plane figure; and the three dimensions of length, breadth, and height, are necessary to form a solid. Hence, three is the symbol of the cube—the simplest form of solid figure...Three, therefore, stands for that which is *solid, real, substantial, complete,* and *entire.*

It will be found, as we proceed, that all things that are especially complete are stamped with the prominent number three. For instance, the three great divisions that complete time are past, present, and future. In grammar, three persons express and include all the relationships of mankind—first, second, and third. Further, the three components—thought, word, and deed—complete the sum of human capability. Then, three kingdoms embrace our ideas of matter, namely, mineral, vegetable, and animal. The world is brought before us as earth, sea, and sky and, as we know, the primary colors are three in number: red, yellow, and blue.

THREE IN SECULAR LITERATURE

Secular writings also contain some very interesting allusions to the significance of the number *three.* Macaulay, in *Horatius,* reveals his fondness for the figure in the following lines:

> And straight against that great array
> Forth went the dauntless three....
> Thrice looked he at the city;

Thrice looked he at the dead;
And thrice came on in fury,
And thrice turned back in dread.

In Buddhism, ordination into the order is a simple ceremony, the central part of which is the taking of the threefold pledge:

I go to Buddha for refuge,
I go to the Doctrine for refuge,
I go to the Order for refuge.

This threefold refuge later became known in all Buddhist lands as the Three Jewels, or the Three Treasures.

THREE IN JEWISH TRADITION

It is most profitable to discover the symbolic significance associated with the number *three* in Jewish literature, both biblical and traditional. Rabbinical writings are full of illustrations as to the symbolism of numbers. Dealing with such a subject, the *Jewish Encyclopedia* says:

At an early time in the history of man certain numbers were regarded as having a sacred significance or were used with symbolical force, the origin of their symbolism lying in their connection with primitive ideas about God and nature. Such a use of numbers is found also in the Bible, although biblical authors were hardly conscious of their origin. In later Jewish literature, however, with the Pythagorean doctrines, was introduced the use of numbers as symbols, based on their mathematical qualities.

God rebuked Israel for knowing Him with their lips but having hearts far removed from Him. (See Isaiah 29:13.) The fear they had toward Him was not fostered by His Word but by the precepts of men. And, for centuries, Israel followed the precepts of men in what is known as the Talmud, a gigantic literary work that embodies various traditions and which is popularly known by three names: Gemara, Talmud, and Shas.

The word *Shas* consists of the two Hebrew consonants *Sh* and *S*, the initial representing the phrase *Shishoh Sedorim*, meaning the six orders or tractates of the Talmud. Thus, there are six major divisions of the Talmud, each minor division called a *Maskhet*, meaning "treatise." There are sixty-three *Masektos*. One of the most outstanding treaties in the Talmud is the *Ethics of the Fathers* tractate, in which the number *three* is prominent. The great rabbi, Simon the Just, declared, "Upon three things the world is based: upon the Torah, upon the Temple service, and upon the practice of charity."

Furthermore, Rabbi Simeon, son of Gamaliel, uttered the dictum, "By three things is the world preserved: by truth, by judgment, by peace."

Rabbi Judah Hanasi emphasized another triad in his advice: "Reflect upon three things and thou wilt not come within the power of sin: know what is above thee—a seeing eye and a hearing ear—and all thy deeds written in a book."

Another Rabbi, Akabya the son of Mahalel, had this trinity to offer:

> Reflect upon three things, and thou wilt not come within the power of sin: know whence thou earnest, whither thou art going, and before Whom thou wilt, in future, have to give account and reckoning.

Whosoever has these three attributes is of the disciples of Abraham our father, but whosoever has three other attributes is of the disciples of Balaam the wicked. A good eye, a humble mind, and a lowly spirit are the tokens of the disciples of Abraham—an evil eye, a haughty mind and a proud spirit are signs of the disciples of Balaam.

Jesus made it clear that if we are to enter heaven, our righteousness must exceed the righteousness of the scribes and Pharisees. (See Matthew 5:20.) Having no righteousness of our own, we must be found clothed in His righteousness.

Three is prominent in the ancient rite of circumcision as well. (See Genesis 17:10.) The three chief heroes in the rite are the body, the father, the mother, while the three main actors in the rite are the *mohel*, the one who performs the operation; the *sandek*, the one who holds the child on his knees during the ceremony; and the *quatter*, the one who carries the child to the *sandek*. Furthermore, the rabbinical rite connected with circumcision consists of three distinct parts: the *prio*, the uncovering; the *milo*, the actual circumcision; and the *metzizo*, the sucking.

Thirty days after the birth of the first son, the redemption of the firstborn is celebrated. (See Exodus 13:2.)

The rabbis say that there were three things Moses asked of God: (1) that the *shekinah* (glory) might rest on Israel; (2) that it might rest on none but Israel; and (3), that God's ways might be made known to him.

A distance that could be traveled in three days became the standard by which distance was measured. (See Genesis 30:36; Exodus 3:18.) Likewise, a three-day period was considered a fair allowance of time for a decision to be made. (See Genesis 40:10, 12; 1 Kings 12:5.)

A threefold division of the Old Testament was recognized by the Jews: the law, the prophets, and the writings. (See Luke 24:44.)

In the Decalogue, or Ten Commandments, there are three commands of a very positive nature, telling the people what they must do: (1) *"I am the* Lord *thy God...You shall have no other gods before me"* (Exodus 20:2–3); (2) *"Remember the Sabbath Day"* (Exodus 20:8); and (3), *"Honor thy father and thy mother"* (Exodus 20:12). The rest of the commandments are of a prohibitive nature, telling us what not to do. But the prophet Micah expressed positively, and in a threefold way, the essence of the commandments: (1) to do justly, (2) to love mercy, and (3) to walk humbly with God. (See Micah 6:8.)

Before the giving of the Law, God ordered three days of preparation for the people of Israel. They were required to make themselves clean in three ways: (1) hygienically, (2) morally, (3) and spiritually. (See Exodus 19:10–15.)

Jewish rabbis divided the Pentateuch—the first five books of the Bible—into fifty-four portions and ordained that the Jews study one of these portions each week. (See Acts 15:21.) They studied each portion three times during the week, twice in Hebrew and once in Aramaic. Orthodox Jews considered themselves subject to three sets of laws: (1) the Ten Commandments; (2) the Law of Moses, which they called "The Written Law"; and (3), the Traditions of the Fathers, which they called "The Oral Law."

Furthermore, as a people set apart, the Jews had three popular names in Scripture: (1) the Hebrews (see

Genesis 14:13); (2) the Israelites (see Exodus 4:22); (3) and the Jews (see Esther 2:5).

Then there were three political epochs in Old Testament history: (1) the epoch of leaders (see Joshua 1:5; etc.); (2) the epoch of judges (see Judges 6:11; 13:24–25; etc.); (3) and the epoch of kings (see 1 Chronicles 3:9–10; etc.). In the course of its national existence, Israel had three kinds of spiritual leaders: (1) the priests (see Malachi 2:7); (2) the prophets (see Judges 6:8); (3) and the scribes (see Ezra 7:6). As this three-fold, God-appointed spiritual leadership became weak, it was replaced by three major political parties: (1) the Pharisees (see Matthew 23:14); (2) the Sadducees (see Matthew 22:34); (3) and the Herodians (see Matthew 22:16).

In its delineation of Israel, Scripture uses three emblems to emphasize the nation's privileges and blessings: (1) the vine (see Psalm 80:8); (2) the olive tree (see Zechariah 4:2–3); (3) and the fig tree (see Joel 1:7).

The tabernacle and its furniture carries quite a number of threes—the candlestick with its six branches, three on one side and three on the other (see Exodus 25:31–36), and three cups (see Exodus 25:33). Three times each year, all males had to appear before the Lord God. (See Exodus 34:23–24.) Three witnesses ratified a decision. (See Deuteronomy 17:6.)

The Holy Land is referred to in Scripture by three names: (1) Canaan (see Acts 7:11); (2) Palestine (see Exodus 15:15); (3) and the land of Israel (see Matthew 2:20). Additionally, Jerusalem is given three symbolic names: (1) Ariel, lion of God (see Isaiah 29:1); (2) the Holy City (see Nehemiah 11:1); (3) and the holy mountain (see Daniel 9:16).

As God addressed men through the prophets, He used the method of threefold repetition for emphasis. For instance, through Jeremiah, God said, "*Trust ye not in lying words, saying, The temple of the* LORD*, the temple of the* LORD*, the temple of the* LORD*, are these*" (Jeremiah 7:4). The same prophet, as the divine mouthpiece, uttered the call, "*O earth, earth, earth, hear the word of Jehovah*" (Jeremiah 22:29). Ezekiel also uttered the cry of divine judgment when he cried, "*I will overturn, overturn, overturn it*" (Ezekiel 21:27). Creatures are shown as addressing God in a threefold way. (See Daniel 9:19.) Seraphim exclaim, "*Holy, holy, holy*" (Isaiah 6:3).

There are ancient illustrations of the symbolic use of the number *three* in Joseph's experience as a prisoner of Pharaoh. In the dream of the butler, the vine, with its three branches, represented the last three days before the Pharaoh had favor on him. In addition, the baker's three baskets represented the three days before he was to be hanged by Pharaoh. (See Genesis 40.)

David came to recognize that he had sinned greatly in the eyes of God when he numbered the people. Such reliance on the flesh deserved divine judgment. God gave the repentant king the choice of three alternate forms of punishment: (1) three years of famine; (2) three months to be destroyed before his foes; or (3), three days of "*the sword of the Lord, even the pestilence*" (1 Chronicles 21:12). When David left the choice to God, a disastrous pestilence overtook Israel and he earnestly prayed that God would spare the sheep, having once been a shepherd himself.

As we have seen, there are many instances throughout Israel's history that allude to this curious "threefoldedness," including legislative enactments and other precepts such as Solomon's dictum, "*a threefold cord is not quickly broken*" (Ecclesiastes 4:12).

THREE IN CHRISTIAN TRUTH

As we come to the teaching of Christ and Christian truth, we find many threefolds of grace binding us to Him, and threefolds of love that also should bind us to Him. Facts and promises remind us of our Christian privilege, duty, or danger. It is because these Bible triads, or trinities, make the Bible more precious and Christ more dear to our hearts, and disciples more eager for a closer walk with God, that we now consider their representation of truth.

Devotionally and practically, preachers and teachers use this particular form of Bible meditation because it enables them to see three constituent elements of truth. In the following expositions, it is easy to see that triads in single verses have a vital connection, like three branches of a tree. Triplets of truth are also found in laying together words, verses, or phrases from widely separated portions of God's Word. Thus, a divine message compacted in a threefold form presents the truth in an orderly and emphatic way, also aiding the memory. Alexander Maclaren was a great advocate of what he called "the three-decker sermon," using three points in a message. Likewise, the writer hopes that within the triads cited, preachers will find a reason to use a "three-decker sermon."

In the introduction to her small brochure on biblical trinities, Mary Bazeley cited this most apt poem:

A threefold cord will stand the test,
And will not soon be broken;
This precious truth, through God's own Word
Has been most clearly spoken.

The Holy Trinity of God,
In perfect Oneness blending;
Mysterious, yet all-divine,
To fallen man descending.

Showing us how to reach the goal
Of mystic sweet communion;
Illuminating heart and mind,
Providing perfect union.

A threefold cord is also seen,
When God and I together
Are used to bring a lost one home,
To dwell with Him forever.

Yet other trinities there are,
The truth to us unsealing;
Removing all our doubts and fears,
God's purposes revealing.

Proving how wonderful His grace,
Our weaknesses transcending;
Fragrant with messages of love,
And mercy never-ending.

And so, like golden strands of light,
God's precious truth entwining,
Alive with everlasting hope,
Each threefold cord is shining.

We all agree that the number *three* is the first of the four perfect numbers of the Bible. Bullinger reminds us that *three* denotes divine perfection or completeness, *seven* denotes spiritual perfection, *ten* denotes ordinal perfection, and *twelve* denotes governmental perfection. *Three*, then, is a prominent number that indicates what is real, perfect, substantial, complete, and divine. *Three* is not only the number representing that which is perfect, entire, and consummate—as we shall discover later on.

A SYMBOL OF THE RESURRECTION

In the days of His flesh, Jesus raised three persons from the dead: the twelve-year-old daughter of Jairus (see Luke 8:41–42, 49–56), the young man of Nain (see Luke 7:12–15), and the friend at Bethany whom Jesus loved (see John 11:43–44).

Jesus used Jonah's "burial in the sea" for three days and three nights as a sign of His own burial in the tomb for the same period of time. (See Matthew 12:39–40.) Referring to His body as a temple, He prophesied that after three days, it would be raised again. (See Matthew 27:40.) It was at the third hour that Jesus was crucified, and for three hours, darkness shrouded the naked form of the divine Sufferer and Redeemer.

> Well might the sun in darkness hide,
> And shut His glories in,
> When Christ, the mighty Maker died
> For man the creature's sin.[1]

The two witnesses slain by the beast because of their faithful witness were raised from the dead after three days by the life-giving Spirit. (See Revelation 11:11.) These witnesses were "perfected" on the third day by the Savior. (See Luke 13:32.) After Elijah stretched himself out on the dead son of the widow three times, the boy came to life again. (See 1 Kings 17:21.)

---

1. Isaac Watts, "Alas and Did My Savior Bleed," 1707.

A SYMBOL OF PERSISTENCE

Christ illustrated the symbol of persistence in Gethsemane, setting the example in the garden, where He prayed three times that the bitter cup might pass from Him: (1) His first prayer (see Matthew 26:39); (2) His second prayer (see Matthew 26:42–43); and (3), His third prayer (see Matthew 26:46). It should be noted that Jesus used the same words in these three pleas and that He won the power to endure all that the cup symbolized through His persistent prayer. These are not *"vain repetitions"* (Matthew 6:7), which are condemned by Christ. The victory He gained through His threefold prayer is exemplified in the strong way He rose from His knees to meet His enemies, amazing and subduing them with His calm demeanor. Too often, the world rudely breaks in on our prayers. Never were devotions so roughly interrupted as when the sacrilegious Judas sought Jesus. Yet Jesus was not afraid of the face of His betrayer—He had seen the face of God.

The apostle Paul prayed three times for the thorn in his flesh to be removed; however, his threefold petition was not granted. (See 2 Corinthians 12:8–9.) God *always* answers prayer, even if it is with a "no." Paul had to offer his weakness and infirmities to God so that He could use them to display His grace and strength.

Then we have the record of Daniel, whose life was an example of persistent and steadfast devotion. In spite of the decree that forbid anyone to petition except the king, Daniel *"kneeled upon his knees three times a day, and prayed"* (Daniel 6:7, 10, 13 NAS). This was customary for pious Jews who attended three periods of devotions: in the morning, before sunset, and after sunset. (See Psalm 55:17.) Private home devotions also occurred three times a day. Rising early in the morning, the Jew would say his *moide*; retiring to bed at night, he would repeat his *kriasshma*; and breaking his sleep in the middle of the night, he would sit on the floor and say the *khatzois*. In this midnight prayer, he would lament over three tragedies: the destruction of the temple; the exile of Israel; and the loneliness of the Shekinah.

A further illustration of the patience and persistence associated with the number *three* is found in our Lord's parable of the barren fig tree. (See Luke 13:6–9.) The owner of the vineyard wanted to destroy the fruitless tree, because, after three years, no figs appeared and the tree was considered barren. But the dresser still pleaded with the owner to spare the tree for one more year.

Another hint of persistence is found in Luke 11:5–8, with the three friends and the three loaves. We will have more to say about this when we come to the lesson Jesus adduced from this charming story on the importance of endurance in prayer. *"Men ought always to pray, and not to faint"* (Luke 18:1).

CHAPTER 1

THREE IN ONE

God...Christ Jesus...the Spirit.
—1 Thessalonians 5:18–19

Entering upon an examination of triads of truth as found in verses of Scripture, we begin with the greatest of all three-fold cords: God, the three in One. While the term *Trinity*, as related to the three persons forming the Godhead, is not found in Scripture, the fact of it is clearly evident from beginning to end. *Three* has always been the number associated with the Godhead. Three times, the seraphim cried, *"Holy, Holy, Holy"* (Isaiah 6:3; Revelation 4:8)—one for each of the three persons in the Godhead. This is the same application Bishop Heber embodied in his renowned hymn of worship:

Holy, Holy, Holy! Merciful and mighty!
Early in the morning our song shall rise to Thee;
Holy, Holy, Holy! Merciful and mighty!
God in Three persons, blessed Trinity!

Three times the divine benediction is given by Moses: *"The* LORD [the Father] *bless thee and keep thee; the* LORD [the Son] *make His face shine upon thee; and be gracious unto thee; the* LORD [the Holy Spirit] *lift up His countenance upon thee, and give thee peace"* (Numbers 6:24–26). Each of these benedictions is twofold, so that there are two members in each, while the name Jehovah occurs three times. This marks the blessing as being divine in source. No merit drew it forth; the origin was grace and the result was peace.

Verses and portions containing the truth of the Trinity are *ad infinitum*. Perhaps the most outstanding is that of the apostolic benediction: *"The grace of the Lord Jesus Christ, the love of God, and the communion of the Holy Spirit"* (2 Corinthians 13:14).

A characteristic feature of the epistle to the Ephesians is the way each chapter emphasizes the Trinity. For example, the three persons are wrapped together in the verse, *"God... the Father of glory, our Lord Jesus Christ, the spirit of wisdom and revelation* [imparted by the Spirit]" (Ephesians 1:17).

> Well might we sing,
> Holy and blessed Three Glorious Trinity,
> Wisdom, love, might...

Coming to the last chapter of the Bible, we have the one-in-three mystery of the Godhead united in the glorious task of redemption—God the Father, *warning* (see Revelation 22:18–19); God the Son, *witnessing* (see verse 16); and God the Spirit, *wooing* (see verse 17).

John Donne, of the fifteenth century, could write of the "Three Person'd God." Rudyard Kipling, however, was critical of the mystic Godhead, for in *Lispeth* he wrote,

> The Three in One, the One in Three?
> Not so! To my own Gods I go.
> It may be they shall give me greater ease
> Than your cold Christ and tangled Trinities.

But to the believer, while the Trinity cannot be wholly comprehended by natural reasoning, faith accepts the revelation and sings,

We praise Thee, bless Thee,

Worship and adore, Father, Son, and Spirit evermore.[2]

The modern official emblem of Israel, one of the Jewish national emblems, is the six-pointed star known as the Star of David, or Shield of David. The emblem consists of two triangles, one pointing upward and the other pointing downward. Many Hebrew Christians understand this emblem to represent the Holy Trinity of the Father, Son, and Holy Spirit (see Matthew 28:19); on the other hand, it also can represent the human trinity of man's spirit, soul, and body (see 1 Thessalonians 5:23). Pythagoras calls *three* the perfect number—expressive of the beginning, middle, and end—which symbolizes the deity.

As a substance, water is manifested in the threefold way as rain, snow, and ice; and the ministry of the Trinity operates in three beneficial ways.

The Father, in a past eternity, conceived the plan of salvation for the world of sinners, lost and ruined by the fall yet dearly loved by Him. (See John 3:16.)

The Son, at Calvary, executed the divine plan, and by doing so, manifested and expressed God's love. (See Galatians 2:20.)

The Spirit, sent by the Father and Son, reveals the sacrificial love of both to the hearts of men (see 1 Corinthians 2:10–12), and orchestrates the divine plan of redemption in the lives of those who repent of their sins. How comforting to know that we are equally loved and cared for by all three persons of the Trinity. A carol by J. Mason Neale expresses our praise of the Trinity in these words:

---

2. R. G. Greene, doxology, 1896.

Laud and honor to the Father,
Laud and honor to the Son,
Laud and honor to the Spirit,
Ever Three and ever One;
Consubstantial, coeternal,
While unending ages run.

CHAPTER 2

THREE CROSSES
ON CALVARY

They crucified him and two others with him.
—John 19:18

These *three!* What a remarkable triad this is! Why were there only *three* on that crucifixion day? And why these particular three? On that hill, long and gray, outside the city wall, God's arranging hand is seen in the way the three sufferers were placed. Man meant only to increase the shame of the sinless Christ by putting Him between two notorious criminals as if He were the worst of the three, *"On either side one, and Jesus in the midst"* (John 19:18 NKJV). In placing the two thieves on either side of Jesus, however, God represented the two classes of humanity both now and in eternity—the saved and the lost.

The King of Love hung on the center cross, numbered among transgressors; and on the other two crosses hung slaves of sin, dying for their sins. Because all three victims died together, they depicted three relative truths. In fact, the spiritual suggestions of this grim triad are numberless.

One dies *for* sin; one dies *to* sin; one dies *in* sin. The two thieves were dying for their own iniquities, but the Son of Man was dying for the other two men and for all they represent. Thus, we have a dying *saint*, a dying *Savior*, and a dying *sinner*. As we view these grim crosses, we find ourselves hanging on one of the three, for such a scene presents the separation Christ illuminates.

THE CROSS OF REDEMPTION

We take a look at the center first—the greatest of the three—not only because of its central revelation in Scripture, but also its central point in history. The heart of Christianity is the Bible, and the heart of the Bible is the cross, and the heart of the cross is the very heart of God who was in Christ, reconciling the world unto Him. Crucifixion, the form of capital punishment conceived by the Romans and abolished by Emperor Constantine, forms the darkest blot on the pages of history as meted out to Jesus, the sinless One. At the old rugged cross, we see man at his worst—but God at His best.

What infinite condescension on the Lord to make Himself of no reputation, reckoned among transgressors, and thought of as the chief of the three dying that day! There He was in agony and shame dying *like* sinners, dying *among* sinners, but dying *for* sinners. No wonder the old divines revered the cross as "The Divine Academy of Love." At Calvary, we see, at least, a fourfold accomplishment:

A LOVE MANIFESTED

> We sing the praise of Him who died,
> Of Him who died upon the cross;
> The sinner's hope let men deride,
> For this we count the world but loss
> Inscribed upon the cross, we see,
> In shining letters, God is Love.[3]

---

3. Thomas Kelly, "We Sing the Praise of Him Who Died," unknown.

Nature eloquently extols God's power and wisdom, but it is silent about His love for sinners. It is only at Calvary that we learn that He loves us without stint and reserve. In the surrender of His beloved Son as the sinner's substitute, God broke His alabaster box of precious ointment.

> Love so amazing, so divine,
> Demands my soul, my life, my all.[4]

A LAW SATISFIED

By His death, Jesus met and discharged the demands of the divine law, decreeing death for disobedience: "*The soul that sinneth, it shall die.*" (Ezekiel 18:20). Along with the condemnation, came a curse: "*Cursed is every one who continueth not in the book of the law*" (Galatians 3:10). But Jesus took our condemnation and curse and took them upon Himself. He bore our curse and carried our penalty so that we can sing,

> Free from the law, O happy condition,
> Jesus has bled, and there is remission.[5]

That middle cross is the charter of our pardon, the guarantee of our acceptance and heirship with God. Delivered from the guilt, penalty, and reign of sin, we are enthralled in glad bondage to our Redeemer.

A LIBERTY SECURED

While it may appear somewhat repugnant to refined yet Christless minds to sing about being "washed in the blood of the Lamb," it is nonetheless true that there is power in the ruby blood shed by the Savior for sinners. John was not ashamed

---

4. Isaac Watts, "When I Survey the Wondrous Cross," 1707.
5. Philip Paul Bliss, "Once For All," 1873.

to join in the Calvary doxology, *"Unto him that loveth us, and loosed us from our sins in His blood"* (Revelation 1:5 ASV). Although we cannot understand the miracle of it, we believe the fact that the red blood of Jesus is able to make a black heart whiter than the snow. And we have seen too many sin-bound captives gloriously emancipated to doubt the efficacy of Christ's finished work. Ours is the solemn obligation to *"stand fast...in the liberty wherewith Christ hath made us free"* (Galatians 5:1).

A LIFE TO BE LIVED

It is one thing to believe in a crucified Christ, and a different matter altogether to live a crucified life; yet the latter should be the fruit of the former. The provision of the cross not only cancels out our past but covers our present. Christ died that we might live—live in the fullest and highest sense. This was the truth Paul emphasized when he declared that the crucified, risen, and exalted Christ lived in him. (See Galatians 2:20.) As we know, Paul's epistles are drenched with the message and mission of the cross, for he was one who *"determined to know nothing among you save Christ, and him crucified"* (1 Corinthians 2:2 NAS). In one verse, he gave a marvelous triad to summarize his teaching on the cross. This triad is found in his Galatian epistle, every chapter giving us a different glimpse of Calvary. Just as there were three crosses outside the city wall, so Paul wrote of three crosses: *"God forbid that I should glory save in the cross of our Lord Jesus Christ, by whom the world is crucified unto me, and I crucified unto the world"* (Galatians 6:14). Here, we have *Christ on a cross, the world on a cross,* and *the believer on a cross.*

The first cross was the Lord's, and what a dreary desolation it was for Him! Yet it produced life and peace for us.

Blest cross! Blest sepulchre!
Blest rather be, the Man that
There was put to shame for me.[6]

The second cross carries the present world which was dead in so far as Paul was concerned. The world, with all its glitter, used to be "a sight which, day and night, filled an eye's span," but now to the apostle it was a "hollow thing, a lie, a vanity, tinsel and paint." The world's idols fell from their high estate and higher motives governed his life. Can we say that the world is crucified—dead, having no appeal to us?

The third cross is the realization of the mystic truth found in being crucified with Christ, imitating His sacrifice, and sharing His death. Paul wrote to the Philippians conforming to Christ's death. Is ours the crucified life? Are we dead to the world's appeal? Do we know what it is to be raised again in the grace of Christ, leaving behind all sins that once held us captive?

Dying with Jesus, by death reckon'd mine;
Living with Jesus a new life divine...[7]

THE CROSS OF RECEPTION

This was the cross of the thief, whose spiritual biography was brief but blessed. In the morning, he was lost and condemned in nature; at midday, his black past erased in grace; by midnight, he was sharing bliss with the One who had redeemed him in glory. That dying thief, who rejoiced seeing the fountain opened for sin and uncleanness, was the first trophy of Christ's

---

6. John Bunyan, *The Pilgrim's Progress*, 1678.
7. Daniel Webster Whittle, "Moment by Moment," 1893.

redemptive work. Had He not declared, "*I, if I be lifted up, will draw all men unto me*" (John 12:32)? Well, here was the first fulfillment of that prophecy. Here we find Christ illustrating His threefold office of prophet, priest, and king. As the prophet, He said to the daughters of Jerusalem, "*Weep not for me, but for yourselves…and for the days that are coming*" (Luke 23:28). As the priest, He prayed, "*Father forgive them*" (Luke 23:34), and cried in triumph, "*It is finished*" (John 19:30). As the King, He opened the door of Glory for a believing soul to enter. "*Today shalt thou be with me*" (Luke 23:43).

What a manifestation of omnipotent saving grace we have in this repentant thief, exchanging his deep-dyed scarlet for a robe of righteousness that is whiter than snow! Here we have a Savior "*able to save to the uttermost*" (Hebrews 7:25 ASV), and He bids us despair for no one. *One* of the two thieves was saved, that none might despair; but *only* one, that none might presume.

We arrive at two truths in considering the cross of reception, which perhaps was on the right side of the middle cross, seeing that the right hand of the Lord brings salvation.

THE TRIUMPH OF FAITH

The Good News says, "*He that believeth and is baptized shall be saved*" (Mark 16:16). Yet the dying thief only believed and still, a naked faith in Christ's promise saved him. Had he lived, he would have confessed his Lord in the waters of baptism. Sinners are saved by grace, through *faith*. Furthermore, when Jesus said, "*Today shalt thou be with me*" (Luke 23:43), He implied that there would be no unconscious period between death and glory, as some believe. The thief did not have to pass through purgatorial fires before he could enter paradise. He departed with Christ, and reveled in His presence for the three days that Christ was absent from earth.

THE TRIUMPH OF GRACE

This thief was saved at the eleventh hour; no, more accurately, on the stroke of twelve. Certainly we believe in deathbed conversions, that whenever and wherever a sinner repents and turns to the Savior, an immediate salvation occurs. *"Him that cometh to me I will in no wise cast out"* (John 6:37). But it is suicidal to put off the matter of our soul's eternal welfare until our deathbed, for we may never have one. Ours may be a sudden death. Furthermore, if bedridden, we may come to our last days bereft of reason—unconscious, and utterly unable to hear, appeal, and respond. Some of my saddest moments have been when I'm standing by the bedside of the dying, knowing that they were not able to hear and appreciate my words.

Then, is it not mean and contemptible to give the best of our lives to the devil and the ragtag of a wasted life to Jesus at the end? Yet, there is no limit to His mercy. Although the dying thief and murderer had just enough time to cry, *"Lord, remember me"* (Luke 23:42), grace prevailed and the blood that Jesus was shedding made the vilest clean.

THE CROSS OF REJECTION

Standing beneath this dark, tragic cross, we learn that the only impediment to salvation and eternal peace is a hard, impenitent heart. The second thief died just as he lived, namely, in callousness and sin. This unrepentant criminal was just as near to Christ as the repentant companion and could have received the same assurance of pardon as the first—but did not cry for mercy. Jesus *can* save the unholy, the unfit, and the unclean; but the *unwilling* He cannot save. In His compassion, He never asks a man about the extent of his sin, only his desire for freedom from iniquity forever.

Consequently, a thief from one side of the cross goes to paradise, while the one on the other side goes to perdition. Here the universal law is enacted—Christ is either the savor of life or death. On that lone hill of Calvary, we have a picture of how the cross of Christ divides the world. Wherever He is still lifted up in testimony and offer, there are those who repent and believe on one side, and those who scorn and disbelieve on the other. The preaching of the cross is either the power of God unto salvation, or it is foolishness. We do not know. Perhaps those two thieves were natural brothers, cradled at the same knee and brought up in the same good home. However, they engaged in a life of sin and suffered together for their crimes. The difference is that one received the Savior and one did not. Additionally, there is another scene showing two companies. At the judgment throne, the sheep and the goats are found, *"on either side one, and Jesus in the midst"* (John 19:18). The sheep go into eternal glory, but the goats into eternal grief.

This sad and somber cross of the unrepentant thief emphasizes two inescapable thoughts:

HE WANTED A CHRIST WITHOUT THE CROSS

Both of the thieves cried, *"If thou be the Christ save thyself and us"* (Luke 23:29). The one who believed discovered that Christ could save him from sin, although He did not deliver him from the penalty of sin. He confessed of the dying Savior, *"This man hath done nothing amiss"* (Luke 23:39); and he received Him as the sinner's substitute. But the other thief clung to his desire of the bloodless Gospel. If the bleeding Savior is the miracle-working One, then let Him come down from His cross and save us.

The modern cry is for a Christ without His blood-stained cross. Therefore, we hear a great deal about the ethical Christ, the social Christ and Christ the Teacher, the Exemplar. But Christ and His cross are eternally inseparable. Paul said, *"We preach Christ crucified"* (1 Corinthians 1:23), and this is the only preaching the Spirit blesses and can use for conviction of the sinner's conscience; *Christ crucified* is the only preaching that shows the sinner the loathsomeness of his sin and deliverance from it. The preaching of the cross is always the power of God unto salvation.

HE DIED WITH HIS SIN'S REMEDY AT HAND

It was impossible for Christ to be any nearer to either of the thieves than He was. The thief that did not receive his blessing was just as close to the Savior, but he failed to accept the proffered mercy. There may be some excuse for the heathen who never heard of God's redeeming grace and power, those who have no law by which they can realize their lost and hopeless condition; but those who live in a land of Bibles, churches, and Christian influences are without excuse. They are constantly reminded in so many ways of their perilous state without Christ, and are often exhorted to forsake their sin. But they prefer to stay on their cross of rejection, dying in their sin. If only they would transfer to the cross of reception, and experience the cleansing and deliverance of the One who died on the middle cross.

From pain to pain, from woe to woe
With loving heart and footsteps slow

> To Calvary with Christ we go.
> Was ever grief like His?
> Was ever sin like ours?[8]

There is no sin so black and disastrous as callous rejection, and no end so dark and hopeless as that of one deliberately refusing Jesus as the only Savior. May we be found singing like the poor mentally impaired boy, hardly able to speak ten intelligent sentences, but following the Spirit repeated, "Three in One, and One in Three, and the One in the middle died for me."

Many years ago, in the now defunct *Sunday School Times*, W. Everett Henry published a poem summarizing the truths suggested by the three crosses:

THE CROSS OF IMPENITENCE

The wood was hard and held the nails;
The soft flesh gave with aching pain.
Dread mockery beat down the wails
Of stricken friends; there came again
In dripping bitterness a voice,
"If thou be Christ, then save us three
From Death." His hardened heart made choice
Of darkening death's black certainty;
His twisted soul could not relent;
He knew no word that spelled "repent."

THE CROSS OF PENITENCE

The wood was hard and held the nails;
The soft flesh gave with aching pain.
Some tears dropped down, and gales

---

8. Christopher Upton, "At the Stations of the Cross," unknown.

Of ribald mirth could not restrain
The plea, "Remember me, Thou King to be."
And hard against the clash
Of darkest sins, with sovereign ring
Came words of gentleness to smash
Sin's shackles off the soul: "Thou'lt be
Today in paradise with me."

THE CROSS OF MERCY

The wood was hard and held the nails;
The soft flesh gave with aching pain.
A shameful shame the Son assails,
And sin's black waves roll on amain;
But majesty rests on Christ's brow,
Compassion dwells in his distress;
Omnipotence rides in the now
A humble penitent to bless.
The Lord of mercy, flaming Light,
Endows the cross with ageless might.

CHAPTER 3

THREE LANGUAGES INSCRIBED ON THE CROSS

This title...was written in Hebrew, and Greek, and Latin.
—John 19:20

Lingering at Calvary, we are arrested by the trinity of languages used to announce Jesus' identity. The three tongues used to write the inscription on the cross indicate the completeness of man's rejection of Christ. Apart from the fact that in the Middle Ages, many believed that a thorough knowledge of Hebrew, Greek, and Latin was necessary to understand theology, we might ask the question: What was the significance of writing, *"This is Jesus, the King of the Jews"* (Matthew 27:37), in these three languages? The title was a little gospel written in the three great languages of that time. Since then, the fuller story has been expressed in every tongue.

Behind Pilate's determination to write the title in a triad of languages was the overruling providence of God; for the historic marvel is that Christ's lifetime was the epoch when Hebrew faith, Greek eloquence, and the Latin empire could most naturally combine to serve the propagation of the evangel. Surely the Lord came in the fullness of time! (See Galatians 4:4.) Pilate wished that all who were present at the Passover could read the inscription; and he knew that if they could read at all, they would know one of these three languages. However, providence intended something else, for these were the three representative languages of the ancient world. Hebrew was the tongue of religion; Greek was the tongue of contemporary culture; and Latin was the tongue used in law and government. Wonderful, is it not, that Christ was declared King in them all? On His head are many crowns. He is King in the religious sphere—of salvation, holiness, and love. He is King in the cultural sphere—of art, song, literature, and philosophy. He is King in the political sphere—or all trade and commerce, social relationships, and all activities of men.

Those three great languages individually represented a whole panorama of world history. The Scottish preacher James Stewart in *The Gates of New Life* goes into more detail about this topic and describes how the crucified King would influence the nations represented by the three languages. Hebrew, Greek, and Latin were at the cross to proclaim that *"This is Jesus the King"* (Matthew 27:37). Can you see what Providence intended?

Everything that the Greek idea in history stood for—Jesus was King there. Everything that the Roman idea in history stood for—Jesus was King there. Everything the Hebrew idea in history stood for—Jesus was King there. For this reason, we will now take a closer look at these three languages and the national traits they represented.

IN HEBREW

In Scripture, the term *Hebrew* first occurs in Genesis 14:3 with the battle between "four kings with five" in the vale of

Siddim: *"And there came one that had escaped, and told Abram the Hebrew…."* The translators of the Septuagint rendered this phrase from Greek term meaning *"passer-over,"* "passenger," or "immigrant." Whatever the reason, the descendants of Abraham became known as the Hebrews, distinguishing them as a people. In particular, the term was used by foreigners or in speaking of them to foreigners. Likewise, Paul boasted that he was a Hebrew of the Hebrews.

The Hebrew language was a divine revelation and a spiritual religion, and it was the medium Abraham used to express the oracles of God. Our Lord, conversant in the Jewish tongue, had the Hebrew title *"This is Jesus the King"* (Matthew 27:37)written above His head. Not only did it declare that He was supreme in the realm of religion, but also that the Christianity He would produce would be more than a just religious system, but a way of life—even as He Himself was *"the Life"* (John 14:6).In the divine revelation granted to man, He is God's last word to humanity. The world's religions, isms, and ethical codes often leave men cold and without hope; however, what an anchor of the soul that Christ crucified is the Lord of our lives!

IN GREEK

There are many lovers of the ancient Greek language who would agree with Samuel Johnson: *"Greek,* sir, is like lace; every man gets as much of it as he can." In reference to his school days at Harrow, Winston Churchill wrote, "Naturally I am biased in favour of boys learning English; and then I would let the clever ones learn Latin as an honour, and *Greek as a treat."*[9] Few of us, however, agree with Bernard Shaw in

9. Sir Winston Churchill, *My Early Life,* 1930.

Major Barbara when he says, "Nobody can say a word against Greek; it stamps a man at once as an educated gentleman."

He fails to realize that the Greek language is very full, complete, expressive, and precise. The Greek language was established in the East with the emergence of the Roman Empire at the beginning of the second century B.C. Three centuries after the death of Alexander the Great, when practically all of his former dominions became Roman provinces, Greek was the only language that could carry a traveler from the Euphrates to Spain. The Roman Empire had two official languages, *Latin* for Italy and all provinces north, southwest, and west of Italy; and *Greek* for all provinces west and southeast of Italy.

The Romans did not attempt to force the Eastern peoples to adopt Latin, but allowed Greek influence in the region. All of the officials understood and spoke it. Therefore, early Christian preachers used Greek to teach and write the New Testament. The church language remained Greek until about the middle of the second century A.D. Kenneth S. Wuest said that the Greek used in the New Testament was known as *koine*, or "common" Greek:

> Previous to 332 B.C., Greek was confined to the Grecian peninsula. The little country of Greece was divided into its mountain valleys and its districts, each speaking a different dialect of Greek. It was all Greek, but each section spoke the language in a somewhat different way. When Alexander the Great conquered the world, he drew men from each of the districts, and the army found itself with various Greek dialects. In order to function efficiently, it became necessary to merge these dialects into one

language common to all soldiers. This amalgamation of dialects is what scholars call koine Greek. The word means common and refers to the Greek language held in common by the Greek soldiers. The language was spread over the then known world in the conquest and occupation of the various countries, and became the world language of international exchange, as English is today...

The New Testament was written in this *koine* Greek. It was written in the language, not of the scholars and writers, but in that of the people on the street, in the marts of trade, in the homes, in the workshop. There is nothing poetic about it, nothing polished, just matter-of-fact statements as the ordinary speaker of the first century would utter them. The New Testament writers were not men of higher education, except Luke and Paul who were university men, yet the two latter spoke the language of the man in the street like the others.

The original Greek, however, was the language of culture; the products of ancient Greece, in the zenith of her greatness, represented the pinnacle of art, poetry, thought, and intellect. In their genius, the Greeks created the finest civilization in the world. Athens was spoken of as "the eye of Greece, mother of arts and eloquence." Alexander's ambition was to make all men Greeks and, although failing in his quest, succeeded in sowing the seeds of this rich culture everywhere. Greek historical and mythical literature, along with the Greek version of the Old Testament and New Testament, make the world a debtor to Greece. No wonder historians love to extol the glory of Greece!

Was it not fitting, then, that the title over Christ's cross was written in Greek? Did it not proclaim that man with all his acquired refinement, knowledge, and culture is still a lost sinner? Acknowledgement of Christ as King is the road to a superior culture. The present age is overloaded with educated pagans who believe that man is king and needs no heavenly Sovereign. John Owen, the renowned Puritan theologian, once said that the main barrier between the human soul and Christ is simply pride—the self-sufficient, superior feeling which refuses to cry, *"God be merciful to me a sinner"* (Luke 18:13).

When culture and cleverness are elevated above Christianity and genius elevated above grace, Christ's ethical standards are nullified. Man sadly errs when he judges himself by standards of his own creation. In all things—whether in art, literature, ethics, politics, or society—the one infallible standard is the character and claims of Christ who was born King, died as King, and commands man's utter allegiance.

IN LATIN

English poet of the sixteenth century, Samuel Butler, suggested that Latin is not as difficult to master as Greek. Describing an ecclesiastic, he wrote:

> Beside, 'tis known he could speak Greek,
> As naturally as pigs squeak:
> That Latin was no more difficile,
> Than to a black-bird 'tis to whistle.

In addition, Ben Jonson said that Latin was "the queen of tongues." In the time of our Lord, only the Latin language had a place in Roman courts and official acts. It was an act of grace on the judge's part when Greek was allowed in court pleadings. Among the twenty-five or so Latin words appearing in the New

Testament in Greek form, the majority are administrative, legal, or military terms. Roman coins— such as the penny—had the Latin name "denarius." Thus, although Greek was the main language of commerce and Hebrew the common language of Jews, Latin was the administrative language of Palestine.

The significance of the edict *"This is Jesus the King"* (Matthew 27:37), in Latin proclaims that Christ, through the cross, became the King of nations and had His own law and government. It is clear that within both secular government and national and international affairs, Christ's ethical and spiritual laws are often excluded. To Him, there is no line between the spiritual and secular. Where He is King, true justice reigns. If the government is upon His shoulder, then peace and righteousness reign supreme in both individuals and nations.

Before long, He will take over the government and the majesty of His empire will be unsurpassable. With His brow adorned with many crowns, all will recognize His sovereign right.

James Stewart tells the story of one Palm Sunday in the City of Florence 450 years or so ago; Savonarola was preaching to a great multitude and suddenly cried aloud, "It is the Lord's will to give a new Head to this city of Florence!" Then pausing for a moment, he relieved the crowd's suspense: "The new Head is Christ! Christ seeks to become your King!" At this, the whole multitude was on its feet shouting, "Long live Jesus, King of Florence! Long live Jesus the King!" What our broken, bleeding world needs is a new head, because it is evident that governments are failing to govern! Let us not lose sight of the fact that He is coming back to clean up the mess of faulty rulers.

CHAPTER 4

THREE PORTRAITS
OF THE SHEPHERD

I am the good shepherd.
—John 10:11

…great shepherd…
—Hebrews 13:20

…chief Shepherd…
—1 Peter 5:4

Among the three hundred or so names of Jesus, actual and symbolical, none is as tender and comforting as *Shepherd*. Charles J. Rolls, in *The Name above Every Name*, affirms that…

> To remove the teaching of the Shepherdhood of God from the Bible, would rob the Scriptures of one of the greatest disclosures of the divine disposition, and certainly deprive mankind of one of the choicest expressions of assured care and comfort. Through the medium of this gracious ministry God guarantees the maximum of guidance and guardianship, sympathy and security, that is known in any literature. That form of skepticism which attempts to deny revealed truth cannot suggest a substitute that would in any wise replace this beneficent vocation of the divine

shepherdhood, which is so interrelated to Saviourhood, Priesthood, and Kinghood of Christ Jesus.

The almost eight occurrences of the term *shepherd* in Scripture are principally in connection with Israel. They remind us that the Israelites were a pastoral people and would therefore understand the association of *shepherd* with Christ. The lowly shepherds were the first to receive the angelic announcement of the incarnation. This was most fitting, seeing that the babe born in Bethlehem came as *"the shepherd, the stone of Israel"* (Genesis 49:24).

> The Shepherd, the Stone of Israel,
> His ancient people will assemble;
> Jacob's dispersion will then be o'er,
> And the Lord be King for evermore.

The prophets foretold many facets of His life as a shepherd. The Shepherd's presence on earth makes it ever more convincing He can care for us in every way. (See Psalm 23:1.) Through grace, He is not only the *"shepherd of Israel"* (Psalm 80:1), but the Shepherd of all those redeemed by His blood. From experience we have proved that *"He shall feed his flock like a shepherd"* (Isaiah 40:11), and that He is our one and only Shepherd. (See Ezekiel 37:24.) The New Testament presents us with *three precious portraits* of Jesus as the Shepherd.

GOOD SHEPHERD

I am the good shepherd.   (John 10:11)

The word *good* is used in contradistinction to the hireling, or the hired man who cared more about money than his sheep.

The hireling had neither love for the task nor a deep concern for the safety of the sheep, seeing how he left them to the mercy of the wolves. Jesus, as the *good* Shepherd, was willing to die for His beloved sheep that knew the tone of His tender voice. As the *good* Shepherd, He illustrated the truth of *redemption*. Despite the fact that we strayed, He willingly gave His life that He might deliver us from our iniquity. The marvel is that He became the sheep and the Shepherd at Calvary: *"He is brought as a lamb to the slaughter, and as a sheep before her shearers is dumb"* (Isaiah 53:7). *"What are these wounds in thine hands... Awake, O sword, against my shepherd"* (Zechariah 13:6–7).

> Lord, whence are those blood-drops all the way
> That mark out the mountain's track?
> They were shed for one who had gone astray,
> Ere the Shepherd could bring him back.[10]

The design and extent of Christ's atoning death are in that He laid down His life instead of His sheep, whose rescue involved His vicarious sacrifice. (See John 10:11–29.) The satanic wolf was waiting to devour the sheep; the only way for Christ to save them was to throw His body before their devouring jaws, so that the swift pursuit of the enemy might be stayed forever and the flock safely gathered into the fold. Once redeemed by the blood, no one can pluck us from the double grip of the Savior and Father.

> Good Shepherd, Thou who once didst give
> Thy life, that all to Thee might live;
> Such wondrous love can ne'er be told,
> Sweet is the peace within Thy fold.

---

10. Elizabeth C. Clephane, *Lord, Whence Are Those Blood Drops All the Way*, 1868.

GREAT SHEPHERD

...[that] *great shepherd of the sheep...*

(Hebrews 13:20)

If redemption is the provision of the *good* Shepherd, adding the title *great* Shepherd emphasizes the resurrection. God became our *"God of peace"* (Hebrews 13:20) because of His the death and resurrection. The blood of the *great* Shepherd is the blood of the everlasting covenant, confirming and sealing the promise of the Father to preserve the sheep for whom the *good* Shepherd died. Do we realize the extent of what the good and great Shepherd accomplished for us through His death and resurrection? May we rest in the His revelation as *"the Shepherd and Bishop of our souls"* (1 Peter 2:25).

Christ's strength to safeguard, sustain, and satisfy His sheep is depicted in His victory over sin, death, and Satan—secured by Calvary and the empty tomb.

> Shepherd and Bishop of our souls,
> Thy Word assures us of Thy watchful, tender care
> Over each one of Thy redeemed; O Lord,
> Implant in each heart Thy holy fear.

The only direct reference to the resurrection of Christ in Hebrews is *"Now the God of peace, who brought again from the dead the great shepherd of the sheep..."* (Hebrews 13:20). The verb in the phrase *"brought again"* was often used as a nautical term referring to the transfer of a vessel from land to water, or putting out to sea. Likewise, Christ became the *great* Shepherd through the blood of the covenant and can assert the power of the eternal covenant of reconciliation and peace freely. By perfecting His flock in every good work to do His will, He works them into a masterpiece in whom He is pleased. As the Shepherd of the Covenant, He guides, tends, and leads His flock into profitable and safe pastures.

> Lord Jesus, the Great Shepherd of the sheep,
> Through the eternal covenant of blood,
> Thou wilt from evil Thy redeemed ones keep,
> Presenting each one perfect before God.

CHIEF SHEPHERD

When the chief Shepherd shall appear...

(1 Peter 5:4 ASV)

The word Peter used for *chief* means "first and foremost" among shepherds, or all those who are called to "*feed the flock*" (1 Peter 5:2). Eventually, Peter realized what it looked like to shepherd his flock under the *good, great,* and *chief* Shepherd. The apostle would never have dreamed of using the title "*chief Shepherd*" for himself, as Rome often claims.

The word *pastor,* allied to *pasture*—like the green pastures and still waters the shepherd provides for his sheep— means "shepherd." One of the Hebrew words for shepherd is *pasturer,* found in Jeremiah 2:8 and Ephesians 4:11. The *reward* is prominent in this portrait of the divine Shepherd, for He promises rewards to all His faithful under-shepherds with an unfading crown of glory. Dr. Roll says,

> The stateliness of His superiority, by virtue of which He sways the scepter of sovereign supremacy over the flock of God, devolves upon His veracious

coronation as Chief Shepherd, at the right hand of the majesty on high.

Through both the gospel and Millennium Age, Christ retains His credentials as *chief* Shepherd, never losing His tenderness toward His flock. All who are called to minister to the flock have a solemn obligation as shepherds to live and labor in the light of the chief Shepherd. Such a blessed hope shines out from more than forty New Testament exhortations to fidelity and endurance. What a pity it is that many never receive a single beam of our Lord's second advent on their pilgrim way; one of the major reasons for this is because pastors fail to preach it.

Scripture has much to say about those who fail to shepherd the flock. Zechariah spoke of shepherds who lack pity (see Zechariah 11:5); Isaiah spoke of those who are avaricious (see Isaiah 56:11); Jeremiah spoke of those who lead the sheep astray (see Jeremiah 50:6); and Ezekiel spoke of those who gorge themselves but did not feed the sheep (see Ezekiel 34:8–10). Christ is the ideal Shepherd, while the coming Antichrist will be the idol shepherd (see Zechariah 11:17), worshiped and adored by the deceived. (See Revelation 13:1–10.)

> The Chief Shepherd hath promised a crown of glory
> To those who feed the flock of God;
> The time is but short to recount the story
> Of Him who shed His precious blood.
> Faint not, but work on, tho' your hair be hoary,
> Willingly feed the flock of God,
> Reward is assured by the Word.

CHAPTER 5

THREE GLORIOUS APPEARANCES

He hath appeared...now to appear...shall appear.
—Hebrews 9:24–28

In this remarkable portion the three appearances form a trilogy, not in the order given but in the order in which they are related to one another in the work of redemption: (1) the past appearing: *"hath he appeared to put away sin"* (Hebrews 9:26) referring to the atonement already secured by Christ; (2) the present appearing: *"now to appear in the presence of God for us"* (verse 24), depicting His advocacy on behalf of the redeemed; (3) and the prospective appearing: *"He shall appear the second time"* (verse 28), declaring Christ's personal advent. What an unbreakable, threefold cord of redemption, intercession, and glorification! These three unify to form one, for we need the whole work of Christ, just like we need the whole Bible.

In the first appearing, which is past and permanent, we receive salvation from the penalty of sin—Christ made the perfect sacrifice for sin. In the second appearing, which is present and progressive, we experience salvation from the power of sin—Christ's plead merits the perfect sacrifice. In the third appearing, which is prospective and perfect, we will be saved from the entire *presence* of sin—Christ presents the fruits of His sacrifice to the Father. Thus, every need of the human heart was anticipated and provided for by this three-fold manifestation of the Lord of glory.

Looking *back*, we see Jesus dying for us. Looking *up*, we see Him pleading for us. Looking *forward*, we see Him returning for us. Let us take a closer look of the Savior and Suppliant, who appears as the all-victorious Sovereign Lord.

HIS PAST APPEARANCE

The design and consequence of the first manifestation is distinctly stated in Hebrews 9:26: "*To put away sin by the sacrifice of himself.*" Truly, no other being was good enough to pay the price of sin, thereby opening the gates of heaven for us. The words *put away* actually mean "to set aside" or "to displace." Therefore, all sin of the believer, outward and inward, is displaced, set aside, and cast behind God's back. (See Isaiah 38:17.) The sin is cast into the depths of the sea (see Micah 7:19), forgiven and forgotten (see Jeremiah 31:34), and separated from him as far as the east is from the west (see Psalm 103:12).

Note the difference between the act of putting sins away and bearing the sins of many. (See Hebrews 9:26, 28.) The first denotes the results of Christ's death toward God (see John 1:29; 12:32; 1 John 2:2), while the second denotes the results of Christ's death toward all believers. Although the atoning sacrifice of the cross is of immense value in the sight of God, it avails nothing whatsoever for the sinner until he or she receives it by faith. Calvary made salvation *possible*, but faith makes it *actual* in the life of the sinner. Thus, a perfect Savior made a perfect sacrifice for all sinners, yielding perfect salvation for all believers. (See Titus 2:14.)

Christ has for sin atonement made;
What a wonderful Savior!
We are redeemed!—the price is paid
What a wonderful Savior![11]

HIS PRESENT APPEARANCE

It is interesting to observe, as W. E. Vine points out in the *Dictionary of New Testament Words*, that there are three different Greek words for the English word *appear*, used three times in previous passage. For instance, the Greek word *phaneroo* is used for the past appearing; it means more than just to appear, also describing the work of the cross:

> A person may appear in a false guise or without a disclosure of what he truly is; to be *manifested* is to be revealed in one's true character: this is especially the meaning of *phaneroo*. (See John 3:21; 1 Corinthians 4:5; 2 Corinthians 5:10–11; Ephesians 5:13.)

Emphanizo is the word for Christ's present appearing before the face of God on our behalf. It means "to shine in," and is used to describe a physical manifestation (see Matthew 27:53; John 14:22), or a metaphorical manifestation. The metaphorical manifestation is seen in John 14:21, when believers abiding in His love experience Christ through the Holy Spirit.

Optomai means "to see" and is used in reference to Christ's future appearance to the saints. It is from this Greek word that we have the English word *optical*. Objectively, the reference is to a person or thing that is seen. (See 1 Corinthians 15:5–8.)

---

11. Elisha A. Hoffman, "What a Wonderful Savior," 1891.

Subjectively, the reference is to an inward impression, a spiritual experience (see John 3:36), or a mental occupation, as in *"look ye to it"* (Acts 18:15); *"See thou to that"* (Matthew 27:4) and *"see ye to it"* (verse 24), giving the responsibility to others.

How comforting and assuring it is to know that Jesus appears in the presence of God as our Advocate, making intercession for us! Although we are secure standing before Him, our state on earth is characterized by failure to walk in the light as He is in the light, and our communion with Him is thereby disturbed. It is His desire that we do not sin (see 1 John 2:1), but if inbred sin manifests itself in actual sin, then, as we repent and confess, our mighty Intercessor pleads the efficacy of His atoning blood and we are cleansed. (See 1 John 1:9.) We have two divine Advocates in the mercy of God, as well as abundant provision: we have an Advocate present among us to keep us from sin—the Holy Spirit making intercession for us. (See Romans 8:26–27.) And if we do sin, we have an Advocate above, the Savior, to restore our broken fellowship with God. (See Hebrews 7:25; 1 John 2:1–3.)

> There is a way for man to rise
> To that sublime abode;
> An Offering and a Sacrifice,
> A Holy Spirit's energies,
> An Advocate with God.[12]

HIS PROSPECTIVE APPEARANCE

A study of Hebrews provides many reminders of the truth of our Lord's return for His true church. It is here that we are exhorted to exhibit patience as we wait for the

12. Thomas Binney, "Eternal Light," 1826.

fulfillment of this promise. *"Yet a little while, and He that shall come will come and will not tarry"* (Hebrews 10:37). The declaration of His future appearance refers to two times—*"once"* and *"second time"* (Hebrews 9:28). He was *once* offered to bear the sins of many, and that one sacrifice was sufficient, for in it He tasted death for every man. (See Hebrews 2:9–14.) But He is to appear a *"second time,"* that we might have the final installment of our salvation—the final abolishment of sin. Then it will be evident that His church will sin no more. Thus, the crucifixion and the coming are bound together.

Whether we are looking for Him or not, He will appear. If, however, we are among the few who love the thought of His appearing and live and labor in light of it, then a special reward will be ours for keeping hope alive in our hearts. (See 2 Timothy 4:8.) It is regrettable that while some Christian circles give full attention to the first two appearances, they treat the third appearing as a forbidden topic. The precious and prominent truth of "the blessed hope" exerts little or no influence in the hearts and lives of those who call upon the One who said, *"Surely, I come quickly!"* (Revelation 22:20).

> Thou lovely bright and Morning Star
> Wilt bring the dawn right soon;
> Faith pierces the veil from afar,
> And prays, Lord Jesus, come!

CHAPTER 6

THREE GLEAMS OF PEACE

...peace with God...
—Romans 5:1

...peace of God...
—Philippians 4:7

...peace from God...
—2 Corinthians 1:2

The Bible has a lot to say about *peace*, occurring some four hundred times throughout its sacred pages. In fact, the inspired Word is sometimes called God's "Testament of Peace," operative in many realms. Much is said about peace in both divine and human relationships—peace within ourselves, peace among fellow-believers, peace among nations, peace as an expression of the perfect rest and felicity in heaven. In the exhortation to *"follow peace with all men"* (Hebrews 12:14), we have a hunting allusion—"Follow peace, as the hound does the hare." All true peace springs from *"the God of peace"* (Hebrews 13:20). In *The Book of Common Prayer*, Thomas Cranmer writes,

> The Author of peace and Lover of concord, in knowledge of whom standeth our eternal life, whose service is perfect freedom.

Quaint George Herbert sang of Him as the "King of Glory, King of Peace." Sifting the numerous references to *peace*, we learn that there is peace *with* God, which His beloved Son secured for men; peace *of* God, which is imparted by the Holy Spirit within the saint; and peace *from* God, which is a full expression of grace from the Godhead.

PEACE WITH GOD

What exactly is the virtue we call *peace*? The dictionary says that "it is a fact or agreement to end hostilities between those who have been at war or in a state of hostility; a state of tranquility or quiet." When Paul wrote that *"being therefore justified by faith, we have peace with God through our Lord Jesus Christ"* (Romans 5:1), he was thinking of those who were at war with God, but who also agreed to end hostility and enter into a peace covenant with Him.

> At peace with God! How great the blessing
>   In fellowship with Him to be,
>   And from all stains of sin set free,
>   How rich am I such wealth possessing.[13]

This particular aspect of peace is not a feeling or mere emotion, but a permanent state or condition, which the justified experience through Christ's death and resurrection. The justified experience the breadth of His work through faith alone. It is important to recognize that peace *with* or *toward* God is not something worked up or felt but a gift obtained for us by another.

Furthermore, we err when dealing with sinners and the dying when we ask them whether they made peace

---

13. Richard Slater, "At Peace with God, How Great the Blessing."

with God. However good the soul-winner's intentions, the fact is that peace has already been made—accomplished almost two millenniums ago when Jesus died as our peace. "[He] *made peace through the blood of his cross*" (Colossians 1:20 ASV).

A guilty sinner can no more make peace with God than a base rebel with a benignant sovereign, or a condemned criminal with the law. Peace is not something, but Someone. "*He is our peace…and came and preached peace to you which were afar off*" (Ephesians 2:12–17). Thus, to all who are in open insurrection against the rightful authority of the Father, we preach "*peace by Jesus Christ*" (Acts 10:36). The only legacy Jesus left to His mother, relatives, and disciples was *peace*. "*Peace I leave with you, my peace I give unto you;*" then He went on to describe the quality of such a bequest, "*not as the world giveth, give I unto you*" (John 14:27). The peace of the world is unstable, uncertain, and easily disturbed. This is not the case with Christ, who is peace personified.

As a result, our feelings have nothing to do with how peace was made, although they do affect our enjoyment of it. For instance, two nations that have been at war declare peace and enter into a new relation toward each other. Certainly parents and wives who had been in constant agony over their sons and husbands have feelings of joy when there is a peace settlement. The sin-hating God met the sin-bearing Christ at Calvary, and forever answered the question of sin for every believer. Thus, we come to experience "peace *and joy* through believing." The blood of Jesus whispers peace within, once we are at peace with God.

> I hear the words of love,
> I gaze upon the blood;

I see the mighty sacrifice,
And I have peace with God.[14]

PEACE OF GOD

Here we see a different facet of peace. Peace *with* God is the legacy of the *crucified* Christ, and is the peace of conscience we receive when we accept Him as our reconciler.

Peace *of* God is the gift of the *living* Christ. It is the peace of heart that can be found in full, unhindered fellowship with Him. Peace before Christ is simply *peace*, but in the latter Christ calls it *"my peace"* (John 14:27). This solidifies the precious promise, *"Thou wilt keep him in perfect peace, whose mind is stayed on thee"* (Isaiah 26:3 ASV). This is the aspect of peace Paul had in mind when he wrote to the saints in Philippi, *"The peace of God, which passeth all understanding, shall keep* [guard, or garrison] *your hearts and minds through Christ Jesus"* (Philippians 4:7). Such peace is beyond our understanding to comprehend, seeing it is divine in nature. It is able to pass all *misunderstanding* as well.

Our minds are garrisoned through this peace, preserved from unnecessary fear, agitation, or worry. Tribulation may surround us, but in Him we have peace.

Like a river glorious, is God's perfect peace,
Over all victorious, in its bright increase;
Perfect, yet it floweth, fuller ev'ry day,
Perfect, yet it growth, deeper all the way.[15]

---

14. Horatius Bonar, "I Hear the Words of Love," 1861.
15. Frances R. Havergal, "Like a River Glorious," 1876.

PEACE FROM GOD

At the beginning of nearly all the epistles, we have the apostolic salutation, *"Grace to you and peace from God our Father and the Lord Jesus Christ"* (Romans 1:7; Ephesians 1:2; 1 Thessalonians 1:1; 1 Peter 1:2–3; etc.). When individuals instead of churches are addressed, the form of invocation is generally changed, adding the word *mercy: "Grace, mercy, and peace, from God our Father and Jesus Christ our Lord"* (1 Timothy 1:2; Titus 1:4; 2 John 3). All of the apostles recognized what debtors they were to divine mercy. Grace! Mercy! Peace! This is a magnificent triad of divine blessings for our needy hearts!

Peace *from* God—the One we rebelled against—is an expression of His grace and mercy. If grace and mercy create the unfailing fountain, then the gift of peace is the everlasting stream. By the unmerited favor of God, grace is the source of all good received both here and hereafter. Those who are at peace with God through the acceptance of His son experience peace as a measure of His favor. As the God of hope and peace, He fills us *"with all joy and peace in believing, that ye may abound in hope, through the power of the Holy Ghost"* (Romans 15:13). His peace is unchanging and eternal, characteristic of Himself.

'Tis everlasting peace,
Sure as Jehovah's name;
'Tis stable as His steadfast throne,
Forever more the same.
My love is oft-times low;
My joy still ebbs and flows;
But peace with Him remains the same,
No change Jehovah knows.[16]

---

16. Horatius Bonar, "I Hear the Words of Love," 1861.

CHAPTER 7

THREE FORMS OF REST

I will give you rest.
—Matthew 11:28

Ye shall find rest.
—Matthew 11:29

There remaineth therefore a rest.
—Hebrews 4:9

In *Concordance*, Crudence speaks of *rest* as "a calmness, composure, and tranquility of spirit, and a cheerful confidence in the promises and providence of God." We might cry with the psalmist, *"Return unto thy rest, O my soul"* (Psalm 116:7). The English word *rest* occurs some three hundred times through Scripture and is used to translate different terms in both the Hebrew and Greek. In our turbulent age, man's deepest need is rest for the heart. Elizabeth B. Browning expresses this need well in the last stanza of "Rime of the Duchess May":

Oh, the little birds sang east,
And the little birds sang west,
And I smiled to think God's greatness
Flowed around our incompleteness,
Round our restlessness, His rest.

Only in God can we find the rest our spirits yearn for. In this particular trinity of truth, we are to examine the phases of rest we have in and from Him who came as the embodiment of eternal rest.

First, there is rest for the mind which brings relief to the troubled conscience. It is directly connected with Jesus as the Savior of sinners.

Second, there is rest for the heart which brings recovery to the troubled heart. It is more immediately connected with the Holy Spirit as our abiding Comforter.

Third, there is the rest for the believer. It is associated with the joy of God's immediate presence in the house of many mansions where the weary are ever at rest.

THE REST WE RECEIVE

Jesus' invitation for rest to the heavy laden is the most beautiful and moving passage in the Bible, if not in the whole realm of literature. It is so full of pity—so lowly, yet so great. How wonderful it was for Him to extend such a gracious invitation to those who abused His mercies! Truly, it outshone any of the works He performed in Capernaum!

"Come unto me, all ye that labour and are heavy laden, and I will give you rest" (Matthew 11:28). Without Him, every soul labors and is heavy laden. The double phrase He used refers to weight of life's loads, and smallness of our strength to carry them. Saints and sinners alike are *laden* with duties, regrets, fears, temptations, sorrows, cares, darkness, and evil tendencies; and their small souls "labor," strained by these burdens. Above all other things, the saints need rest.

Furthermore, in this sweet call, Jesus did not say, "Come unto me *after* your labor has accomplished something that satisfies you" or, "Come when you have thrown off your burden by your own strength"; but, "Come, *while* laboring, *while* heavy laden." Neither did He say, "I will *sell* you rest, or grant it upon certain conditions"; but, "Come as you are without delay and I will *give* you rest." Actually, He used the verb that translates to, "Come *hither! Here! This way!*"

Many are sorely perplexed when thinking about how to come. They stress about coming in the wrong manner. But Jesus said nothing about the mode of coming. In fact, He diverted the attention from the act of coming to simply Himself, focusing solely on His outstretched arms. *Coming* is equivalent to *looking, believing, trusting,* and *receiving*—all expressions intended to direct our thoughts not to self but to Him. He knows how utterly incapable we are of improving our spiritual condition through our own labor.

> Not the labor of my hands
> Can fulfill Thy law's demands.[17]

With a beautiful intimation of His deity, He invites us into His rest—rest He offers as a *gift.* (See Hebrews 4:3, 10.) There is, of course, another application we can make. The true rest He gives is not *letting us off* our duty, but giving us the strength to accomplish a greater duty. William Cowper once wrote,

> Absence of occupation is not rest
> A mind quite vacant is a mind distres'd.

It was Evan H. Hopkins, early theologian of the wide-spread Keswick Movement, who taught multitudes of saints to sing,

---

17. Augustus M. Toplady, "Rock of Ages," 1776.

My Saviour, Thou hast offered rest.
Oh, give it then to me;
The rest of ceasing from myself,
To find my all in Thee.

THE REST WE RECOVER

We must not lose sight of the double rest in this royal invitation. There is the rest we receive as *a gift,* and then the rest we *find* as we journey on to know the divine giver better.

"Take my yoke upon you, and learn of me; for I am meek and lowly in heart: And ye shall find rest unto your souls" (Matthew 11:29). Referring to anyone else, such language would be arrogant assumption. How we would shrink from a man saying, "Look at me, I am meek and lowly in heart." But Christ was God and had every right—the only right—to say, *"Come to me...and I will give you rest...and ye shall find rest unto your souls"* (Matthew 11:28–29).

What does the rest we *find* imply? The shelter of the cross gives sinners half of the rest; they receive the remainder through their service under Christ's yoke. Many who have accepted rest as a gift have failed to *find* rest for their souls. The yoke He asks us to carry is not like the oxen's yoke, dragging a great weight under a driver's lash; on the other hand, His yoke is easy because He bears the heavier part. What He asks of us is fellowship in His service and suffering—to walk in loving communion with Him in all lowliness and meekness.

Having received rest, can we truthfully say that we are *finding* rest? Finding true rest requires the denial of self and our old nature; it requires a holy separation from the world.

O Lord, I seek a holy rest,
A victory over sin!
I seek that Thou alone shouldst reign
O'er all without, within.[18]

THE REST THAT REMAINS

Although the word *rest* occurs eight times in Hebrews 4, the meaning of the word as it appears in the phrase "*There remaineth therefore a rest to the people of God*" (verse 9) is unique. It differs also from the meaning of the word Jesus used in His invitation to the laboring and the heavy laden. The word he used for *rest* in this verse is *up-rest*. The noun *rest* is used six times in Hebrews 4, exactly translated as "down-rest." In the phrase "*There remaineth a rest*," however, the word means *Sab-baptism*, or "Sabbath-keeping." So in "*God rested on the seventh day from all his work which he had made*" (Genesis 2:2), the significance is that the seventh day had *no evening*—which is doubly typical. This is also typical of the millennial day when "*at evening…it shall be light*" (Zechariah 14:7).

God's creation rest was soon disturbed by sin, as was His Canaan rest by Israel's unfaithfulness. Since then, He has been working in grace. (See John 5:17.) But the persons of the Godhead are working onward to the rest that remains, which will become ours when Christ and His church rest together in the Father's blest abode. Meantime, we hear His voice saying, "*Arise ye, and depart; for this is not your rest*" (Micah 2:10). Why? "*Because it is polluted*" (verse 10).

There is a land of pure delight,
Where saints immortal reign;

---

18. Eliza H. Hamilton, "My Savior, Thou Hast Offered Rest," 1909.

Eternal day excludes the night,
And pleasures banish pain.
There everlasting spring abides,
And never withering flowers;
Death, like a narrow sea, divides
This land of rest from ours.[19]

19. Isaac Watts, "There Is a Land of Pure Delight," 1707.

CHAPTER 8

THREE TENSES OF SALVATION

Ye are saved.
—Ephesians 2:5

...being saved...
—1 Corinthians 1:18

Now is our salvation nearer than when we believed.
—Romans 13:11

Salvation is not only one of the grandest themes of Scripture, but also the source from which all blessings flow for the spiritual security of the saved. Too often, we limit the implication of the term salvation to what transpires when a person repents of his sin and accepts Christ as Savior and humbly confesses, "Thank God, I am saved!" But if anyone should stop you and kindly ask, "Excuse me, are you saved?" You would be quite right to reply, "Do you mean have I been saved, or am I being saved, or have I yet to be saved?" This is because the New Testament emphasizes the past, present, and future tenses of salvation.

There is a salvation which the believer in Christ has *now*, which he received the hour he saw Christ hanging on a tree for his sins.

There is a salvation which continues in the saved person in this present life, through the power of the Holy Spirit.

There is a salvation yet to be revealed and experienced, that will be ours when the Savior returns to deliver His people from the sinful world.

SALVATION PAST

Salvation is a gift we receive when, convicted and penitent for our sin, we open the avenue of our being for the Savior Himself to enter and make our heart His throne. *"Thy faith hath saved thee"* (Luke 7:50); *"Unto us which are saved"* (1 Corinthians 1:18); *"By grace ye are saved"* (Ephesians 2:5); *"According to his mercy he saved us"* (Titus 3:5). Along with numerous other examples, these verses refer to a past, decisive act of salvation that was accomplished and is never repeated. What God does is forever; nothing can be added to or taken away from our salvation. (See Ecclesiastes 3:14.) The basis of our faith, that once saved we are saved eternally, is the authoritative word of God: *"He that...believeth him that sent me, hath everlasting life, and cometh not into judgment"* (John 5:24 asv).

It is not presumptuous for a sinner, who trusts God to wipe away his sins, to say that he *knows* he is saved. It would be the height of presumption *not* to say it, for his doubt about the irrevocable work of the Spirit would be a foul dishonor to his loving Savior. Furthermore, what makes such a transformation permanent is the fact that salvation, or eternal life, is not *something* but Someone. Because Christ is the Author of mankind's eternal deliverance, He is sometimes called *Salvation*, which is the equivalent of Savior. *"Behold God is my Salvation*" (Isaiah 12:2). Then there is John's remarkable statement, "*This is the record, that God hath given to us eternal life, and this life is in His Son. He that hath the Son hath life*" (1 John 5:11–12).

Eternal life, therefore, is not only found *in* God's Son, but *is* the Son Himself. So it happens that when He enters the believing soul, salvation remains forever. (See John 14:16.) It was He who said, "*He that cometh unto me I will in no wise cast out*" (John 3:27). Just so, it is also true that when a soul comes to Him and is born anew by the Spirit, no one can cast Him out. He becomes our eternal Inhabitant. How unceasingly grateful we should be if,

> We have heard the joyful sound,
> Jesus saves! Jesus saves![20]

SALVATION PRESENT

The gospel is not only the power of God unto salvation for those who exercise faith in the hour of decision for Christ; it is also the power of God in daily salvation for those who have believed and keep on believing. Christ is the Savior of lost sinners *and* saved sinners. He is "*the Saviour of all men, specially of those who believe* [or have believed]" (1 Timothy 4:10). The *inwrought* salvation must be *outwrought*. We have to work out our salvation with fear and trembling (See Philippians 2:12–13), and show it forth from day to day. (See Psalm 71:15.) This brings us to the passages that speak of the saved as *being saved*. "*Unto us which are being saved*" (1 Corinthians 1:18 ESV); "*in them that are being saved*" (2 Corinthians 2:15–16 RV). Thus, the complete salvation

20. Priscilla Owens, "Jesus Saves," 1868.

the sinner receives at conversion becomes a *continuing* salvation. This is what Toplady calls "the double cure" in "Rock of Ages":

> Let the water and the blood,
> From Thy riven side which flowed,
> Be of sin the double cure,
> Cleanse me from its guilt and power.[21]

The *blood* cleanses us from all past guilt and iniquity, and the *water*—a type of the Holy Spirit—keeps us clean throughout our earthly pilgrimage.

Exhortations such as *"By which also ye are saved, if ye keep in memory what I preached unto you, unless ye have believed in vain"* (1 Corinthians 15:2) and *"What doth it profit...though a man say he hath faith, and have not works? Can faith* [such faith—his saying he has faith] *save him?"* (James 2:14) were written to remind us that the salvation worked *in* the believer must be worked out; that the salvation received must be daily and progressively exhibited in a life of obedience to the Lord. Furthermore, we must continue advancing in the knowledge, joy, and practice of salvation, which is freely and fully bestowed on us by our close fellowship with the Holy Spirit.

We were saved from the guilt and penalty of all past sin through our initial surrender to Christ. But such a salvation did not eradicate the old, Adamic sinning nature within. We are recipients of a new and divine nature; therefore, we have two natures: the one in which we were born, characterized by inbred sin, as well as the one the Holy Spirit imparts, characterized by a heart that avoids sin. Paul dealt at length with these opposing natures in Romans 6 and 7, describing his

21. Augustus M. Toplady, "Rock of Ages," 1776.

struggle that when he did well, the old evil Saul of Tarsus was ever with him. But he claimed salvation from the government and power of sin because he knew that sin must not have dominion over him. *"Thanks be unto God, which giveth us the victory"* (1 Corinthians 15:57).

The tragedy is that far too many have been saved but are not being saved. They have one-half of the Gospels, that is, deliverance from a sinful past; but they neglect the other half, including sanctification and deliverance from a sinning present. There is no place in God's kingdom for sinning saints. Paul combines this double salvation in this remarkable passage: *"For if, when we were enemies, we were reconciled to God by the death of his Son, much more, being reconciled, we shall be saved by his life"* (Romans 5:10). Note that we receive salvation by the *death* of His Son, and a further salvation by the *life* of His Son. Is there a contradiction here? Certainly not! By dying, Jesus bore our sins.

> My sin, O the bliss of this glorious thought!
> My sin, not in part, but the whole,
> Is nailed to His cross...[22]

Paul says that there is *much more* than being saved *from* sin. *"We shall be saved by His life"* (Romans 5:10). So what are we saved from? Why, from sin's dominion and seductive influences! So how does this further salvation become ours? It becomes our by *His life*. What life? Not His earthly life, for there is no salvation in His exemplary life among men, or by mere imitation of Him. No, the life Paul wrote of is Christ's present throne-life, where He is glorified and exalted. He is able to make a saved person *"more than a*

---

22. Horatio G. Spafford, "It Is Well with My Soul," 1873.

conqueror" (2 Corinthians 4:10), because of this risen life. (See Psalm 119:94.)

> Bless, bless the Conqueror slain!
> Slain by divine decree!
> Who lived, who died, who lives
> Again, for thee, His saint, for thee.[23]

SALVATION PROSPECTIVE

Actually, the gospel is three-pronged in that it covers our salvation, sanctification, and glorification. Although we are saved by grace and receive daily victory over temptation, we are still sinful because we have inherited a sinful nature. Also, we live in a sinful world which is always in opposition to the saints. What we must have is salvation from the root of sin within and its appeal in the world. This is the future tense of salvation Paul had in mind when he wrote, *"Now is our salvation nearer than when we believed"* (Romans 13:11). Did we receive salvation when we first believed? Yes! Do we experience salvation as we keep on believing? Yes! Then what aspect of salvation is nearer than when we believed? Paul is dealing with the return of Christ in this narrative, and, because the night is far spent and that glorious day is at hand, he exhorts them to rouse of their spiritual slumber and live in the light of Christ. (See Romans 13:11–14.) This is equivalent to *"the redemption of the body"* from the grave that Paul speaks of in Romans 8:23. Our redeemed soul lives in the old body, characterized by an inherent sinning nature; but we must have a body corresponding to the renewed soul. When Jesus comes again, we will receive the final installment of our redemption or salvation, for we shall be sinless like Him.

---

23. Samuel W. Gandy, "His Be the Victor's Name," 1838.

Paul refers to the three chains in another epistle. He links the past, present, and future together in 2 Corinthians 1:10: "*Who* [hath] *delivered us from so great a death, and doth deliver: in whom we trust that He will yet deliver us.*" God never begins a work without completing it. "Love perfecteth what it begins."[24] He is not like the man in the gospel story "*began to build and was not able to finish*" (Luke 14:30). Our *Alpha* will be our *Omega* as well. If "[His] *hands…have laid the foundation of this house, His hands shall also finish it*" (Zechariah 4:9). We may use past deliverances as reminders of the track already traveled and as headlights to show us mercies still ahead. All that God has been and is, He will be in the future. He has promised never to leave us and at the end of time, will deliver us from a groaning creation. As a writer of the last century expressed it:

As the crescent moon with ragged edge, barely lighting the surrounding clouds, but beautiful even in its imperfection, is the prophet of a complete and resplendent orb, that will illuminate all the wintry skies, so, if the outset of my heavenward way is right, and every step thereafter is taken in faith, a glorious ending is sure.

> Yes, through life, death, through
> Sorrow and through sinning
> He shall suffice me, for He hath sufficed:
> Christ is the end, for Christ was the beginning,
> Christ is the beginning, for the end is Christ.[25]

---

24. Jean S. Pigott, "Lord Jesus, Thou Dost Keep Thy Child," 1876.
25. Frederick W. H. Myers, "Hark, What A Sound," 1867.

CHAPTER 9

THREE PARABLES OF RESTORATION

I have found my sheep which was lost.
—Luke 15:6

I have found the piece which I had lost.
—Luke 15:9

Thy brother was...was lost, and is found.
—Luke 15:32

G. Campbell Morgan, in *Great Chapters of the Bible*, says that Luke 15...

> stands out among the mountain peaks of the biblical literature, first on account of its matchless pictorial beauty, but ultimately and principally because it brings to focus truths concerning God and man which are fundamental in these matters.

Dr. Morgan goes on to say that the key to interpreting this chapter is hanging at the front door, *"This Man receiveth sinners, and eateth with them"* (Luke 15:2). Publicans and sinners crowded around Jesus to hear him define discipleship—much to the chagrin of the Pharisees and scribes. So when we read *"he spake a parable unto them"* (Luke 18:1), the pronoun *"them"* refers principally to His foes. These self-righteous men were just as sinful as the publicans and sinners.

We are accustomed to speak of this great chapter as containing *three* parables. In actuality, it constituted only *one* parable—*"He spake unto them this parable."* The *three* stories constitute one. They form a *triptych*—all needed for the revelation of the compassionate God.

The parable has a threefold movement, showing first, a shepherd suffering in his quest for a lost sheep; second, a woman seeking for a lost coin until she finds it; and third, a father singing with joy when his boy returns to him. The parable is unified in that it deals with lost things—a lost sheep, a lost coin, a lost son—and in that the lost things were sought, found, and restored.

This trilogy of Jesus does not give us isolated drawings but one picture with three panels, merging and blending into one another. The three illustrations are not repetitions but declarations of the same truth, each revealing a different phase of it. As C. H. Spurgeon expressed it,

> The three parables are three sides of a pyramid of gospel doctrine, but there is a different inscription upon each....Each one of the parables is needful to the other, and when combined they present us with a far more complete exposition of their doctrine than could have been conveyed by any one of them.

The whole chapter, then, is *a* parable, not *many* parables. Here we have three jewels in one casket—one complete suite—say, for instance, a pair of earrings and a brooch, all studded with numberless glistening diamonds—two small and one larger, yet each required to complete the whole; the one but the miniature of the other, and the latter but the former magnified.

W. Y. Fullerton goes on to say,

> These ornaments always bear a certain relation to each other in form, in style, and in pattern; and so do the three jewels which adorn this gospel page in Luke's gospel.

What wonderful sermonic material Luke 15 offers ministers of the Word! Here are a few briefs from this chapter:

1. The parable describes sheep, silver, and the son; these three are one in that they represent man as God fashioned him: a sheep, innocent, obedient, and precious; a silver coin, intrinsically valuable and bearing the image of Christ; and a son, partaking of God's nature while in relationship with Him.

2. The parable beautifully represents the Trinity combined and engaged in man's salvation.
   The shepherd portrays Christ in His willingness to give his life to recover the lost sheep. The woman with the light can typify the church, through which the Holy Spirit shines. Many passages represent the church as a woman, and the Spirit as light. "*The Spirit and the Bride say, Come*" (Revelation 22:17), not only to Christ, but to the wanderer. And the compassionate Father is not willing to see anyone perish. Thus, the Father, Son, and the Holy Spirit as One agree in the scheme of redemption. Christ died for the lost; the Spirit convicts the sinner of his need for Christ and His Christ's efficacy to meet that

need; and the Father joyfully receives the convicted and repentant sinner.

3. Furthermore, there are several degrees in the relationship of each to each, leading us up to a greater appreciation of the loss: The sheep—one out of a hundred; ninety-nine left behind. The silver—one out of ten; nine held secure. The son—one out of two—a far more acute loss. As is seen both by the chosen figures and the numbers, Christ, the incomparable storyteller, depicts an increasing value of the human soul: The sheep—one was not much to a farmer who had ninety-nine left—yet he left the majority to search for the lost. The silver piece was more to a woman who had only nine pieces left. The son was the most a father could lose.

4. The ways of becoming lost vary: *"We have turned every one to his own way"* (Isaiah 53:6), and suggest varying phases of man's sin. The sheep, apt to go astray, was lost foolishly. The woman unconsciously lost the silver, realizing one day that it was gone. The Son was lost deliberately, demanding his portion. Is this not all a portrait of those Jesus came to seek and save? We are lost in inherited sin like the silver, without any act at all; we are lost foolishly, as the sheep led astray by others; and we are lost deliberately, when inherited sin becomes practical sin.

5. Another aspect of the parable is the position of the sheep, silver, and son when discovered: The sheep was lost at a distance; the silver was lost in the house amid dust and dirt; and the son was actually degraded and debased by his prodigality. All three, however, were alike in that they were lost. This teaches that although some people are outwardly moral and beautiful, they still can be far from

God; therefore, they need found like sheep. Others may not sin *greatly*; yet, they are still lost in the dirt and sin of the world like the silver coin. Still, others wander and squander, all like the son; yet the Father's heart yearns for their return.

CHAPTER 10

THREE ROBES OF DEATH

It is appointed unto man once to die.
—Hebrews 9:27

She that liveth in pleasure is dead while she liveth.
—1 Timothy 5:6

This is the second death…
—Revelation 20:14

Man's last enemy casts a very heavy shadow over the Bible, evidenced by how many times the words *die*, *dead*, and *death* occur throughout Scripture—over one thousand times! Although *death* is used to describe with both animate and inanimate objects, the majority of references are connected with physical death. There are three features of death, however, and it is essential to distinguish between these so far as man is concerned.

There is physical death, the separation of the soul from body and the cessation of natural life on earth.

There is spiritual death, the separation of the soul from God caused by sin in our present life.

There is also eternal death. In this tragic death, we are eternally separated from God's soul. *The Christian Worker's Manual* describes it as follows:

Death is the separation of a person from the purpose or use for which he was intended. It deprives him of that for which he was created. This definition will fit the word death in whatever connection it is found. Man was created to live forever—physically. Physical or natural death deprives him of that. He was intended for the presence of God—spiritually. Spiritual death separates him from that. He was created to dwell with God forever—eternally. Eternal death robs him of this privilege.

Now we will take a closer look at the features of the phases of the death triad, as found in scripture.

PHYSICAL DEATH

As soon as a child is born, it begins a pilgrimage to the grave. "He that begins to live begins to die."[26] Bishop Hall declares, "Death borders upon our birth, and our cradle stands in the grave." Deny it though we may, death is the greatest fact in life.

> Thou, O Death
> What is thy meaning?
> Some there are of men
> Deny thee quite—"There is no death" they say;
> But ever with veil'd aspects com'st thou still.

Scripture declares that physical death was introduced into this world by sin—that it came as the penalty and wages of sin. While the death of the body differs from the death of the soul, both are the results of sin. The difference is that

---

26. Francis Quarles, *Hieroglyphics of the Life of Man*, 1637.

the former is the dissolution of man's physical nature and the latter is severance from God. *"In the day that thou eatest thereof thou shalt surely die"* (Genesis 2:17); *"Depart from me, ye that work iniquity"* (Matthew 7:23).

The following passages combine sin with mortal death: *"Everyone shall die for his own iniquity"* (Jeremiah 31:30). *"The soul that sinneth, it shall die"* (Ezekiel 18:4). *"The wages of sin is death"* (Romans 6:23). *"Sin, when it is finished, bringeth forth death"* (James 1:15). *"It is appointed unto man once to die"* (Hebrews 9:27). *"Thou takest away their breath, they die, and return to their dust"* (Psalm 104:29).

Bodily death, then, commenced as soon as our first parents sinned. The consequence of Adam and Eve's sin is that all are subject to death—*"In Adam all die"* (1 Corinthians 15:22).If the world God created remained sinless, then there would have been no death and all would be translated to heaven at God's call, just as Enoch and Elijah—the only two in the Bible who did not taste death. (See Genesis 5:24; 2 Kings 2:9–12; Hebrews 11:5.) A great number of the saved will escape death at the return of Christ, for Paul speaks of those *"which are alive and remain,"* (1 Thessalonians 4:15–17) and who will meet Him first without dying. (See 1 Corinthians 15:51–52.)

Christ destroyed physical death—the consequence and the penalty of sin—at Calvary when He tasted death for every man. (See Hebrews 2:9, 14–15.) But although redeemed by the blood, the saved person must still pass through death into life eternal. The sting is removed, however, and He destroyed the power of death to alarm and agonize forever. (See 1 Corinthians 15:55–57.) Death became a factor in the development of the purposes of redemption through the transforming power of Christ's death; and when it stops contributing to redemption, it is abolished absolutely, for *"the last enemy that shall be destroyed is death"* (1 Corinthians 15:26). Paul describes death's ultimate phase with these words: *"swallowed up"* (1 Corinthians 15:54).

If the believer goes home by the way of the grave, death is called "sleep." This is not soul-sleep, however, because personality is active in another realm. The Bible does not affirm that death is the end of existence. On the contrary, it teaches that although the body dies, the soul and spirit live on in another state and condition. "Sleep" is only associated with the body which may be awakened from the dust at any moment. (See Philippians 3:20–21; Daniel 12:2; John 11:11.) Christ's gift of resurrection life is an assurance of His victory over the grave. Thus, to him death is gain, seeing that it ushers him into heaven where there are no graves. (See Philippians 1:21.)

In addition, there is no purgatory after death to make departed souls more fit for heaven. The Roman Catholic doctrine of purification by fire to cleanse believers from any remaining sin after death has no foundation whatsoever in Scripture; it practically denies the efficiency and efficacy of Christ's blood. Our eternal destiny is fixed before we die. If we die in the Lord, then we go to Him immediately—*"to depart and be with Christ"* (Philippians 1:23). There is no intermediary period between death and glory, *"caught up...to meet the Lord"* (1 Thessalonians 4:17). There no second chance for the sinner dying in sin—no hope beyond the grave. There is only judgment for them. (See Hebrews 9:27.)

SPIRITUAL DEATH

The death of the soul is a death in sin, but Jesus offers salvation which is life from death. (See Galatians 2:19–20; Colossians 3:3.) Spiritual death is actually the separation of the spirit from God, who is the only source of life. *"To be carnally minded is death; but to be spiritually minded is life and peace"* (Romans 8:6). *"She that liveth in pleasure is dead while she liveth"* (1 Timothy 5:6). *"We were dead in sins"* (Ephesians 2:5). Being *"dead in sins"* is not characterized by unconsciousness or powerlessness; it simply means that sinners are as powerless to save themselves from sin as a dead body is to rescue itself from physical death. To be spiritually dead, therefore, implies that the natural or unregenerate man is alienated from God and destitute of the Holy Spirit. (See Ephesians 4:18–19.) The sinner is incapable of knowing and enjoying God because of his trespasses and sin. (See 1 Timothy 5:6; 1 John 3:14; 5:12.)Spiritual death is a state of eternal separation from God in conscious suffering, which, as our next section indicates, is called *"the second death"* (Revelation 2:11).

The believer is dead *to* sin because of his co-crucifixion with Christ—dead to the law and the world. (See Romans 6:2; 6:14; Galatians 6:14.) While both physical and spiritual death is penalty for sin, the Holy Spirit frees believers from the self-life and sin loses its power. Thereafter, they are dead to sin so long as they remain Spirit-filled and Spirit-controlled. Death is the absence of life, and spiritual death is the absence of Christ who said, *"I am...the life"* (John 14:6). *"He that hath the Son hath life"* (1 John 5:12). If we are resurrected from spiritual death, then it is our obligation to live as those who are dead or crucified to the world. *"Why seek ye the living among the dead?"* (Luke 24:5).

ETERNAL DEATH

The first death humans experience is physical death, while *"the second death"* is the ultimate penalty for sin. The second or *eternal* death refers to *"the lake of fire"* (Revelation 20:10; See 14–15), or eternal punishment. *"He that overcometh shall not be hurt of the second death"* (Revelation 2:11). *"On such the second death hath no power"* (Revelation 20:6). *"Which is the second death"* (Revelation 21:8). *"Die in your sins: whither I go, ye cannot come"* (John 8:21).

Here we have the most solemn truth a preacher's lips can proclaim. One needs a Calvary heart to warn sinners of the terrible consequences of dying in their sin and reaping eternal woe!

There was a remarkable affectionate bond between Scottish ministers Robert Murray McCheyne and Andrew Bonar, who wrote that spiritual classic every Christian should read and reread, *Memoirs of Robert McCheyne.* McCheyne said to Bonar in a Monday meeting, "I felt led to preach on hell yesterday." Bonar replied, "I hope, Robert, you preached such a message with *tears.*"

The consummation of *spiritual* death is *everlasting* death, that is, the final banishment from God's presence—complete separation from Him. *Physical* death ends the opportunity of salvation. It is necessary, therefore, to focus appeals to repentance in the *present.* (See Luke 19:42.) As it says in 1 Corinthians 6:2, *"Now is the day of salvation."* Scripture gives no hope of salvation *after* death; on the contrary, it teaches the tragedy of death by sin. (See Hebrews 10:26–27; John 8:21). *"It is a fearful thing to fall into the hands of the living God"* (Hebrews 10:31).

Furthermore, the contention that there is no immortality after death—that when we die physically, we die totally—is contradictory to Scripture. If, for the Christian, there is an *"inheritance incorruptible and undefiled, that fadeth not away"* (1 Peter 1:4), those who die without Christ will experience *"the blackness of darkness forever"* (Jude 1:14). John speaks of the wrath of God enduring toward the sinner. (See John 3:36.) Luke 16:19–31 teaches that the wicked are alive and conscious after death, having both memory and regret. *Eternal,* used to describe the quality of life for both the believer and unbeliever as he suffers everlasting condemnation, has been defined as "having neither beginning nor end of existence, from everlasting to everlasting; having no end, that will endure forever, everlasting; having no beginning."

There is no annihilation then for man, whose soul is worth more than the world; he never ceases to be. The absurdity of substituting *annihilation* for death is understood if we restructure this verse to read, "She that liveth in pleasure is *annihilated* while she liveth." Life continues after death for both the saved and the lost, but the sphere in which life continues depends solely on their relationship with Christ during their earthly sojourn. (See Isaiah 14:9; Revelation 21:7–8.) Hell is a place as well as a condition; it is for the unsaved what heaven is for the saved, although totally different in character. In summary, the physical and spiritual death of the lost eventuates in eternal death—the final consummation of the penalty for their sin. (See Daniel 12:2.)

It is interesting that the Jews have three terms for "dying." The Jew refers to the death of an ordinary Jew as *geshtorben*—"he died;" the death of a righteous Jew as *niftorgevoren*—"he was released;" but the death of an extraordinarily saintly Jew as *nistalekgevoren*—"he was taken away." The Jews also have three Hebrew names for a cemetery: the house of the graves—which it is for the sinner; the house of eternity—which it is for the repentant sinner, through which he enters eternity; and the house of life—which it is for the godly, for he passes through into eternal life.

CHAPTER 11

THREE BENEDICTION GIFTS

The grace of the Lord Jesus Christ, and the love of God and the communion [fellowship] of the Holy Ghost.
—2 Corinthians 13:14

Among all the benedictions and triads of the Bible, the most prominent is the one apostle Paul gave the church, which she has used through the centuries to conclude the sanctuary worship. In this trinity of truth, we have the most comprehensive and compact statement of the gospel of peace in Scripture. A common practice among saints since the early times has been giving benedictions and blessings. The origin of the benediction can be traced back to the tabernacle of the Old Testament. The benediction Moses gave the Israelites is the first priestly blessing recorded in Scripture. Priests, thereafter, blessed people with lifted hands. We read that Jesus *"lifted up his hands and blessed them"* (Luke 24:50). He also ascended into heaven this way, symbolic of His priestly ministry for the church until He returns for her—*"he ever liveth to make intercession for us"* (Hebrews 7:25).

As we consider the apostolic benediction Paul closes with in 2 Corinthians, we must note its association with the occasion and object of the larger epistle. Without a doubt, this was the most agitated, stormy letter Paul wrote. It is full of rebuke and condemnation for the worldly condition of Corinth's church, yet he closed it with the most beautiful benediction ever composed.

It is like the calm of a subdued evening after a stormy day. It embodied Paul's longing for the carnal church to experience and emulate the Trinity's grace, love, and fellowship. The apostle wanted three unwelcome traits to be rooted out of the church.

THREE UNWELCOME TRAITS

A LACK OF CHRISTIAN LIBERALITY

When the people lacked effort for the work of the sanctuary, Paul tried to show that giving to the Lord's work was not only a sign of receiving God's grace, but was in itself a Christian grace. He used the illustration of Christ's grace, manifested in His willingness to abandon riches and become poor *"for our sakes"* (2 Corinthians 8:8–9). Here we see His sacrificial and beneficial grace. He gave the uttermost that we might be blessed; such giving is the true incentive in Christian stewardship.

A CAUSE OF ACUTE SUFFERING

We cannot read 2 Corinthians and the biographical references in Paul's letters without grasping the physical pain and weariness he experienced. Along with the thorn in his flesh, he bore spiritual pains and burdens as he cared for all the churches. (See 2 Corinthians 11:28.) What anxieties and infirmities Paul had to endure! Yet he was upheld and sustained by the unchanged love of God through all his trials.

A REASON FOR GREAT ANGUISH OF HEART

The epistle was occasioned by legalizing teachers who questioned Paul's power and authority as an *apostle*. Coupled with the division, these disrupters invited a spirit of bitterness that disturbed the peace and fellowship within the church.

For this reason, he exhorted the members to *"live in peace"* (2 Corinthians 13:11), and to strive after a deeper experience of *"the fellowship of the Holy Spirit"* (verse 14).

The benediction or prayer sums up the teaching of the epistle. Paul strongly defended his calling as an apostle, called the people to a higher standard of Christian giving, and confuted errors of false teaching, exposing its destructive effect on Christian fellowship. The grace of the Lord Jesus Christ was to be this great example and inspiration; the love of God, the motive power that makes such a life of graciousness possible; and the fellowship of the Holy Spirit, the inevitable outcome of grace and love.

Another aspect of this wonderful benediction is the proof it provides on the *Trinity*—three in One. We can draw three facts from this blessed trinity of truth.

It addresses each as a person. The names were not mere influences, but divine persons to be worshiped. It is right and proper to offer worship to Christ and the Spirit as well as God. Each person should be treated with due reverence.

It treats each with equality. The divine order of the divine names is significant. Instead of the regular order of Father, Son, and Spirit, Christ is named first. But such inversion of order does not suggest any inequality, for all Three are coeternal and coequal.

It ascribes different qualities to each—from God, *love*; from Christ, *grace*; from the Holy Spirit, *fellowship*. However, this does not imply that each quality is exclusive to one person. The quality related to each person teaches the outstanding ministry of each. As G. H. Knight expressed it,

> Though three blessings are mentioned here, they are, like God Himself, three in one. Grace is mentioned

first, for all saving and sanctifying experience must begin with that. Love of God is what grace reveals, and the grace is communicated to us by the Holy Spirit. Christ is God revealing Himself; the Spirit is God communicating Himself; the love of God is the deep, invisible, eternal fountain of grace; in Christ, it appeared visibly as an outflowing stream; and the Holy Spirit is the friend who, pitying my helpless inability to reach the stream, lifts the water, cup after cup, and puts it to my thirsty lips. The grace of the Lord Jesus unfolds the love of God, and then the Holy Spirit makes me a conscious partaker of it. Christ pours out—the Spirit pours in.

THE GRACE OF THE LORD JESUS CHRIST

This gift is mentioned first, and rightly so, because it is through Christ's grace that God's love and the Spirit's truth are fully revealed. Paul was not giving any premier place to Christ, for He is coequal with the Father, but was simply revealing the method of salvation. The Father ever occupies the central place. We can illustrate the benediction by a father with his two children, one on either side of him. It helps to note that Paul uses the term *grace* in at least three connections: in the humiliation of the Savior (see 2 Corinthians 8:9), in the provision of salvation (see Acts 4:12; 13:47; 16:17), and in frequent salutations and benedictions. (2 Thessalonians 3:18; etc.) That *grace* is a favorite Pauline word is proven by the fact that he used it some one hundred times in his epistles. The word has a threefold implication:

1. Undeserved, unmerited *favor* is displayed by God to man. Our salvation is because of grace, lest anyone should boast. We are all beggars, dependent on divine charity. *"By grace ye are saved through faith; and that not of yourselves: it is the gift of God"* (Ephesians 2:8). The grace, salvation, and faith are all included in the *gift* of God.

2. The *gifts* that follow the reception of grace are designed for the life of those who are saved. Whatever need may arise, it is met by divine grace—*"My grace is sufficient for thee"* (2 Corinthians 12:9). There is always a need for grace, and there is always grace to meet every need.

3. The *effects* of these gifts in the recipient's life are visible. If we are saved by grace and constantly experiencing its sufficiency, then we shall be *grace-ful*, exhibiting a beautiful character that glorifies Him. Actually, the word Paul uses here for *grace* means "graciousness"—a quality we need more of in our lives!

It is also significant how the apostle used the Master's full name—a glorious triad of designations.

LORD

Associated with His preexistence and deity, this title is His risen, glorified name. *"To this end Christ both died, and rose, and revived, that He might be Lord both of the dead and living"* (Romans 14:9).

JESUS

This birth name represents the humanity of the Savior. He experienced the sufficiency of divine grace through all His earthly trials and temptations. *Jesus* is sweet to a believer's ear because it reminds him of the One who was tested in all areas just like himself. In the Father's estimation, Jesus is the name above every other name. (See Philippians 2:9-11.)

CHRIST

Here we have His official name as the sin-bearer. *Christ* means "the Anointed One," associating Him with the prophecies in the Old Testament that spoke about imminent suffering. His followers also share in this name—Christ-ians!

THE LOVE OF GOD

Truly, this is the greatest phrase ever penned by man. Paul gives the divine love the central place in his benediction because it is central in all divine purposes. Scripture's central truth is the love of God revealed through Christ. *Love* holds out two hands. From one hand we receive the Lord Jesus Christ, and all His grace and graciousness; from the other we receive the fellowship of the Holy Spirit. It is through the love of God that we are saved by the grace of Christ and kept saved through the communion of the Spirit. Man will never be able to exhaust the truth of these four words—the *love of God*.

> Could we with ink the ocean fill,
> Or were the skies of parchment made;
> Were every stalk on earth a quill,
> And every man a scribe by trade,
> To write the love of God above,
> Would drain the ocean dry:
> Nor could the scroll contain the whole,
> Though stretched from sky to sky.[27]

27. Frederick M. Lehman, "The Love of God," 1917.

It was sacrificial love that was expressed on the cross. (See John 3:16; 1 John 4:9–10.) It was an ennobling, yet inexplicable love—a love that always finishes and perfects what it begins. (See 1 John 3:1.) It is the love that forms the very atmosphere of a believer's life (see Romans 5:5), and we should strive to remain in it (see Jude 21). This love gives an example of life and is the proof of true discipleship. (See 1 John 3:16; 4:11; John 13:34–35.)

> For the love of God is broader,
> Than the measure of man's mind;
> And the heart of the Eternal,
> Is most wonderfully kind.[28]

THE COMMUNION OF THE HOLY SPIRIT

We now come to the blessed, inevitable outcome of grace and love. If we have experienced Christ's grace and grow to appreciate God's love, then we know the fellowship and partnership of the Holy Spirit. Many believers have taken the gift of Christ with one hand, but are ignorant of the second gift from the Spirit. The word *communication* springs from *communion*; and communication with the Holy Spirit enable us to participate in the fullness of the gospel.

It is the Spirit who weaves grace and love into the reality of our lives. At the heart of the word *communion* is the notion of "having a thing in common," implying a common participation in all the Spirit has for believers. This explains the phrase "be with you *all*." The Holy Spirit is the birthright

---

28. Frederick W. Faber, "There's A Wideness in God's Mercy," 1878.

of every believer. The Revised Version of the Bible gives us the word "fellowship" for "communion." This touches on the unique personality of the Holy Spirit, for it is impossible to have fellowship with mere influence. Fellowship is comprised the two words: *fellow* and *ship*—literally to have contact with the other fellow in the ship. What a privileged fellowship is ours! It is a secret one in that the world outside is ignorant of our partnership with this unseen friend yet it is a public one because it is the fellowship of the saints. This is why we call the Lord's table *Communion*. It is a mutual communion with the Father and the Son, and all else who believe. (See 1 John 1:5, 7.)

When the tide flows out, pools are separate from each other; but when it flows back in, pools are unified into one body of water. Deeper fellowship with the Spirit is the only thing that preserves us from strained fellowships in the church. We have the constant realization of the fellowship and friendship of Him dwells within us. We say that we can only *know* a person by living with him. Are we living in unbroken partnership with the Spirit? If we are, then we have learned the secret of the life that glorifies the Father and the Son.

So we see that this blessed triad is not only a benediction, but a prayer; it's not only a prayer, but a promise—a promise strong enough to carry us through all life-experiences. All we could possibly need on our journey here below is epitomized in this apostolic benediction: "All that the grace of Christ can do, all that the love of God can give, all that the strengthening, enlightening, and comforting that the fellowship of the Holy Spirit can effect are at our disposal." To quote G. H. Knight again,

Scientific botanists tell me that every tree-leaf bears, in its structure, a resemblance to the character of the tree itself, and that when wintry frosts have wasted it till only a skeleton of fibres is left, that will show, when held up to the light, a delicate suggestion of the conformation of the parent tree. So, when the grace of Christ, the love of God, and the communion of the Holy Spirit have done their present work upon the soul, by which it is ripened for its dying, its likeness to Him from whom its life came will be revealed: the grace of Christ shining out in the beauty of the soul that grace has renewed—the love of God reproduced in the love of the Brotherhood on high—the communion of the Holy Spirit revealed in the perfect sanctity of those who are "presented faultless in the presence of his glory" there. All that is in heaven comes down to us out of heaven, that we receiving it may go up to the heaven from which it comes.

CHAPTER 12

THREE DESCRIPTIONS OF HUMAN NEED

The people is hungry, and weary, and thirsty in the wilderness.
—2 Samuel 17:29

Perhaps the most heartbreaking thing David experienced was the rebellion of his handsome and beloved son Absalom. It was not hard to steal the hearts of the men of Israel with all his physical attractions. It must have been pathetic to see David, who in earlier days defied Goliath, flee from his own impetuous son. David had traitors in both his household and ranks, but he also had faithful followers who honored and cared for him in his days of distress and defeat. Some of his these followers brought vessels and victuals for David and his men who were hungry, and weary, and thirsty, in the wilderness.

What a triad of need mentioned by this historian! Driven from home, the fugitives would have yielded in the wilderness without the thoughtful and bountiful provision of Barzillai and his friends. What fresh courage must have come with the beds and butter, the lentils and the lamb!

It does not take much imagination to imagine the people's physical despair with this triad in the wilderness. The saints and sinners were *"hungry, and weary, and thirsty."* It should also be mentioned that sinners are never fully satisfied. They are forever *hungry*, feeding on ashes rather than the Bread of Life. The prodigal son had more than enough bread in his father's home, but he was still hungry, especially out in the world. In addition, sinners are *thirsty*. The waters of the earth, broken cisterns of worldliness, do not quench their thirst. If only they knew of the life-giving stream the Lord offers, how they would say with the woman at the well, *"Sir, give me this water, that I thirst not, neither come hither to draw"* (John 4:15). Sinners are also *weary*. Running away from God produces heavy feet. We read that the men of Sodom *"wearied themselves to find the door"* (Genesis 19:11). Think of the exhaustion sin causes! Yet it is Christ who invites heavy laden sinners to come to Him for rest.

The descriptive triad, however, gives another application. To the saint, the world is a wilderness; heaven is his home. He is a stranger and a pilgrim, constantly pursued by the traitors of the world—the flesh and the devil. Yet his heavenly helper is near, and he is found coming up through the wilderness leaning on the arm of his beloved. How hungry and thirsty he is! There is nothing satisfying in the world for his new nature. He *hungers* and *thirsts* after righteousness and is filled.

> I hunger and I thirst,
> Jesu', my manna be.
> As living souls are fed
> O feed me, or I die.[29]

The psalmist speaks of his soul panting for God as the heart pants for water. O for a deeper thirst for God! If you feel that you are filled to capacity with all the good things that the Lord has for you, ask Him to enlarge your capacity so that you can appropriate even more!

29. John S. B. Monsell, "I Hunger and I Thirst," 1873.

Those who fled with David were also *weary*. Are we also not often weary? Many saints are weary and long to be freed from the trammeling influences of the flesh. Constant and conscientious service can also wear on the body and mind. *"Jesus, being wearied with the journey, sat on a well"* (John 4:6). He was often weary in His work, though never weary *of* it. It is true that Paul said *"Be not weary in well-doing"* (Galatians 6:9), but the weariness he referred to was despair or disappointments in service. We must never surrender our task. At times, it may seem overwhelming, but as we wait on the Lord, we exchange our weariness for strength. When we see Him in glory, we will serve Him unwearyingly. What a pleasure it will be to carry out His bidding with perfect bodies and never feel tired. Day and night, saints labor unceasingly for the Lord who is never weary. (See Isaiah 40:28.)

CHAPTER 13

THREE EVIDENCES OF DIVINE SUFFICIENCY

I am the way, the truth, and the life: no man cometh unto the
Father, but by me.
—John 14:6

Doesn't this verse stand out as a remarkable trinity of truth? There is a divine threefold cord that neither devil nor man can break. The first overwhelming thought that occurs to us as we look at this verse is that Christianity is summed up in one simple pronoun: "I." "Christianity is more than a creed, a doctrinal system, a code of rules—it is Christ." Here we have the assertion of His deity, for the pronoun is emphatic, meaning "I, and none besides Me."

The person uttering this triad was the divine teacher Himself. No human teacher could claim these attributes without being charged with arrogance and blasphemy. Jesus taught with authority, not as the scribes. They were unable to substantiate their claims as authoritative teachers. But Jesus' ability to use the divine *"I Am"* proves He is coequal with God. This is why His assertions bring such joy to believers. These claims come from the eternal Son, promising believers that He is all-sufficient for both our present needs an our eternal hope.

What an ocean of truth we find in the three metaphors Jesus uses to reveal His qualities. These metaphors explain what Jesus can do if men love, obey, and trust Him! It is true that we must come to the Father through Christ in order to receive His gift of truth and love: *"No man cometh unto the Father, but by me"* (John 14:6). Whether through worship, salvation, or ultimately heaven, we have no access to God apart from the mediation of Jesus. (See 1 Timothy 2:5.) This is why it is vain to try to approach God through other mediators like the Virgin Mary or other saints and angels.

There are various ways we can deal with the three illustrations of Jesus as the way, the truth, and the life. (See John 14:6.) The article *"the"* is emphatic, and is placed before each noun in the original text. He is not *a* way, but *the* way, *the* truth, and *the* life. He alone is the source and embodiment of all three. Without *the* way, there is no going; without *the* truth, there is no knowing; without *the* life, there is no showing.[30]

MEET THE THREEFOLD NEED OF MAN

Because it pleased the Father that all fullness should dwell in His Son, He is able to meet every need in His riches.

Man is lost and in need of a *way*. Ever since the fall, we have forsaken the right way and have gone astray. *"All we like sheep have gone astray"* (Isaiah 53:6; See 2 Peter 2:15). Lost in sin, the sinner tries to pave his own way. Solomon reminds us twice that *"There is a way which seemeth right unto a man, but the end thereof are the ways of death"* (Proverbs 14:12; 16:25). It is obvious that the way that seemed right was wrong because it ended in death! But all who choose Christ as *the* way find eternal life. This verse was actually an answer to Thomas'

---

30. The last two are an expansion of the first.

question: *"How can we know the way?"* (John 14:5). Jesus had just told him beforehand, *"Ye know the way,"* (John 14:4). Well, who was right? Without hesitating we might answer "Jesus," because Thomas had listened to Him speak about the way many times before; but this truth was lying in some dusty corner of his memory. Therefore, Jesus said in effect,

> Go back to the teachings I have given you; look carefully through the inventory of your knowledge; let your instincts, illumined by my words, supply the information you need: there are torches in your souls already lighted, that will cast a radiant glow upon the mysteries to the brink of which you have come.[31]

Even the most abandoned sinners have more truth in their memories than they can readily recall. Thomas insisted that he was ignorant; in response, Jesus declared that he was *the* only way back to God. The only route a sinner can take to God is through the cross. We can have direct, unfettered access to the great invisible God in this way alone.

The figure of a *way* is an instructive one. The Greek word used for *way* speaks of a natural road or the way of a traveler; metaphorically, it speaks of a course of conduct or way of thinking. When we say, "That is not my *way* of doing this," we imply a different mode of operation. It was because Christ was the way personified that the term became associated with His cause—the course followed and characterized by His followers. Paul searched for *"any that were of this way"* (Acts 9:2). Many have discussed the meaning of *"the way"* ever since. (See Acts 19:9, 23; 24:22.) If our feet are not on this way, we are lost—no matter how splendidly paved the other

---

31. Dr. Frederick Brotherton Meyer, *Love to the Uttermost: Expositions of John 13–21*, 1847.

roads may be. Men find other ways more attractive than the blood-stained way of the cross, studded with the nails of the one who became "the way."

> Thou art the Way; to Thee alone
> From sin and death we flee;
> And he who would the Father seek,
> Must seek Him, Lord, by Thee.[32]

Although Christ is the *only* way, He is still all that we need. He excludes all other ways, but includes all who desire to follow Him. Let us now look at the similarities between the term *road* and *way* in relation to Him.

HE IS THE ROAD DOWN

Christ came from above, having been sent by the Father, to provide for those who were lost, ignorant, and dead; and by His death and resurrection He fashioned the road on which the sinner can travel to heaven. "*The veil was rent…from the top to the bottom*" (Matthew 27:51). For all who believe, the incarnation was the road down from heaven and the crucifixion the road up to heaven.

HE IS THE ROAD OUT

We often see the notice "Way Out" in public buildings. As the angel led Lot out of Sodom, so the Savior leads us on the road out of the guilt and power of sin—the road out of the wrath of God and the fear of perdition.

HE IS THE ROAD IN

The previous aspect shows the negative side of Christ's work. The positive side is that when we accept God, we

32. George W. Doane, "Thou Art the Way," 1824.

receive assurance, security, and the fullness of blessing. He is the road into the Word and the hearts of others.

HE IS THE ROAD ON

As we journey on with Christ, we experience an ever-deepening grace and growth in sanctification. What is holiness? Holiness is a better and fuller acquaintance with the road we stepped on at conversion.

HE IS THE ROAD UP

The Lord is our ladder up to prayer—our communion with God. Only through Him do we have access to the Father. (See Ephesians 2:18.) He is our way into eternal rest. (See Hebrews 4:6; 10:19–23.)

HE IS THE ROAD THROUGH

Paul wrote in triumph, *"I can do all things through Christ"* (Philippians 4:13), and what a marvelous medium He is! The ancient prophet assures us that *"When thou passest through the waters, I will be with thee"* (Isaiah 43:2). As the fourth person supported the tree youths in the fiery furnace, so the same Son of God supports us in all our trials, difficulties, sorrows, and graves. Has He not promised that He would never leave us nor forsake us?

A road implies a goal beyond itself, some place to which it leads. If we find ourselves in an unfamiliar area, we often say, "I wonder where this road leads to?" Jesus is no blind road; He is the road that leads us through the present to the goal ahead. The wonderful thing is that He is both the road by which we travel and the goal itself. He is our heaven of heavens!

HE IS THE ROAD HOME

In this passage, the Lord teaches us that He alone is the road to the Father's abode. Thomas was anxious to find the way to the *"many mansions"* (John 14:2), and Jesus pointed to Himself as *the* way, emphasizing that no one can reach heaven apart from Him. Death is a road home for the believer; and when Christ returns for His church, He will be her personal guide to the realms above. (See John 14:1–3.) As a road leads from one place to another, so He takes us out of sin and into grace, out of defeat and into victory, out of earth and into heaven. The distance between sin and holiness, life and death, is covered by Him! *He* is the way; walk ye in Him!

Furthermore, a road unites, or serves as a medium between villages and towns. Two distant places are joined by a serviceable road. We often sing, "Blest be the tie that binds," and in spite of the differing temperaments and personalities of the saints, the Lord Jesus binds them together and makes them one in Himself.[33] When we lose sight of the road, we often lose our unity. Christ is the only one who can keep us in unity of spirit as we travel the dusty lanes of earth to the golden streets of heaven. May grace be ours to keep to the road until traveling days are done!

> Thou are the way—to Thee alone
> From sin and death we flee;
> And he who would the Father seek,
> Must seek Him, Lord, in Thee.[34]

Man is ignorant and needs truth. Man is alienated from God by ignorance. Thus, those who do not know

---

33. John Fawcett, "Blest Be the Tie That Binds," 1740.
34. George W. Doane, "Thou Art the Way," 1824.

God are ignorant of His righteousness. (See Romans 10:3; Ephesians 4:18.) Such ignorance leads to error and false conceptions of the divine will and purpose. The Devil blinds many people; he is the master at keeping his victims from seeing the light of the gospel of Christ. (See 2 Corinthians 4:3–4.) But God commanded light to shine out of darkness; therefore, Jesus came as the *truth* to emancipate the minds of those who do not believe, delivering them from their mental midnight. Earlier Jesus says, *"Ye shall know the truth, and the truth shall set you free"* (John 8:32) and *"If the Son therefore shall make you free, ye shall be free indeed"* (verse 36). Though at first glance these verses seem to contradict each other, they actually complement each other, for the *Son* is *the truth*, and He alone frees men from their beclouded minds and consciences.

Jesus said to Pilate, *"Every one that is of the truth heareth my voice"* (John 18:37). Pilate replied, *"What is truth?"* (verse 38). *Truth* stood before the governor personified in Christ, as he somewhat recognized, for he confessed, *"I find in him no fault at all"* (verse 38). *Truth*, then, is not *something* but *Someone*. He is the one who banished our darkness and revealed the truth of God, salvation, and eternity.

O Everlasting Truth,
Truest of all that's true,
Sure guide of erring age and youth,
Lead me, and teach me, too.[35]

It is Christ who brought God down so near to us that we can hear His voice and feel His touch. Through Him we receive the knowledge of the fatherhood of God that disarms fear and inspires love. Unbelief is turned to belief and errors corrected through His ministration. F. B. Meyer says,

35. Horatius Bonar, "O Everlasting Light," 1858.

Obedience to the *way* conducts us to the vision of the *truth*; ethics to spiritual optics. The truth-seeker must first submit himself in humility and obedience to Christ; and when he is willing to do His will, he is permitted to know.

Nicodemus said of Jesus, *"We know that thou art a teacher come from God"* (John 3:2), and truly He was the most perfect teacher of truth the world has ever known. But He is even more. Hidden in Him are all the mysteries of wisdom and knowledge. "All truth is enciphered in Him."[36]

We are apt to detach Christ's teachings from His person, to distinguish between truth from Him and truth *as* Him. The Gospels contain many truths said about Him, as well as by Him; but we are not saved by truths about Him, not even by the incontestable facts of His death, resurrection, and ascension. We are saved *by Christ alone* who died and lives forevermore. To quote Meyer again:

> This is the ground basis of all true saving faith. The soul may accept truths about Christ, as it would any well-authenticated historical facts; but it is not materially benefited or saved until it has come to rest on the bosom of Him of whom these facts are recorded.

As the perfection and personification of truth, Christ demanded truth in every phase of life by those who accepted Him. If we pledged our allegiance to Him as the King of truth, then as John Bunyan said of "the picture of a very grave person," the law of truth should be written upon our hearts. If the truth is written on our hearts, we will be inspired by an undying love for all that is true and eager to fellowship with

---

36. Dr. Frederick Brotherton Meyer, *Love to the Uttermost: Expositions of John 13–21*, 1847.

truth-lovers and truth-seekers everywhere. May we ever be found walking in the truth. (See 3 John 3; Psalm 86:11.)

> Thou are the Truth—Thy Word alone
> True wisdom can impart;
> Thou only canst instruct the mind,
> And purify the heart.[37]

Man is dead and needs *life*. The Bible clearly teaches that apart from Christ, man is spiritually dead. Paul wrote Ephesians to those *"who were dead in trespasses and sins"* (Ephesians 2:1), but who had been quickened by Him who is *the* life (see verse 5). Those who are physically dead cannot walk on any way. There is no path from a cemetery. Likewise, none who are spiritually dead can please God. However, Jesus came not only as light to lighten our darkness, but as the life. *"In him was life; and the life was the light of men"* (John 1:4). When He appears the second time, it will be as *"our life"* (Colossians 3:4). John reminds us that *"this life* [eternal life] *is in his Son"* (1 John 5:11). *Life*, then, is not only in and from Him; He is *"the life"* in all its fullness.

The compassionate father could say of his prodigal son, *"He was dead and is alive again"* (Luke 15:24). It is through Christ's physical resurrection that the repentant, believing sinner experiences a spiritual resurrection. Then he comes out of the grave of sin, robed in *"the life."* Christ said, *"Because I live, ye shall live also"* (John 14:19). The three metaphors together—the way, the truth, and the life—suggest a picture of a traveler who has lost his way and needs direction to the right road; who is ignorant of the country and needs a true guide; who is exhausted, lacking strength for the journey, and needs new life. As travelers to eternity, our threefold

37. George W. Doane, "Thou Art the Way," 1824.

need is met in Christ. In Him we find the way home. When we are lost in ignorance and error, we can look to Him, the true guidepost. Dead in our sin, He offers Himself as life forevermore.

> Thou art the Life—the rending tomb
> Proclaims Thy conquering arm;
> And those who put their trust in Thee,
> No death nor hell shall harm.[38]

Christ is the way to God, the truth of God, and the life from God. A sinner, conscious of his condition in spiritual death, that wants life must be warned not to seek *it*, but *Him* who is *the* life—not the stream, but the fountain; not the word, but the speaker; not the fruit, but the tree. *"He that hath the Son hath* [the] *life"* (1 John 5:12). Then, how solemn is the exclusion, *"He that hath not the Son of God hath not the life."*

> Thou art the Way, the Truth, the Life—
> Grant us to know that Way,
> That Truth to keep, that Life to win,
> And reach eternal day.[39]

PRESENT A FULL REVELATION OF CHRIST

Not only does this triad emphasize our threefold need, but it also points to three rungs on the ladder of divine grace that links earth below to heaven above. It is only as we set a firm foot on the first rung that we can reach the second and only as we set a foot on the second that we can reach the third.

38. George W. Doane, "Thou Art the Way," 1824.
39. Ibid.

As the *way*, He is the atoning Christ who reveals that only the cross leads home. Access to God is possible only through atonement.

As the *truth*, He manifests the wickedness of our sin, as well as His ability to deliver us from it. Thereafter, He becomes the teaching Christ.

As the *life*, He dwells inside of us and makes us sharers of His risen, exalted life, in which there is no death.

As the *way*, He gives me the pardon and peace I need. As the truth, He gives me the knowledge and wisdom I seek. As the life, He gives me the holiness I desire.

The question of paramount importance is: Are we daily walking along this blessed way? Are we daily learning more about God by listening to the voice of truth? Are we daily growing more like God by imbibing more of the blessed life He gives?

> O blessed Life, heart, mind, and soul,
> From self-born aims and wishes free
> In all at one with Deity,
> And loyal to the Lord's control.[40]

---

40. William Tidd Matson, "O Blessed Life—The Heart at Rest," 1866.

CHAPTER 14

THREE LAWS OF HEAVEN FOR EARTH

What doth the Lord require of thee, but to do justly, and to love
mercy, and to walk humbly with thy God.
—Micah 6:8

Hebrew prophecy attained its peak in these sublime words, summarizing the divine requirements.

In the eighth century before Christ, in the heart of idolatry, a Hebrew prophet put forth a conception of religion which is as wonderful an inspiration of genius as the art of Phideas or the science of Aristotle!

The passion for righteousness that burned in Micah's heart inspired these words and revealed the prophet's contention that right *doing* must always precede right ceremonies. Although Micah's words are no less wrathful than those of the other prophets, he is known as the prophet of mercy. The opening chapters of his prophecy begin with judgment, but end with mercy, sweet refreshment for a parched and blasted land.

This trinity of truth sums up God's requirements simply, revealing that God's vision is not grievous. Furthermore, He enables us to do whatever He commands. *"Faithful is he who calleth you, who also will do it"* (1 Thessalonians 5:24). Transparency of character, a heart of mercy, and a lowliness of heart—these are the three things God asks of His followers. And He empowers them attain it. Micah implies outer profession, inner disposition, and upper communion in this marvelous statement.

DO JUSTLY

Both Micah and Amos—his faithful disciple—declared that ritual can never substitute for righteousness. The Lord demands integrity in all our relations, both public and private. As Christians we must be scrupulously fair and just in our thoughts, feelings, and actions. We must share the prophet's passion for righteousness. The foundation of God's throne is *justice*, and He is just in all His ways. And He expects us to reflect His character.

The gospel teaches that we should act toward others as we expect them to act toward us. We look for others to be honorable, fair, and just as they deal with us; therefore, we must be prepared to treat them according to the same standard. But are we as scrupulously just as we should be? Are we clear and transparent in all our dealings with those who surround us, both in our public and private lives? We must be just because we are divinely justified. What society would look like if we were all as upright and just as God calls us to be! But, alas, equity has fallen in the streets, and injustice is glaringly obvious in these godless days.

LOVE MERCY

Justice can be as cold as it is correct. God does not want us to be merely just, but to show mercifulness and tenderness in all our dealings with others. Mercifulness of feeling must transform into mercifulness in act; and this, not from compulsion of conscience only, but from a generous heart. We are to *love* mercy. Mercy was more than justice to Micah. We are to *do* the latter, but *love* the former. If justice compels us to go one mile, mercy freely goes two. If justice says, *"Pay... that thou owest"* (Matthew 18:28), mercy listens to the suppliant's cry, *"Have patience with me"* (verse 29), and forgives him *"all that debt"* (verse 29). God delights in mercy; therefore, we must go the extra mile of mercy in addition to the first mile of justice. Although justice is mentioned first, we still must be merciful in heart and habit. A mere show of mercy is hypocrisy. In addition, mercy must be mixed with love to be effective.

Tenderness is the inward disposition that makes possible mercifulness possible. Justice without mercy would crush us altogether. Mercy without justice would fail to alleviate our need. In God, both attributes must act in unison; He requires us to preserve the same harmony between them. We must not be hard, harsh, unfeeling, and unbending as we strive *"to do justly."* Tender mercy must be combined with integrity. God is *just,* and the justifier of all who believe, but at the same time He is *"very pitiful and full of tender mercy"* (James 5:11). Just as we are fully dependent on divine mercy, we must also exhibit grace to win transgressors from their evil ways. The Master exhorted us to, *"Be ye therefore merciful, as your Father also is merciful"* (Luke 6:36).

WALK HUMBLY WITH THY GOD

Micah insists that a humble walk with God is the crown of true discipleship. *"He hath showed thee, O man, what is good...to walk humbly with God"* (Micah 6:8). Was there ever a better definition of the true religious life than this? Such a privileged walk, however, is only possible if we are in heart-fellowship with the divine travel-companion: *"Can two walk together except they be agreed?"* (Amos 3:3). Furthermore, such a walk will inevitably transform our character and conduct to match the Lord's.

This is the last strand in our threefold cord related to communion or direct obligation to God. The secret of doing justly and of having tender mercy is our walk *with* God, following in His footsteps. We may question whether a close fellowship with God is possible in such a corrupt time. The trammeling influences of the flesh and the world militate against a holy walk. However, just as Enoch and Noah walked with God despite the terrible degeneracy of their time, so we can too by God's grace.

The manner of such a walk must not be overlooked. We are to walk *humbly* with God. We must have the humility that Saint Augustine called "the crown of all the virtues." Walking in the white light of a purity in which our best actions are still tainted with self, our walk with God will be, above all else, a walk in lowliness of heart. The nearer we are to Him who is infinitely holy, the less room there will be in the heart for pride. Pride is the deadliest of sins; it always precedes the fall. Pride brought about the fall of Satan and is at the root of every sin. Then, what actually is sin? Is it not the heart's refusal to bow down to the commanding, arranging will of God?

Pride can assume a thousand forms. We have pride of face, pride of lace, pride of grace, pride of race. How God hates any semblance of pride! He condemns it all throughout His Word. Jesus came as *"meek and lowly in heart"* (Matthew 11:29) and was willing to *"humble himself"* even to *"the death of the cross"* (Philippians 2:8).It makes no difference whether it is pride of position, pride of nationalism, pride of power, pride of wealth, pride of speech, pride of life. God hates any high look. If we walk with Him, we must be prepared to clothe ourselves with all humility.

We may be tempted to think of God's threefold requirement as beyond us—too idealistic. It is true that if it was left to us, the situation would be hopeless, but what He requires of us, He enables us to do. By His grace, He can enable us *"to do justly."* Through His mercy, He can inspire us to show mercy and love. In His humility, He can empower us to walk humbly as well, teaching us that the highest position we have can is low at His feet.

CHAPTER 15

THREE SANCTUARIES IN MAN'S NATURE

The very God of peace sanctify you wholly; and I pray God your whole spirit and soul and body be preserved blameless unto the coming of our Lord Jesus Christ.
—1 Thessalonians 5:23

What an impressive triad of Scripture! Surely there is no more comprehensive prayer to offer for ourselves than this one Paul offered for his Thessalonian converts. There is no experience comparable to that of being wholly sanctified, or of having every part of our threefold nature in complete agreement with the will of God. When we are sanctified in thought, feeling, imagination, ambition, speech, and life, then our personality is indeed a holy temple for His praise.

Man is a tripartite being, a trinity in unity, consisting of spirit, soul, and body. We are whole only when the three are together, not separate. At creation, the Trinity of God formed the trinity of man, as the first reference to man's threefold nature. The body of man was created from the dust of the earth. The spirit of man came from the Creator's breath. The soul of man—a "mixture of dust and deity"—became the medium between body and spirit.

The body is connected with the material world, without and around. The spirit reaches after and responds to God, within and above. The soul, or personality, controlled by the Spirit expresses itself through the body's five senses.

The scriptural illustration of our complete nature, both by Christ and His apostles, is of a tabernacle or temple with their three sanctuaries in one.

Our spirit is like the Holy of Holies. It has intercourse with the unseen; it is the innermost sanctuary where we hear God's voice and feel His presence. The spirit of the believer stands for *God-consciousness*, and contains all the faculties for prayer, worship, and adoration. Until the Holy Spirit takes possession of man, he cannot fully function in his threefold being as God intended him to.

Our soul can be compared to the Holy Place, a portion of the tabernacle less mysterious, more varied, and with more constant service than the Holy of Holies, but still secluded from public gaze. The high priest alone could enter the Holy of Holies, but priests ministered in the central compartment of the tabernacle. We have all the powers that make up personality in the soul. My soul is myself, and can therefore represent *self-consciousness*.

Our body can be likened to the outer court, open to the sky. There all the people could see everything that was done. Through the medium of our body we are connected with the world around us by the five senses: *seeing, smelling, tasting, hearing,* and *touching.* The body, then, speaks of *world-consciousness*.

Paul prayed that the saints at Thessalonica might be wholly sanctified, or holy in their relationship with God, self, and man. When we are whole in these three areas, then we live a well-pleasing life unto Him. *All* we are and have must be brought into complete conformity to the divine will.

O, Spirit of God and of Jesus,
Blest Trinity, come and possess
My body, my soul, and my spirit,
And fill me with Thy holiness.

A SANCTIFIED SPIRIT

It is significant that Paul speaks first of the sanctification of the spirit-part of our nature. In his "Magna Carta of the Resurrection," the apostle says, *"Howbeit that was not first which is spiritual, but that which is natural: Afterward that which is spiritual"* (1 Corinthians 15:46).

But the order in creation is reversed in sanctification. It was then that the spiritual is first. It is only when our spiritual relation to God is right that we continue in the sanctification of soul and body. Once the godward attitude is settled, the self-ward and man-ward attitudes correspond. If the spirit-part has been quickened by the Holy Spirit in regeneration, then the sanctification of this Holy Place means the realization of God-inspired worship, praise, prayer, and intercession. Jesus taught that God must be worshiped *in spirit*, as well as in truth.

A SANCTIFIED SOUL

The soul is the hub of man's universe, and because of its centrality, is influenced by two opposite attractions. There are the attractions of the world which reach my soul through my body, and the attractions of heaven which reach my soul through my spirit. Within the soul we have another trinity— the heart, mind, and will. With the mind we think, with the heart we love, with the will we act. The tragedy is that we often try to regulate our ways by the principles and precepts of the self-life. Paul would say, *"I live; yet not I…Christ liveth in me"* (Galatians 2:20). Here we see that his personality was controlled by a divine personality. If the spirit is sanctified, then all phases of the self-life will harmonize with the divine will.

A SANCTIFIED BODY

Paul pled with the believers at Rome to present their bodies as a living sacrifice, holy, acceptable unto God, as a reasonable service, because God depends on our bodies to reach the world around us. (See Romans 12:1.) Therefore, they must be sanctified so that out of our bodies, like rivers of living water, can flow to refresh the thirsty souls of men. (See John 7:37–39.) Too often, the body-part of our being is the last part to be wholly sanctified. We strive to live in harmony with the divine will, but the body—with all its senses, passions, and activities—is not under the Spirit's control. Bodily habits prevent the Lord from making our bodies a channel of blessing to other bodies. Is He the Lord of your body?

If we profess to be the Lord's, we must ask ourselves: are we willing to be sanctified *wholly*, and to have the apostle's prayer answered on our behalf? Are we ready to yield our *spirit*, with all its heavenward aspirations; our *soul*, with all its affections and ambitions; and our *body* with all its pleasant activities and passions to Him who has a redemption-claim on our entire being? May we be delivered from the folly of pretending that our *all* is upon the altar, when, like Ananias and Sapphira, we are guilty of keeping part of the price!

It is comforting to know that the one who desires our entire sanctification is *the God of peace*. Even so, He wants to bring our spirit, soul, and body into a complete and glad uniformity to His will. Let the words be written in letters of gold, "Great peace have they who joyfully set God upon the throne of their heart and life, and dare not attempt to put Him in any lower place." Knowing the utter inability of the believer to sanctify himself wholly, Paul added the encouraging words, *"Faithful is he that calleth you* [to complete sanctification] *who also will do it"* (1 Thessalonians 5:24).

St. Augustine's commented on this blessed verse: "Give what Thou commandest, then command what Thou wilt."

He meets our insufficiency with His all-sufficiency, our helplessness with His almightiness, our defeat with His victory. Sanctification, like salvation, is all by grace, lest any man should boast. We are blessed to know that He who is our Savior is also our sanctifier. Charles Wesley taught us to sing,

> Finish, then, Thy new creation,
> Pure and spotless may we be;
> Let us see our whole salvation
> Perfectly secured by Thee:
> Changed from glory unto glory,
> Till in heaven we take our place;
> Till we cast our crowns before Thee,
> Lost in wonder, love, and praise.[41]

---

41. Charles Wesley, "Love Divine, All Loves Excelling," 1747.

CHAPTER 16

THREE REFERENCES TO MAN AS A WORM

Man, that is a worm…the son of man, which is a worm.
—Job 25:6

I am a worm, and no man.
—Psalm 22:6

Fear not, thou worm Jacob.
—Isaiah 41:14

Out of the twenty or so references to *worms* in the Bible, three passages use this somewhat repulsive creature as a metaphor of man, who is most lowly. Applying the name of this small, creeping, limbless object to man conveys contempt. Of all the figures of speech used to describe humans, none is as repugnant as the worm. Yet there is grace for man at his worst. Isaac Watts reminds us of this of this grace in the Calvary hymn—

Alas! and did my Savior bleed?
And did my Sov'reign die?
Would He devote that sacred head
For such a worm as I?[42]

---

42. Isaac Watts, "Alas! And Did My Savior Bleed," 1707.

Charles Wesley expresses a similar truth when he wrote of "the vilest of the sinful race" becoming the "meanest vessel of His grace":

> If so poor a worm as I,
> May to Thy glory live,
> All my actions sanctify,
> All my words and thoughts receive:
> Claim me for Thy service, claim
> All I have, and all I am.

WORM—MAN'S CONCEPTION OF HIMSELF

In order to fully appreciate Job's comparison of himself to a worm, we must interpret his phrase *"Man...a worm"* in context. After discussing how the bright moon and twinkling stars were not pure in God's sight, Bildad said, *"How much less man, that is a worm"* (Job 25:6). The moon and stars are created things—material, not spirit—and are therefore not stained with the sin of man. Yet the heavens are still not pure in His sight because they reside in an atmosphere that is polluted by the presence of Satan as *"the prince of the power of the air"* (Ephesians 2:2). But man is inherently sinful. Over his fallen and ruined nature is the inscription, "Here God once dwelt." Through grace, however, God comes to dwell inside of us. Although worm-like, the sinner discovers his corruption and appropriates by faith the Redeemer's transforming power when exposed to eternal light.

Those who, like humanists, have a "guild conceit" of themselves and have no need of God's grace, spurn the idea of man as a worm. Many share the view of a speaker at a church congress who said that he had no use for a theology that taught man to regard himself as a worm. Any theology that does not include this idea of man is not only painfully superficial and shallow, but anti-scriptural, for the whole tenor of the Bible is that puny, sinful man is nothing in comparison to a thrice Holy God.

WORM—MAN'S DESCRIPTION OF HIMSELF

The lowly cry of David was, *"I am a worm, and no man"* (Psalm 22:6). A person may include this estimation in his theology and yet feel nothing of its humbling power in his life. David meant what he said of himself with all the force of his great and emotional nature because of his grievous sin. Nor was it false modesty to call himself a "worm"—one who was contemptible in the sight of both God and man. Yet David was not the only one who put his head in the dust.

Abraham must have been one outstanding figure for God to say to Himself, *"Shall I hide from Abraham that thing which I do"* (Genesis 18:17). How glorious he was when he *"stood yet before the LORD"* (Genesis 18:22)! He was far above his fellows when he became an intercessor for Sodom. After he began pleading, he took yet another step and asked God to reduce the number of the righteous souls needed to spare Sodom. He does not assume a place of greater familiarity with God when he does this; on the other hand, he realizes his lowly position even more acutely and cries, *"I am but dust and ashes"* (Genesis 18:27)—a mere worm daring to approach the Creator!

Psalm 22 is the most profound messianic Psalm in that it paints a unique picture of Calvary centuries before Jesus died. When David said, *"I am a worm and no man"* (Psalm 22:6) he gave us, as C. H. Spurgeon expressed it, "a miracle in language." Those who despised and rejected Jesus saw no desirable beauty in Him. Furthermore, if as our sin-bearer He thought of Himself as a worm as He bore our sin, is it unseemly of us, whose sins He bore, to think of ourselves as such?

WORM—GOD'S ESTIMATION OF MAN

What compassionate grace is wrapped up in the remarkable verse, *"Fear not, thou worm Jacob...I will help thee, saith the LORD, and thy redeemer, the Holy One of Israel"* (Isaiah 41:14). What a contrast there is between *worm* and the *Holy One!* God recognizes our lowly condition and takes for granted our state as worms. Yet He builds His glorious promise on such recognition, and in so doing magnifies His grace. The very fashion of the promise extols such a contention. Our threefold condition is that of (1) helpless exposure to hostile forces, (2) complete bondage to evil powers, and (3), the inner sin, which has brought them about. But His grace is seen in that to the first, God refers to Himself as Jehovah: *"Thou hast destroyed thyself,"* He says, *"but in Me is Thine help"* (Hosea 13:9). To the second condition, He refers to Himself as the Redeemer, rescuing us from bondage and routing our foes. To the third condition, He reveals Himself as the Holy One of Israel. In His holiness, we despair in our wretched condition; yet He it is our refuge when we rest in the righteousness of God in Christ.

In his pride, man may scorn being associated with a worm; but we cannot afford to reject the reality of this position. God declares that it is true, yet surrounds us with gracious promises. One of the marvels of salvation is that although we are *worms* in His sight, He can use us to thresh mountains if we yield to Him. *"Thou worm...I will make thee a new sharp threshing instrument having teeth"* (Isaiah 41:15). What is this, but the symbol of a crushing victory? How God loves to take the weak to confound the mighty!

CHAPTER 17

THREE PROMISES OF CHRIST

I will send him [my Spirit].
—John 16:7

I will build my church.
—Matthew 16:18

I will come again.
—John 14:3

The Bible abounds in great and precious promises. In fact, we can look upon the Bible as God's promise-box. What spiritual treasures we discover as we feed on His unfailing promises—fully capable of fulfilling every one. There are, of course, promises made by man to God, and by angels and Satan to man. But those of inestimable value are those the covenant-keeping God has given to man. A distinction must be drawn between conditional and unconditional promises. God has promised to *"direct our steps,"* but only in the condition that we *"acknowledge him in all our ways"* (Proverbs 3:6). Too often we speak rather glibly of "the promises of God," as if there was some magical quality to them and that all we had to do to claim them was to press some magical button. Tremendous conditions, however, are often attached to divine promises before we can inherit them. They are of little value until we obey the commands they come with.

Without doubt, *"all the promises of God in him are yea, and in him Amen"* (2 Corinthians 1:20), but the *"yea"* must be born of obedience. When in obedience we say *Amen* to a promise, then that promise is ours. The Lord promises to carry it out: *"There failed not...any good thing which the Lord had spoken...all came to pass"* (Joshua 21:45).

> Standing on the promises that cannot fail,
> When the howling storms of doubt and fear assail,
> By the living Word of God I shall prevail,
> Standing on the promises of God.[43]

The Lord Jesus made many wonderful promises while on earth. *Three* of them are co-related and form a divine trinity. They are also *unconditional*, in that the recipient need not fulfill any condition to receive them. These promises were the advent of the Holy Spirit, the building of the church, and the divine promise of the second advent.

PROMISE TO SEND THE HOLY SPIRIT

We place this promise first because the coming of the Spirit was prerequisite to the fulfillment of the second promise, regarding the building of the church. This is confirmed by Jesus' statement that it was necessary to return to heaven so that He could send the Spirit to men. On earth, He could not be in more than one place at any given time because of the limitations of His humanity. However, He is able to be present everywhere through the Spirit—thus fulfilling His promise to build the church.

---

43. Russell K. Carter, "Standing on the Promises," 1886.

The Spirit fulfilled the promises of both the Father and the Son when He came at Pentecost. Jesus said to His disciples, "*I will send Him unto you*" and declared that the Spirit would come in answer to "*the promise of the Father*" (Acts 1:4). At Pentecost, we witness the fulfillment of this double promise; the Spirit came in His totality as a divine person. The disciple's instruction to "*wait for the promise*" had nothing to do with the redemption of the promise. The Holy Spirit could not come until Jesus was glorified, and so the waiting was related to His exaltation. (See John 7:39.) As soon as He entered the majesty on high, He sent the Holy Spirit.

> Our blest Redeemer ere
> He breathed His tender, last farewell,
> A Guide, a Comforter bequeath'd
> With us to dwell.[44]

PROMISE TO BUILD HIS CHURCH

In many ways, Peter's confession in reply to the Lord's question, "*Whom say ye that I am?*" (Matthew 16:15), and the revelation of Christ's purpose to build His church were the most important episodes in the New Testament. Here we have the first mention of the church which bears the name of Christ. The word used for church is *ecclesia*, which means "an assembly of called-out ones." In his defense, Stephen spoke of "the church in the wilderness" before the Sanhedrin. The Hebrew use of the word *church* marked Israel as a separate people, distinct from surrounding nations in that she constituted a theocracy, or God-governed people. God's purpose

---

44. Harriet Auber, "Our Blest Redeemer, Ere He Breathed," 1829.

was the creation of a spiritual theocracy with Himself as the Head. The emphasis, then, is on the personal pronoun *My*.

The term *build* means more than the act of building. The verb is made up of the noun *oikos*, or "a house," and *demo*, "to build," indicating the idea of a house-builder. As the perfect builder, our Lord speaks of the safe foundation He would create for the church. *"Upon this rock I will build my church"* (Matthew 16:18)—the rock not referring to Peter, as the Roman Church teaches, but on Peter's confession—Christ's deity. *"Thou art the Christ, the Son of the living God...upon this rock I will build my church"* (Matthew 16:16, 18). G. Campbell Morgan points out that the significance of the word *rock* is that it is never used in Hebrew Scripture to symbolize man, but always God. This is why we hear Paul refer to the church as *"God's building"* (1 Corinthians 3:9), that *"other foundation can no man lay than that is laid, which is Jesus Christ."* (3:11).

> The church's one Foundation
> Is Jesus Christ her Lord:
> She is His new creation.[45]

Pentecost is often described as "the birthday of the church." This *"habitation of God through the Spirit"* (Ephesians 2:22) is impregnable and invincible, for God said, *"The gates of hell shall not prevail against it"* (Matthew 16:18).

The modern use of the term *church* denotes any particular denomination of religious people distinguished by particular doctrines or ceremonies, such as the Roman Catholic Church, the Greek Orthodox Church, the Anglican Church, the Baptist Church, the Methodist Church, etc. But Christ said, *"I will build my church"* (Acts 2:42), the constitution of

---

45. Samuel J. Stone, "The Church's One Foundation," 1866.

which, according to the record of its establishment, is composed of men and women born anew by the Spirit and who continue in apostolic teaching and fellowship. *Only* those who came to experience the Lord's saving grace and power were added to the church. (See Acts 2:47.) It has been said, "God made the church—men made denominations." How true! Church today is not the spiritual, dynamic force she was when she turned the world upside down by the Spirit. Why? Because it is made up of many unregenerate members. They belong to the church, yes; but they are not members of His body.

PROMISE TO RETURN FOR HIS CHURCH

If Pentecost marked the commencement of the church, then Christ's return will mark her completion. His promise to send the Holy Spirit was final. (See John 14:26; 15:26.) The promise to build His church was initial and progressive. The promise to return for His church will mark the end of her sojourn in the world as a channel of expression through the Spirit. It is John who records the Lord's promise to come again for His own; nothing could be more clear and explicit than His statement, *"I will come again, and receive you unto myself; that where I am, there ye* [His true church] *may be also"* (John 14:3). As the first promise *has been* fulfilled, and the second promise *is being* fulfilled, so this third *will be* fulfilled, for Christ is not a man that He should lay.

If He is not to return as He said He would, then He is not the truth He declared He was. But He cannot act contrary to His nature or being. *"He that shall come will come, and will not tarry"* (Hebrews 10:37), and we are looking for the man who promised to return! The Lord's last recorded word in the Bible is a confirmation of His original promise to the disciples—His church in representation: *"Surely* [a word that implies the certainty of realization] *I come quickly"* (Revelation 22:20). No wonder John replied, *"Even so, come, Lord Jesus."* The question is, are we living and laboring in the light of that day—when the Lord will descend from heaven and snatch us away from a godless world to be with Himself forever? (See 1 Thessalonians 4:13–18.) May we never forget that He wishes to bring the blood-bought church along with Him, that she may behold and bask in the glory of the Father. (See John 17:24.)

> Mid toil, and tribulation,
> And tumult of her war,
> She waits the consummation
> Of peace forevermore;
> Till with the vision glorious
> Her longing eyes are blest,
> And the great church victorious
> Shall be the church at rest.[46]

---

46. Samuel J. Stone, "The Church's One Foundation," 1866.

CHAPTER 18

THREE FORMS
OF RESURRECTION

God…hath quickened us together with Christ.
—Ephesians 2:4–5

Awake thou that sleepest, and arise from the dead.
—Ephesians 5:14

The dead in Christ shall rise first.
—1 Thessalonians 4:16

These verses show that there are three different aspects of *resurrection*; yet they all refer to the same persons, that is, the redeemed of the Lord. There is a resurrection all believers have experienced and now have: a resurrection to which they are called, if they have walked away from the spiritually dead, and a resurrection awaiting them if they are in their graves when Christ returns for His own.

The first resurrection is *spiritual,* and it links us to the risen Lord along with the finished work of the cross. (See Ephesians 2:1–7.)

The second resurrection is *mystical,* in response to the solemn and tender summons of the Holy Spirit. (See Ephesians 5:9, 14–18.)

The third resurrection is *physical*, and will commence with the dead are raised to life again. (See 1 Corinthians 15:51–57.)

SPIRITUAL RESURRECTION

As *"the chief of sinners,"* Paul—brought out of the grave of sin by the power of the risen Lord—had much to say about *"the power of his resurrection"* in delivering the dead. (See Philippians 3:10.) *"God...hath quickened us together with Christ...and hath raised us up together"* (Ephesians 2:4–7). Again we read, *"Ye are risen with Him through the faith of the operation of God, who hath raised him from the dead"* (Colossians 2:12). Then we have the exhortation, *"If ye then be risen with Christ, seek those things which are above, where Christ sitteth on the right hand of God"* (Colossians 3:1). Evidently, all who are born anew are already risen, for it is often stated that those who are risen from the dead are in Christ. In addition, only by the Spirit can the spiritually dead rise to a higher, better life in Him *"who was dead, but is alive forever more"* (Revelation 1:18). The moment the sinner, long dead in sin, is born anew by the Spirit, he is immediately *"accepted in the beloved"* (Ephesians 1:6), not because of anything he has done himself, but because of all he becomes in the risen Savior. The father could say of his prodigal son, "[He] *was dead, and is alive again"* (Luke 15:24). Once having been dead in sin, the repentant, believing sinner now experiences what it is to be dead to sin.

MYSTICAL RESURRECTION

When resurrected from a sinful past, we did not leave inbred sin or the old Adamic nature in the grave of iniquity, but became the recipients of a new nature. Paul vividly describes this conflict between natures within the believer in Romans 6 and 7. Notwithstanding our resurrection from the past and our life in the future heaven, we still live in a world where the Wicked One rules. When Paul wrote, *"Awake thou that sleepest, and arise from the dead, and Christ shall give thee light"* (Ephesians 5:14) he was not addressing himself to the unsaved, but to the saints in the risen Christ.

Paul was quoting from Isaiah 60:1, of which Betty Eadie says,

> The prophecy is primarily addressed to Zion, as the symbol of the church. Nor do we apprehend that the application is different in Paul's use of the quotation, as the words are still to the church.

Later on, Christ said that the church of Ephesus had *"left her first love"* (Revelation 2:4). Spiritual slumber had overtaken her, so the solemn voice sounded, *"Awake!"* The word here translated "Awake" is nearly always translated "Arise!" in the New Testament. If the church had gone back to some of the dead things of the world, then she needed the restorative ministry of the Holy Spirit. God does not want His living ones mixed with the company with the dead: *"Awake thou that sleepest—not thou that art dead, but thou that sleepest—and arise from among the dead, and Christ shall give thee light"* (Ephesians 5:14). Alas! Many worldly-minded Christians should hear the divine voice asking, "What doest thou among the dead and in darkness, O child of God, risen with Christ to manifest the life He has given, and to walk in the light as He is in the light?"

How solemn the apostle's question is: *"How shall we, that are dead to sin, live any longer therein"* (Romans 6:2)? The measure of Christ's separation from the world is the precise measure of our separation. He gave Himself to "*deliver us from the present evil world*" (Galatians 1:4); therefore, we should not return to it for satisfaction and enjoyment! How base such a thought! A preacher of a past generation said, "*Let the dead bury their dead*" (Luke 9:60).

If Lazarus to whom Jesus gave life had preferred to return to the damp and gloom of the grave, if the fierce demoniac to whom He gave liberty had longed to return to his dwelling among the tombs, it would have been less shocking than the humiliating sight of a soul, claiming redemption through the blood of Jesus and oneness with our risen Lord, descending to the charnel house of the world to seek its ghastly amusements, and to nourish the fleshy nature with its corruptions.

PHYSICAL RESURRECTION

How impressive is the ring of certainty in Paul's declaration, "*The dead shall be raised incorruptible*" (1 Corinthians 15:52). Not "perhaps" or "may be" but "*shall be*"! The New Testament has much to say about the immortality of human nature, for man is not a perfect man without a body. A reconstruction of the whole man—body, soul, and spirit—is in the plan and purpose of Christ's redemption. Having a redeemed soul, we await the redemption of the body. Sin and death will not triumph over man, even to the extent of the material body. It will be transformed into a body resembling that of the risen Christ Himself. (See Philippians 3:21.)

When the Lord descends from heaven with a shout, the dead in Him will be the first to respond to the joyous call, *"Arise, my love, my fair one, and come away"* (Song of Solomon 2:10). On the contrary, the fate is sealed of those who died in sin. *"The rest of the dead lived not again until the thousand years were finished"* (Revelation 20:5), when they were raised to stand before the great white throne for the ratification of their condemnation. Although we linger now amid the shadows, mourning the loss of our dear ones, we hold onto the hope that we will be caught up *together with them* when Jesus comes, living together with Him forever.

> Gone forever parting, weeping,
> Hunger, sorrow, death and pain;
> Lo! her watch Thy church is keeping;
> Come, Lord Jesus, come to reign.[47]

---

47. Henry Downton, "Lord, Her Watch Thy Church Is Keeping," 1866.

CHAPTER 19

THREE DETERMINING WILLS

I will come to you shortly, if the Lord will.
—1 Corinthians 4:19

What will ye?
—1 Corinthians 4:21)

One cannot read Paul's epistles without escaping his constant use of threefold cords. How he loved expressing truth in triadic form! His trinities abound and afford preachers and teachers ready-made points to unpack.

We have a further illustration of Paul's unique ability to express truth in triple form in the text above. He was reminding the saints in Corinth of the *three wills*: (1) the will of the Lord—*"The Lord will"* (1 Corinthians 4:19); (2) the will of the believer—*"I will"* (verse 19); and (3), the will of the church—*"What will ye?"* (verse 21).

What a divine gem this is! It gives us such insight into the three great conditions of fruitful service! When we think of Paul's indomitable faith, unflinching courage, utter humility, extreme sacrifice, and holy yearning after souls, we might ask to know the secrets of such an outstanding character and career in the history of the Christian church.

THE WILL OF THE LORD

Paul was willing to go to Corinth to correct irregularities among the church, but only if the Lord willed it. The apostle heartily agreed with James' sentiment: *"For that ye ought to say, If the Lord will, we shall live, and do this, or that"* (James 4:15). Are we as careful in our walks to live within the orbit of the divine will? Peter affirmed that the main objective of our lives should be harmony with God's will. (See 1 Peter 4:2.) Dwight L. Moody's motto, which was engraved on his tombstone, was John's assertion that *"he that doeth the will of God abideth for ever"* (1 John 2:17).

When I was a student in Glasgow, Scotland in 1910, S. D. Gordon, author of the *Quiet Talks*, came to lecture on the gospel of John. I asked him after one of his sessions to write his favorite passage in my autograph album. Kindly obliging, he penned, "The greatest passion that can burn in the human heart is to know the will of God, and get it done." Without doubt, the knowledge and accomplishment of God's will is the greatest passion that can burn in both your heart and mine. The chief end of life is not to be good, or even to win souls, but to ascertain and achieve the divine will. Did not Jesus, who delighted in the will of God, teach us to pray *"Thy will be done"* (Matthew 6:10)?

But what, exactly, is the nature of God's will? The *will* is the center of our being; it is what our whole being revolves around, just like the sun rotates on its axis. Thus, as the will is the center of being, God's will represents all that He chooses, prefers, and eternally purposes. Furthermore, all the relations of men to God are determined by the attitude of man's will toward God's will. A. T. Pierson once said,

If we take the system of the heavenly bodies as an illustration, the sun may represent God moving round on the axis of His own will forever more, and all obedient souls may represent the planets that move about this central sun in the orbit of obedience, and all unholy and disobedient souls may be represented by wandering stars that will not move in the orbit of obedience to God, and to whom is reserved the blackness of darkness for ever.

A very real problem facing God's children is ignorance of His precise will in matters concerning personal life and service. Paul prayed that the believers at Colosse *"might be filled with the knowledge of his* [God's] *will in all wisdom and spiritual understanding"* (Colossians 1:9). F. B. Meyer used to say that our problem is simply that we are not *willing* to be made willing to know and do the will of God. *Willing* to be made willing! Is unwillingness really the cause of spiritual failure? We are not long in discovering God's will when we decide to *choose* His will instead of our own in any matter that arises. Are there any signposts that indicate how we can find God's will? We think there are. Let us consider some of these.

THE WITNESS OF THE WORD OF GOD

If anything is laid down clearly in the Word, it is that God will never give us any further light outside of the Word, which outlines our duty. He has revealed His will concerning man and the nations in Scripture. If God says to the sinner, *"Repent and believe the gospel"* (Mark 1:15), the sinner needs no further instruction of what is required of him. If He says to the believer, *"Be ye holy"* (1 Peter 1:16), then we know that

He wills us to be sanctified. No matter what question rises, Scripture gives the answer of God's divine will.

THE LIGHT OF CONSCIENCE

Then there is the light given by a conscience enlightened by the Word and the Spirit of God. All we need to do when we are compelled to make a choice is compare conscience with the will of God found in the Word; if there is harmony between them, we will know what our duty is. The psalmist speaks of guiding our affairs with discretion or *"judgment"* (Psalm112:5). With a sound mind or sanctified common sense, a balanced consideration of all facts will help us clearly understand the will of God in any situation.

THE LIGHT OF THE HOLY SPIRIT

Furthermore, the Holy Spirit is ever present to act as our infallible Guide. He prompts us to discern the soft whisper of the divine voice. Paul, who wrote most powerfully about the leading of the Holy Spirit, knew from experience the necessity of obeying His inner prompting. He wished to preach the Word of God in Asia after establishing churches in Phrygia and Galatia, but the Holy Spirit did not allow him to go; it was not His will. After, Paul made up his mind to witness to Mysia when he arrived, but *"the Spirit suffered him not"* (Acts 16:7). Again, the higher will intervened. The vision of Macedonian man explained everything. Certainly there were souls that needed saved and saints that needed edified in Asia, but not through Paul at that particular time. He discovered that the Lord's will for him was to preach the Gospel in Macedonia. (See Acts 16:1–13.) Paul saw God's will when he stopped doubting. Carefully heeding the voices of the Spirit and saints, we come to know the divine will, purposing to live in it.

Thy will, O God, is life,
Thy life and ours is one,
Be Thou our master in the strife,
Until Thy will be done.

THE WILL OF THE BELIEVER

Once we discover God's will, only then are we ready to say, "I will." What precious truths reside in the phrase, *"If the Lord will, we will."* It has about it the sound of marriage bells, "Wilt thou?—I will." The man full of leprosy pleaded with Jesus saying, *"Lord, if thou wilt, thou canst make me clean,"* and Jesus replied, *"I will"* (Luke 5:12). When two wills are fused into one, peace and security prevail. It is interesting to observe what Paul said, *"I will come to you shortly, if the Lord will"* (1 Corinthians 4:19). This word *"shortly"* actually means *straightway* or *directly*. If we call Him, *"Lord! Lord!"* (Matthew 7:21), it is incumbent on us to do His will without any hesitation. Too many of us have vague intentions to do the Lord's will…some time, in the future…but our response is very indefinite and uncertain. How did Paul react to the vision of God's will to preach in Macedonia? *"I was not disobedient to the heavenly vision"* (Acts 26:19). Paul waited to know the will of God, and then acted upon it without delay.

It is perfectly right for us to wait until we clearly understand God's will in any given situation, but the moment we understand, we are to respond without delay to perform His blessed will, which is ever good and acceptable to those who are willing to obey. Cheerfully and spontaneously we must obey the divine will. We must ask ourselves if we are prepared to say with our whole heart,

> In that resplendent will of Thine I calmly rest;
> Triumphantly I make it mine,
> And count it best.[48]

THE WILL OF THE CHURCH

Paul asked *"What will ye?"* (1 Corinthians 4:21) to the four conceited classes of men in the church at Corinth. There were those that gave themselves to rhetoric, logic, wisdom, and sophistry.

But the apostle's message to these men was clear and direct, *"I determined not to know anything among you, save Jesus Christ, and him crucified…And my speech and my preaching was not with enticing words of man's wisdom, but in demonstration of the Spirit and of power"* (2 Corinthians 2: 2, 4). The art of speaking to a godless world about the truth of the gospel is the art of commanding the power of the Holy Spirit. When Paul reached to Corinth, it was not to preach salvation but to administer rebuke. For that reason he asked, *"What will ye? Shall I come unto you with a rod, or in love, and in the spirit of meekness?"* (1 Corinthians 4:21). We are not told what the rebuke of those puffed up Corinthians was. We do know, however, that loving rebuke is part of the Bible, not detached from it. To quote A. T. Pierson again,

> The same word that is a rod of rebuke to the sinner is a staff of support to the saint. The same message over which a rebel sinner falls and stumbles is a stepping stone to the saint, and the same word that Paul spoke in rebuke to those in Corinth that were apart from God or backslidden from Christ became a word of

48. James Mudge, *The Will of God*.

help and strength and support to those that were truly God's.

What will ye? The wants of a congregation often unconsciously guide the preacher's message. The spiritual impulse of the true herald is to meet the needs of the congregation. Perhaps it was not Felix's inner will to listen to Paul's reasoning about God's righteousness, temperance, and judgment, but that was the message he needed—and it made him tremble! What a different story he would have had if he willed to do God's will.

Those who are called to minister the Word must never lose sight of the three wills operating where the gospel is preached. Preeminently, the Lord's will is to save all who repent and believe, for He has no pleasure in the death of a sinner. Then there is the will of the preacher, which reflects the divine will of God's salvation. In full harmony with the redemptive purpose of the Savior, he pleads with men to reconcile themselves to God. Now, the will of the lost often resists the other two wills. Jesus said to those He was willing to bless, "*Ye will not come to me, that ye might have life*" (John 5:40). He shed tears over sinful Jerusalem because they rejected His love: "*How often would I have gathered thy children together...and ye would not*" (Matthew 23:37).

When God fashioned man, He gave him the most precious gift of free will. The reason for the sin and sorrow throughout the ages is that this gift was used against the giver.

> Our wills are ours we know not why:
> Our wills are ours to make them Thine.[49]

---

49. Alfred Tennyson, *In Memoriam A.H.H.*, 1849.

By endowing man with freedom of choice, God never coerces him to will the divine will. His position toward all who hear His message is, *"Choose you this day whom ye will serve"* (Joshua 24:15). Sinners, therefore, will their *own* salvation or damnation; and saints will their *own* spiritual stagnation or sanctification. All who are responsible for facing the lost must realize the necessity of proclaiming God's love— that His arm is stretched out to save and that He never sends a sinner to hell for sin. If the sinner goes out into darkness forever, it is on his own volition.

CHAPTER 20

THREE APOCALYPTIC FROGS

I saw three unclean spirits like frogs.
—Revelation 16:13

What a fascinating and dramatic book Revelation is! There are those who find it so mysterious and impossible to understand that they leave it alone entirely. But as it is called *"The Revelation of Jesus Christ"* (Revelation 1:1), there is nothing cryptic about it. It is not an incomprehensible conglomeration of unintelligible symbols, but a divine revelation of the person and purposes of Christ. While it is prophetic and emblematic in content, it has no figure of speech that is not explained in some other part of Scripture.

It is not within the scope of this volume to offer an exposition on the book of Revelation.[50] Our intention here is to consider the significance of John's triad, under the emblem of "frogs," which we can also call "the trinity of hell." This trinity is not under the control of the Antichrist and does not form part of the kingdom that will be gathered at the Battle of Armageddon.

A previous statement speaks of *"the way of the kings of the east…[being] prepared"* (Revelation 16:12). Revelation draws an intimate connection between the drying of the Euphrates and the mission of the three unclean spirits. Both

50. For more material on Revelation, see author's *Studies in the Book of Revelation*, published by Zondervan.

are preparatory to the war of God Almighty: the drying of the river prepares the way for the king's march of the East and the unclean spirits gather the kings of the earth together at Armageddon. The three unclean spirits are the dragon, the beast, and the false prophet. These demon spirits work miracles, inspire nations, and mobilize vast armies to prevent the establishment of Christ's earthly kingdom. Furthermore, they work through the mouths of the dragon, beast, and false prophet. Throughout Revelation, the mouth is regarded as the source and means of destructive action. (See Revelation 1:16; 2:16; 9:17; 19:15; Isaiah 11:4.)

What a diabolical trinity these three form!

The Dragon not only works actively to effectuate his plans, but his two prime ministers share in his hellish work— the Beast, the vast apostate civil and political power of Rome; the False Prophet, who, by his lies and influence more readily acts upon the nations.

Thus, we have a combination of satanic power, apostate force, and malignant influence employed in the daring but hopeless task of thwarting the divine purpose. (See 1 Kings 22; Psalm 2.) In an effort to show how these three spirits are codependent on one another, Abraham Kuyper says that they indicate "the three great world powers of philosophy, politics, and pseudo-religion." Furthermore, John refers to these three evil spirits as frogs. This image is not at all mysterious, for we know that these are despised, small creatures. Joseph Seiss commented on hell's trinity as having not the shape, but the nature of frogs:

> These demon-spirits are the elect agents to awaken the world to attempt to abolish God from the earth;

and they are frog-like in that they came forth out of the pestiferous quagmires of the universe, do their work amid the world's evening shadows, and creep, and croak, and defile the ears of the nations with noisy demonstrations, till they set all the kings and armies of the whole earth in enthusiastic commotion for the final crushing out of the Lamb and all his powers.

Dean Alford uses the phrase, "The uncleanness and the pertinacious noise of the frog," to describe these creatures. Their croaks emit one keynote only. Such croaking is deadly monotonous and leads to nothing fuller or higher. Though the demoniac trio belongs together, it is profitable to consider them separately.

THE DRAGON

John identified the Devil as a great red Dragon: "...*the dragon...which is the Devil, and Satan*" (Revelation 20:2). This picture is of Satan in his worst character. However, Pharaoh and Nebuchadnezzar were also called "*great dragons*," because of their cruel and haughty independence. (See Jeremiah 51:34; Ezekiel 29:3.) Ten times over the word *dragon* appears in Revelation and it is the most fitting symbol of God's chief adversary—the relentless persecutor and murderer of the saints and sinners. Jesus named the devil, "*a murderer from the beginning*" (John 8:44). As the Dragon, he will lead all hideous and horrible schemes; he is also responsible for insatiable violence, represented by Job as the "*king over all the children of pride*" (Job 41:34).

Red, the color of blood, can symbolize the Devil's murderous nature. In addition, the adjective *great* suggests his preeminence in realm of evil. In fact, if you take away the *d* from *devil*, you are left with his creation—evil! Legend portrays the dragon as a monster in form and appearance, a combination of superhuman craft and cruelty. What a sad day it will be on earth when this hellish dragon is released!

Changing the symbol, John also calls the devil *"that old serpent,"* alluding to Genesis 3. Such a description draws on his subtlety, deceit, and craft. (See 2 Corinthians 11:3.)

THE BEAST

Revelation 13 solely portrays the nature and activities of two fearsome and awe-inspiring beasts. The term *beast* is sometimes used as a name for a power or kingdom, or of the personal head of each. It is often used interchangeably for an empire or its ruler. Scripture seems to carry a double meaning of the word: (1) the folly of acting without feeling responsibility toward God (See Daniel 4:16); and (2), the refusal of imperial powers to acknowledge God. (See Daniel 7.)

The Greek word used for "the beast out of the sea," is not *zoa*, "the living one," used in Revelation 4:6: *"the four beasts full of eyes."* On the contrary, the Greek word for "the beast out of the sea" is *therion*—meaning "wild beast"—describing the bestiality, demonism, rage, and reign of terror of the Beast and False Prophet. The beast John mentions in Revelation 13:1–10 is not only Satan's masterpiece, but the most awesome personage of himself ever to inhabit earth— the embodiment of misrule and anarchy, the personification of iniquity. The symbol of the *sea*, where this first beast emerges, represents what will be the agitated, turbulent, and unsettled condition of the world at the time. It also symbolizes the chaotic, revolutionary forces which produce such a brutal dictator.

It should be noted that John is not merely describing a principle or force, but an actual person. The ultimate doom in the lake of fire proves this. (See Revelation 19:20; 29:10.) This counterfeit christ—satanically controlled, energized, and sustained—will be the last Gentile ruler of the Gentile government. However, after the Beast is overthrown, Christ will fashion the kingdoms of this world into His own world-kingdom and reign supreme "where'er the sun doth its successive journeys run."[51]

THE FALSE PROPHET

Like the companion frog, the Beast, this unclean spirit presents himself more like a pretender lamb, coming out of the earth and portraying ordered government. These beasts are faithful allies and act as one, for both are puppets of the devil. Like his companion, the False Prophet is a person and suffers the same doom. He will be more feared than the *political* beast because he is a *religious* one. The arrogant imitation of the divine Trinity is complete when he appears, for the Dragon, Beast, and False Prophet will stand against God, Christ, and the Holy Spirit.

He is described as having *"two horns like a lamb"* (Revelation 13:11), identifying him as the false messiah, an ape of the Lamb of God. But whatever lamblike appearance he may assume, the *dragon* is deep-seated in his heart. He

---

51. Isaac Watts, "Jesus Shall Reign Where'er the Sun," 1719.

feigns to be a lamb so that he may assail the followers of the true Lamb. Our Lord prophesied that false prophets would deceive many, and this False Prophet will be the perfection and completion of all who contradict the original purpose of the *prophet*. When we compare Scripture, we find that he will assume the following activities: he will exercise the power of the sea-beast and carry out his will; he will empower an image of the Beast and demand absolute worship; and he will ultimately share the doom of the beast.

These two dreadful figures, then, will be Satan's chief lieutenants during the end times. The three together will be the "three radical foes of Christ and His righteousness." The dragon represents the hate of evil spirits; the wild beast represents the world-power hostility; and the false prophet represents the antagonism of world-culture and intellectualism. Each sends forth his emissary, appealing to the pride and passions of men. In unity, these spirits make up the wisdom James describes as *"earthly, sensual, devilish"* (James 3:15)—another trinity the preacher can develop. In many of our life-times, there have been *three* similar diabolical and destructive forces like the unclean spirits—Nazism, Fascism, and Communism—to name a few. Can we not look at this trinity of hell as a foreshadowing of the one yet to come? These modern forms of government have already drenched the earth with blood because of their lust for power. It seems that Communism is the epitome of all defiance to God—introduced by the Dragon, Beast and False Prophet.

CHAPTER 21

THREE GLORIOUS NAMES

A Savior, who is Christ the Lord.
—Luke 2:11

Isaac Watts marveled that even if we join all the glorious names of God's beloved Son, they are still...

> All are too mean to speak His worth,
> Too mean to set my Saviour forth.[52]

All of the names of the Lord found in Scripture, whether actual or symbolical, form a fascinating study for lovers of the Lord. In his massive work on the designations of God, Benjamin B. Warfield says in *The Lord of Glory*:

> If we are to take the designations employed in the Gospel narrative as our guide, we would say that the fundamental general fact which they suggest is that Jesus was esteemed by His first followers as the promised Messiah, and was looked upon with reverence and accorded supreme authority as such.

As we can see from this trinity of names, the angelic messenger of the incarnation did not doubt the deity of the babe in Bethlehem and the mission that brought Him from heaven to earth. *"Unto you is born this day in the city of David*

---

52. Isaac Watts, "Join All the Glorious Names," 1709.

a Savior, who is Christ the Lord" (Luke 2:11). Paul wrote of this triad of divine names as well—"*Jesus Christ our Lord*" (Romans 6:23). The difference between the expressions of the angel and the apostle is that in the angel's pronouncement, we see what Christ is to us, and in the apostle's call, we see what He ought to be to us by our own choices. Here we have a complete statement of Christ's *sympathy* with us, His *substitution* for us, and His *sovereignty* over us. What a trinity of profound significance this is for our hearts to ponder!

At the conclusion of his masterly work, Dr. Warfield discussed the three convictions of the early Christian church, which repeated quite often: Christ is the *Messiah*, Christ is the *Redeemer*, and Christ is *God*. These the great and emphatic assertions embodied in their souls. All three are summed up in the angelic announcement given to the shepherds: "*I bring you tidings of great joy which shall be to all people: for there is born to you this day in the city of David a Saviour, who is Christ the Lord*" (Luke 2:8–14). The whole New Testament could be an exposition of this announcement.

THE SAVIOR

The term *Savior* in the Old Testament is applied to both God and men. (See Nehemiah 9:27; Isaiah 45:21.) It appears twenty-four times in the New Testament, where it is used exclusively for the Lord Jesus Christ. Man needed a Savoir from the very first sin he committed, and Jesus was born for this very purpose. *Savior* was given to Him as a title of honor, Christians seeking a *Savior* to deliver them, even the "*Lord Jesus Christ*" (Ephesians 5:20; Philippians 3:20).

HE IS A DIVINE SAVIOR

Some of the ancient "saviors" who delivered Israel from her foes were human. They were instrumental in releasing people from physical dangers and strongholds. (See Jeremiah 14:8; Obadiah 21.) But Jesus was *born* a Savior to emancipate men from sin and Satan's stronghold. Thus, as Warfield says, "The significance of the epithet *Savior* applied to Jesus may perhaps be suggested by the circumstance that it is in the Epistles a *standing epithet of God.*" The phrase, "*the great God and our Saviour Jesus Christ*" (Titus 2:13), should be "our great God and Saviour Jesus Christ," and provides us "with one of the most solemn ascriptions of proper deity to Jesus Christ discoverable in the whole compass of the New Testament." (See 1 Timothy 1:1; Titus 1:3.)

HE IS A PERFECT SAVIOR

He could not be anything less than perfect because He was divine. Prior to creation and incarnation, Jesus was rich and resplendent in divine glory. He held a status far superior to all other created beings with inexpressible titles of deity and dignity. He is unique, supreme, and incomparable; there is no savior beside Him. (See Hosea 13:4.) He provided a perfect salvation for a sinning race through His death and resurrection. There is no other named under heaven whereby the sin-cursed can be saved. (See Acts 4:12; Hebrews 2:10.)

> There was no other good enough,
> To pay the price of sin.
> He only could unlock the gate
> Of heaven and let us in.[53]

---

53. Cecil F. Alexander, "There Is a Green Hill Far Away," 1847.

HE IS A UNIVERSAL SAVIOR

He became the Savior that God dearly loved. (See John 3:16; 4:42.) He was sent from heaven by the Father to be the Savior of the world, the good tidings of His salvation meant for *"all people"* (Luke 2:10). It was not exclusive to the Jews, but was also a free gift to the Gentiles. Christ had no respect for persons, but tasted death—the wages of sin—for *every* man. He died with outstretched arms, symbolic of His desire to embrace every human sinner.

> God loved the world of sinners lost
> And ruined by the fall;
> Salvation full, at highest cost,
> He offers free to all.[54]

HE IS A PERSONAL SAVIOR

Sadly, it is possible to speak of Jesus in a general sense as the Savior of the world, admiring Him for so great a sacrifice, while missing the truth that gripped Paul's heart when he wrote, *"The Son of God, who loved me, and gave himself for me"* (Galatians 2:20). Mary said in the *Magnificat*, *"My spirit hath rejoiced in God my Saviour"* (Luke 1:47). Although He made salvation *possible* for the whole world, it only becomes *actual* when we repent of our sins and receive Him as our personal Savior. C. H. Spurgeon used to say that his theology could be condensed to four words: *"He died for me."*

Furthermore, He is the Savior of the saints as well as the Savior of sinners. Paul assures us that He is *"the Savior of all men, especially of those that believe"* (1 Timothy 4:10). The Lord is able to save to all those for whom He intercedes. (See Hebrews 7:25.) Is ours a present salvation as well as a past one?

54. Martha M. Stockton, "God Loved the World," 1871.

Jesus is stronger than Satan and sin,
Satan to Jesus must bow;
Therefore I triumph without and within:
Jesus saves me now.[55]

THE CHRIST

As the purpose of the written Word is to reveal and extol Him who came as the Living Word, it is evident that Christ alone is the key to all Scripture. Did He not expound on His qualities throughout the Scriptures? Nothing, then, is quite as important for lovers than to study the *Christology*. Christ could say of the Scriptures, "These are they which testify of *me*." The name *Christ* occurs some three hundred times in the New Testament; the kindred name *Messiah* appears four times in the Bible. Both of these names mean *Anointed One*; the often-repeated words *anoint* and *anointed* are all the same in the original. *Young's Concordance* says that the title *Christ* is very significant:

> The official appellation of the long promised and the long expected Saviour, denoting His kingly author-ity and mediatorial position as "the Servant of the Lord." Jesus was His common name among men during His lifetime, and is generally so called in the Gospels; while the Christ or Jesus Christ is generally used in the Epistles.

The distinction is that He was sent as *Jesus*, that He might be *Christ*, the latter His official name as the sin-bearer, anointed as the Priest and Lamb at the altar of sacri-fice where *"he offered up himself"* (Hebrews 7:27). Thus, the

55. A. C. Downer, "Jesus Hath Died and Hath Risen Again."

emphasis is upon this precious name. Christ died, *"the Just for the unjust"* (1 Peter 3:18), to bring us to God. *Christ*, the Anointed One, is *Jesus* as the fulfillment of the messianic hope. (See Matthew 16:16, 20.) Herod inquired of the chief priests and scribes where the Messiah would be born. (See Matthew 2:4.) When John heard in prison about *"the works of the Messiah"* (Matthew 11:2), he sent and asked whether Jesus was indeed the *coming one*. The phrase "Jesus, surnamed Christ" follows a similar mode of speech in the case of like instances of double names, such as, "Simon surnamed Peter."

In ancient times, kings, priests, and prophets were consecrated to their offices by the ceremony of solemn unction with perfumed oil, known as *"the oil of gladness"* (Isaiah 61:3). This was because it occasioned great joy both to the anointed one and the other participants. Christ, the Lord's Messiah, or Anointed One, was set aside by the internal anointing of the Holy Spirit which manifested in mighty, public works—not to be confused with material oil or any external unction. (See John 3:34–35.) Because of this divine unction, no Messianic title is used more than *Christ*. The compound name *Jesus Christ* is rarely used in the Gospels, reserved as an august name and weighted with the implication of all His claims. After the Gospels, however, the combination "Christ Jesus" is used quite often.

When, by divine revelation, Peter made his remarkable confession to the Lord's deity, He instructed His disciples to *"tell no man that he was Jesus the Christ"* (Matthew 16:20). Matthew, having a deep reverence for His title, thought of it as his Master's peculiar property. *"Thou art the Christ"* (Matthew 16:16), said Peter; this declaration was accepted by Jesus Himself. The high priest asked Him, *"Art Thou the Christ, the Son of the Blessed?"* (Mark 14:61); Jesus replied, *"I am!"* (verse 62). When the Samaritan woman confessed her knowledge about the coming of the *Messiah,* Jesus prophesied that He would be the *"coming one."* (See John 4:25–26.) The prevailing messianic designation in Acts is the simple Christ, and Luke tells us that the staple of apostolic teaching is Jesus as the Christ. (See, for example, Acts 5:42; 8:5.)

Phrases common in the Epistles and Revelation such as *Christ Jesus, Jesus Christ,* and *Lord Jesus Christ,* testify to the of the early church's conviction that Jesus was indeed God's Anointed One.

Other combinations of the Lord's titles open us to a line of study which the reader could profit from: (1) The Christ of God, (2) Christ the Lord, (3) Christ a King, (4) Christ the King of Israel, (5) Christ the Son of the Living God, (6) Christ our Savior, and (7), Christ Jesus the Lord.

These august names all declare that the fullness of the Godhead dwells in Christ—whom God anointed with the Holy Spirit. In Him is abundant grace and power to meet every need until we finally awake in His likeness and see Him as the coming one.

> Yes, through life, death,
> And through sorrow and through sinning,
> He shall suffice me, for He hath sufficed:
> Christ is the End, for Christ was the Beginning,
> Christ is the Beginning, for the End is Christ.[56]

---

56. Frederick W. H. Myers, "Christ! I Am Christ's," 1867.

THE LORD

Occurring well over a thousand times in Scripture, this is the highest ascribed name for Him who became the man of sorrows. He died and rose again that He might be the *Lord* of both the dead and living. The disciples nearly always spoke of Him as Lord after His glorification. The Saxon word *Lord*, signifying a ruler or governor is applied to God, Christ, and the Holy Spirit. When Jesus takes control of earth, it will be as the Lord of lords. In prophecy, He is referred to as the coming Lord, a term representing the incommunicable name of Jehovah. (See Isaiah 26:4; Psalm 83:18.) In the proclamation of the birth of Jesus to the shepherds, the angel said that He was "*Christ the Lord*." Dr. Warfield raises the question:

> It seems impossible to suppose that the term Lord here adds nothing to the term the Christ—else why is it added? But what can the term Lord add as a climax to Christ? In Christ itself, the Anointed King, there is already expressed the height of sovereignty and authority as the delegate of Jehovah. The appearance is very strong that the definition of Lord is intended to convey the intelligence that the Christ now born is a divine Christ. Christ Adonai, that is, Christ-Jehovah.

After Christ's ascension, His designation as *Jesus* falls into the background and His Lordship comes forward. This is seen more in Paul's epistles than in Acts. *Jesus* occurs in the epistles seventeen times, while *Lord* occurs one hundred forty-four times—not to mention the ninety-five to ninety-seven uses of Lord in conjunction with the proper name. The frequent use of Lord is not only a formal mark of respect; it is also His definite ascription of universal dominion over the whole universe. (See Philippians 2:11; Romans 10:12.)

Paul recognized Jesus as the Lord of his life. Sure, the apostle knew that Christ would return to exercise His dominion as King of Kings and Lord of Lords, but his constant desire was to have Him reign as Lord over his entire being. He realized, unlike many others, that if He was not Lord of all, then He was not Lord at all. What about ourselves? Where do we stand in respect to His Lordship? We have received Him as Savior, and know He is Christ, but is He the sovereign of our lives, reigning supreme over the empire of thought, love, and desire? His shed blood has won Him the right to be our Lord. Does He have undisputed authority over all our feelings, powers, and possessions? We are no longer our own because we have been bought with a price.

I am the Lord's, then let me gladly tender
My soul to Him in deeds, not empty words;
Let heart and tongue and life combine to render
No doubtful witness that I am the Lord's.[57]

57. Karl J. Spitta, "We Are the Lord's," 1843.

CHAPTER 22

THREE MESSIANIC OFFICES

Jesus…a prophet mighty in deed and word before God and all the people.
—Luke 24:19

That he might be a merciful and faithful high priest.
—Hebrews 2:17

Where is he that is born King of the Jews?
—Matthew 2:2

The proper and symbolic names given to Christ in Scripture are profoundly expressive and "supply a most compelling mass of evidence—to Christ's pre-existence, and to His superhuman dignity," Dr. Warfield reminds us. Solomon informs us that *"a good name is rather to be chosen than great riches"* (Proverbs 22:1), and all of the names of Jesus are good names because they display Him as our "never failing treasury, filled with boundless stores of grace."[58] A man's name is what we use to distinguish him from others. When a name is spoken, it reminds us of a certain character, not always according to the truth, but our idea of the man nevertheless. Just so, we have expressed ideas of each person of the Trinity when we meditate on divine names and designations. When we come across His titles, we can say, "He is that."

---

58. John Newton, "How Sweet the Name of Jesus Sounds," 1779.

Mary named her son *Jesus*, meaning, "the Saving One," for this was the purpose of His incarnation.

He is often portrayed as the *Prophet, Priest,* and *King.* These familiar titles reveal how well he was at harmonizing the prophetic, priestly, and regal aspects of redemption. Furthermore, there is no better way to express Christ's relation to man than through his prophetic, priestly, and governmental work, which is so conspicuous in ancient Jewish history. The *prophet* is the instrument of teaching and instruction; the *priest* represents the ethical relation of man to God; and the *king* describes his role as the sovereign authority.

After the first sin, the Redeemer announced that the seed of woman would overthrow Satan, through who sin originally entered the world to mar God's handiwork. This is where we see the development of the Jewish people moving toward Christ, who they knew would come from the tribe of Judah. Christ reveals Himself through the three offices of prophet, priest, and king. He combined in Himself a threefold dignity to exercise a threefold ministry.

Prophets and priests became prominent in Jewish religious life as the nation emerged from a tribal state and became a national theocracy. The people knew that they would live under kings when the government transformed from a theocracy to a monarchy. Samuel was one of the first individuals to give dignity to the position of a judge. As a prophet, he enjoyed direct communication with the Lord; as a priest, he offered the appointed sacrifices; and as a king, he established the kingly office in Israel's development as a kingdom.

Warfield points out that with the establishment of the Davidic house, the three orders of God's service were completely installed: "the *king* was seated on his throne in Zion; the *priest* was ministering at the one altar of the nation, the *prophet* with the divine message was ever at hand to teach, to guide and to rebuke."

The tragic story of Israel, however, resulted from a deterioration of these offices. *Kings* became idolatrous and corrupt and the kingdom suffered, so much so that external foes threatened the nation's existence. *Prophets* proved to be a mixed bag; those who were true to God were compelled to warn and rebuke the sinful rulers and people. *Priests* were also unfaithful to the truth and purity of the religion they professed at times. Failure to realize these divine ideals produced a yearning in the hearts of the godly for a coming Messiah, who in some mysterious way would gather in Himself all the best hopes resident in the prophet, priest, and king.

CHRIST THE PROPHET

The first promise and prophecy of the Messiah as a prophet is found in Deuteronomy 18:15–19. (See Acts 3:22–23.) The test of a true prophet follows in verses 20–22. Isaiah gave a fuller revelation of the Messiah as the unfailing prophet of Jehovah (see Isaiah 49–53), but he also declared that He would fulfill the penalty of sin by taking it upon Himself (see Isaiah 53:5); and as a mighty victor, He would triumph over all His foes. (See Isaiah 53:10–12.) He appeared as *the* prophet of the Lord in the fullness of time, illustrating the prophetic office in an exalted way. Those that listened to His superb teachings recognized Him as the perfect prophet. They saw Him as a teacher sent from God, still recognized today as the most supreme moral teacher of all time. (See John 3:2.)

There is much evidence of His effective prophetic ministry today. He was designed for the prophetic office by the Father. (See Isaiah 61:1–2; Matthew 17:5; Luke 4:16–21.) He had, as the preexistent one, an intimate knowledge of God. (See John 1:18; 4:24; 16:15; Matthew 11:27.) He was to us the perfection of all wisdom. (See 1 Corinthians 1:30.) He always spoke with authority. (See Matthew 7:29; John 1:9, 17–18; Luke 4:18–21.) He was peculiarly fitted to be the revealer of God to man, His nature a combination of divine and human. (See John 3:34.) He came as the source of God's revelation, declaring Himself as the sinner's eternal life. (See 1 John 5:11–12.) He manifested a remarkable method of teaching through parable and proverb, making His message both powerful and easily understood to all who listened to His gracious words; many exclaimed, *"Never man spake like this man!"* (John 7:46). His testimony is described as the spirit of prophecy. (See Revelation 19:10.)

Jesus was the prophet that Moses predicted would come years earlier; the Lord raised him mighty in word and deed. The solemn obligation of all who profess His name is to hide His teachings in their hearts, that they would not sin against Him. May grace be ours to keep His precepts!

CHRIST THE PRIEST

While it is not within the scope of this study to trace the Moses' priesthood under divine instruction, Scripture still makes it clear that the Lord's priesthood is based on the priestly office found in the Old Testament. The concept of the priest as the mediator between God and humans was ingrained in the mind of every true Jew. The Old Testament picture of the priest teaches that (1) priestly acts were performed on behalf of the worshiper; (2) priests secured divine favor for man through expiation; and (3), priests ordered sacrifices to cover the sin of man. The latter act consisted of acknowledging guilt and satisfying the Law to receivefull assurance of divine forgiveness and God's favor.

The sacrifice the priest commanded and offered was never himself, but always an animal. Jesus, however, became both the priest and the victim. He declared that there should be an offering for sin and offered Himself to God as the spotless Lamb to fulfill this need. He was given the name *Jesus* before His birth, embodying the promise that the Priest would bear the sins of the world. Entering his ministry, He was always careful to observe the authority of the priest, but he also understood that He was the perfection of all the priesthood. (See Matthew 8:4.)

Christ saw Himself as the sacrifice, evident in His frequent references to death as the ransom for many. He spoke of His blood being poured out for the remission of sins. In addition, we find in the book of Acts that the apostles emphasized the sacrificial aspect of the Lord's priestly office. They saw Him as the Anointed One, fulfilling His messianic mission, and for this reason, concentrated their preaching on His death, resurrection, and exaltation. The Epistles reinforce Christ's priestly sacrifice. Paul's writings are drenched with the precious blood of Christ—the high priest after order of Melchizedek. The ultimate message of the apostle's teaching of the cross is that Christ is the only Mediator between God and man because He gave Himself a ransom for all. (See 1 Timothy 2:5–6.)

No New Testament book reveals the priestly conception of the Lord as well as Hebrews—which, if Paul did not write in its entirety, certainly contributed to. *High priest* occurs nine times in the epistle and *priest* occurs eight times—the favorite designation of Christ. There was a distinction between the high priest and the priest in the service at the tabernacle. Only the high priest was allowed to enter the Holy of Holies. In Hebrews, however, the two titles are synonymous when used of Christ, signifying His eminence in priestly character. *High priest*, however, is preferred by the author of Hebrews. He anticipated Christ's entrance into the Holy of Holies on the Day of Atonement. This was the central act of Christ's priestly ministry, that is, His entrance into heaven and His unceasing intercession thereon in. Hebrews is an eloquent exposition of the fundamental doctrine of Christianity: (1) the death of Jesus as the propitiation for sin, (2) the reconciliation of God through His sacrifice, and (3), His eternal intercession for the redeemed.

The following outline serves as a base for meditation for students who want to learn about the conception of Christ's priesthood in Hebrews:

+ He purged our sins through His sacrifice. (See Hebrews 1:3.)

+ He tasted death for every man and now delivers him from its fears. (See Hebrews 2:9.)

+ He is a merciful and faithful High Priest, who made reconciliation for the sins of all people. (See Hebrews 2:17; 3:1.)

+ He is the great High Priest who passed into heaven. (See Hebrews 4:14.)

+ He has all the virtues, authority, and power of the priesthood. (See Hebrews 4:5; 15.)

+ He was a Priest after the order of Melchizedek, which is far more excellent than the Aaronic priesthood. (See Hebrews 5:6–7.)

+ His priesthood is eternal in nature. (See Hebrews 8.)

+ He entered into the Holy of Holies to become the Mediator of a new covenant. (See Hebrews 9:11–15; 12:14.)

+ He continues the intercession he began on earth in heaven. (See Hebrews 5:7; 7:25.)

+ He has consecrated a new way to God for the redeemed. (See Hebrews 10.)

The Lord's priesthood is also discussed in the general Epistles and Revelation. The Scriptures emphasize that He was the sacrifice for our sins everywhere the priesthood is mentioned. He had power to lay down His life, which He did at Calvary; He had power to take it up again, which He did in His resurrection. And He entered into heaven during the ascension with a glorified body, marked by the nails—evidence that He, the Priest, became our sacrifice.

CHRIST THE KING

The first intimation God's purpose to save mankind carries with it the association of concepts of *rule* and *redemption*. The phrase *"Thou shalt bruise his head"* (Genesis 3:15) is the first promise and prophecy of the cross and indicates supremacy. Jacob's blessing of the tribe of Judah, from where our Lord came, reflects His dominion. *"The sceptre shall not depart from Judah...until Shiloh come"* (Genesis 49:10). Divine intimations of the perfect king became more numerous with the establishment of an earthly, visible monarchy. God said that He would set His holy king on Mount Zion. (See Psalm 2.) Royalty psalms are all prophesies of the King who was born in Bethlehem. (See Psalm 45; 72; 110.)

The witness of the prophets to a coming King, who would restore the glory of the Davidic house and His people, are too numerous to mention. The passages from Isaiah to Malachi concentrate on the royal authority of the coming one. *"Of the increase of his government and peace there shall be no end"* (Isaiah 9:7), that is, when Christ finally appears to establish His kingdom. The witnesses of His powerful works acknowledged Christ's assertions of His kingship here below.

Jesus was *born* a king. (See Matthew 2:2.) The phraseology employed here is of great importance: He was *born King*! In a royal household, a son is born a prince only if he is next in succession to the king, upon the abdication or death of the reigning sovereign. Jesus, however, was born a King. This is because He was King before He even entered this earth. He came as *"the King eternal"* (1 Timothy 1:17). There is a fervent expectation of a royalty and kingdom that will be restored throughout the New Testament. Jesus claimed the authority to accomplish the restoration of the kingdom to the Father. In all His parables and teachings on the kingdom, He alludes to His title as King.

Pilate asked Jesus: *"Art thou a king then?"* (John 18:36), to which Jesus replied, *"To this end was I born"* (18:37). Jesus told Pilate that the nature of His kingdom was not of this world, meaning that it was not based on material and external power like the Roman Empire, but founded on truth, righteousness, and peace. All authority was centered in Himself as God's anointed King. The kingdom He came to establish was not merely a righteous kingdom, but *the* kingdom of righteousness—the kingdom of God, not men. The nature of this heaven-founded kingdom was prophesied by Daniel. (See Daniel 7:13, 22–27.) It is noteworthy that Matthew applied Zechariah's prophecy to Jesus as He entered Jerusalem—"*Behold, thy king cometh unto thee*" (Matthew 21:5; Luke 19:38). In the great judgment scene that Matthew depicts, our Lord uses the title *King*. (See Matthew 25:31–40.)

One or two particular phrases in connection with His kingship call for our attention.

THE KING OF THE JEWS

Christ's prosecution was based precisely on His claim to be "*the king of the Jews*" (Luke 23:37–38), and was placed above His head as He died on the cross as a form of mockery. This messianic title also identifies Him with the nation He became a part of when He was born of a Jewish mother. When the Jews look upon the King they pierced, they will be born again as a nation, becoming "*Israel my Glory*" (Isaiah 46:13). Christ will be the glory of His people Israel during His millennial reign.

THE KING OF ISRAEL

This designation is practically equivalent to the *King of the Jews* and describes Jesus as the messianic sovereign. When He sits on His glorious throne, it will be as the King of *all* flesh, not only Israel. Israel was given many prophecies of His coming kingship. In once voice, the prophets proclaimed that the Lord Jehovah would come—that He alone would protect His flock and reign as the King in Zion. Christ would finally be found by Israel.

THE KING OF KINGS

The royal designation, *"The King of Kings, and Lord of Lords"* (Revelation 17:14), is also used in reverse, *"The Lord of Lords, and King of Kings"* (19:16). When the Lord fashions the kingdoms of this world into His own world-kingdom, all the Gentile kings and Lords will submit to His rule. His dominion will be universal as He rules over all earthly kings, stretching from shore to shore. He is the only hope of the sin-cursed world. When He finally comes to reign, all Jewish and Christian longings for a righteous kingdom will be fully realized.

Other designations worthy of consideration are King of Peace, King of Glory, King of Saints, and King in His Beauty.

The prophets, priests, and kings appeared to either help or save the people in some critical period. Whether the people received or rejected him, each one added to the knowledge of God. But when the Messiah came, He brought perfection to all these offices. He came as the prophet to reveal and declare; He came as the priest to offer and intercede; He will return as the King to assume His power to reign. He was a prophet like Moses and a priest like Melchizedek. In the future, He is coming as a King like David, perfect in holiness.

THREE GIFTS

In the trinity of gifts presented to Jesus as His birth, we find a symbolic recognition of His threefold office. *"They presented unto him gifts, gold, and frankincense, and myrrh"* (Matthew 2:11). The word *presented* actually means *offered*— a sacrificial term used to describe the gifts that were dedicated to God for His service: *"offerings to God"* (Luke 21:4).

One interpretation of this threefold sacrifice reads: "*Gold* a Monarch to declare, *frankincense* that God is there, *myrrh* to tell the heavier tale of His death and burial."

GOLD

This gift can represent Christ's royalty as King, seeing that gold is usually associated with kingship. Esther knew that the golden scepter was the emblem of a king's authority and will. Solomon was most lavish in his display of gold to show visitors his kingly position and wealth. Gold is also used to represent the rich and noble character that Christ alone makes possible. (See Revelation 3:18.) In sacrificing their gold, the magi not only wanted to give their best to Jesus, but also to recognize Him as the King of Glory.

Is this the offering we present to God—who, although so rich, became poor for our sakes? We cannot give Him material gifts as the wise men did in their day, but we can give our gold in the persons of others. Likewise, we can give to further His cause and relieve the needy here on this earth. Furthermore, the gift of gold usually stands for the consecration of the most precious things in life. Our material gold is His by right, for the silver and the gold are His. (See Haggai 2:8.) But what about our golden joys, golden love, golden successes—are they not His? If gold represents the *spirit* part of our being—the most precious possession human nature has—does He reign as King within? We see that Mary brought her "gold," for she could say, "*My spirit hath rejoiced in God my Saviour*" (Luke 1:47)! May ours be the glad surrender of the best we have in both person and possessions!

FRANKINCENSE

This white, fragrant tree gum, imported from Arabia, is harvested by slitting bark. Part of this blend of anointing oil was used in sacrifice, but not for the sin or jealous offering. The "incense" offered with the prayers of the saints should be translated "frankincense." This costly gift can indicate that, by divine intuition, they saw the purity of the babe. They sensed the fragrance of this prophet and the holy aroma of His obedience to the will of God.

In the great *"Psalm of the King,"* Christ is pictured as walking out of an ivory palace perfumed with garments of *myrrh, aloes,* and *cassia* (Psalm 45). When Mary poured the precious, perfumed ointment of her alabaster box over the Lord, it was not only its sweet savor that gladdened Him, but the love in which it came. Along with the magi, she saw Jesus as her fragrant master. It was the love of her heart consummated in material form. What can our gift of frankincense mean? According to John, it represents our continual prayers to Him. (See Revelation 5:8.) We must pray to the one who constantly intercedes for us. There are times when our frankincense may help the world more than our gold. If frankincense stands for the soul—the central hub of our nature—then all its powers should act as censers bearing incense before the Lord. May we not disappoint Him by withholding the fragrant frankincense of love, surrender, and prayer. Offering ourselves as *"a living sacrifice"* (Romans 12:1) will enable Him to see the consummation of His sacrifice. Service, prompted by an inner love, will always be *"an odour of a sweet smell, a sacrifice acceptable, well-pleasing to God"* (Philippians 4:18).

MYRRH

This extract, from the *balsamodendron myrrha* tree, was used as a perfume for sacraments and embalming. It was balsamic in color and had a bitter taste. It was also used as an antiseptic, known for its medicinal powers. The word *myrrh* means *suffering*—similar to the name *Smyrna*, where the saints suffered for the Lord. Myrrh, because of its medicinal qualities, can typify the healing powers of the Great Physician. However, when the soldiers gave Him *"wine mingled with myrrh"* (Mark 15:23) on the cross, it was emblematic of His suffering and sacrifice as the priest. Therefore, when the magi offered myrrh to baby Jesus, they saw in Him the Lamb who would die for the sins of the world.

Myrrh was the symbol of Christ's sacrifice, the surrendering of a bruised and broken body. He willingly offered His myrrh of anguish on our behalf. What does such an offering mean for the redeemed? It represents the death of self-ambition, self-pride, self-glory—putting life's glory to death. *Myrrh* can stand for the *body*, the part of our being which toils and suffers. Mary surrendered her *body* to the Holy Spirit saying, *"Be it unto me according to thy word"* (Luke 1:38). The call comes to us also to *"present your bodies a living sacrifice"* (Luke 12:1)—a sacrifice we live out in our daily lives. As myrrh relieved the crucified One of pain, may we be found carrying what J. R. Miller describes as, a flash of sympathy, out of which to pour some drops of consolation into a sufferer's heart, to lighten the gloom of a doleful heart, to cheer all the depressed, and weary, and desponding I am chanced to meet. If I cannot give *gold*, I would at least give some of *the balm of Gilead* to all faint and wounded ones at my side.

If myrrh suggests the sorrows, grievances, fears, tears, and separations of life, then let us take them to the Lord—the all-sufficient Friend who is always at hand to soothe and sympathize. Gold, frankincense, and myrrh are precious and prophetic gifts, none of which should stand alone. May we sacrifice them all to the Lord. G. H. Knight reminds us that...

> It costs less sometimes to give my gold than to give my sympathy. Gold may be given even when the heart is cold; but frankincense and myrrh can only be given by a heart that is warm. The gold without the frankincense and myrrh will not glorify my Lord, and ought not to satisfy me. And yet these last without the gold, if I have gold, will be valueless in His sight. We must go through the world with loving hearts, kindly words, and open hands.

A great hymn also reminds us of these gifts:

> As they offered gifts most rare,
> At the manger rude and bare,
> So may we with holy joy,
> Pure and free from sin's alloy,
> All our costliest treasures bring,
> Christ, to Thee, our heavenly King.[59]

Christ's threefold office can also be traced in His *three appearances*, which were already been mentioned. (See Hebrews 9:24–28.) One of William H. Robertson's poems was on Christ's threefold office:

> God's Word declares that Jesus came,
> A Prophet of God's grace.

---

59. William C. Dix, "All with Gladness Men of Old," 1860.

To cover sin "hath He appeared,"
His love redeemed the race.

The Word reveals that Christ now lives
A Priest before God's throne.
He is for us "now to appear."
By faith, we're not alone.

God's Word foretells our Lord will come,
A King to show God's power,
A second time "shall He appear"
Our hope, in earth's dark hour.

CHAPTER 23

THREE CHRISTIAN GRACES

Now abideth faith, hope, love, these three.
—1 Corinthians 13:13 ASV

Your work of faith, and labour of love, and patience of hope.
—1 Thessalonians 1:3

The English poet, William Savage Landor, wrote of the graces,

> Around the child bend all the three,
> Sweet Graces; Faith, Hope, Charity,
> Around the man bend other faces;
> Pride, Envy, Malice are his Graces.

While the last three qualities can hardly be called "graces," the first three are the graces that should refine the lives of all believers. In the whole realm of literature, there is no language or sentiment as beautiful as the hymn of love Paul wrote in 1 Corinthians 13. Had such a panegyric of love come from John, the apostle of love, we would have considered it natural.

When writing about controversial matters to the Corinthians, Paul preceded his approach through close, logical argument. Yet out of the blue and in the middle of a protracted argument, there flowed this remarkable poem on *love*, proving he was not all cold logic. Charles John Ellicott reminds us that this is an insight into the depths of his character: "The clear, vigorous intellect and the masculine energy of the great apostle are united to a heart full of tenderness." Paul made it clear that all moral and intellectual gifts are valueless unless a man has *love*—the love of God in our hearts, the love for one another, and the love for a lost, perishing world.

A remarkable trinity of graces concludes the apostle's argument—*"Now abideth faith, hope, love, these three; but the greatest of these is love"* (1 Corinthians 13:13 ASV). The word *now* does not refer this present time, but is actually used in contrast to the future. It is not temporal, but rather logical, and implies that the three graces are imperishable and immortal. Many of the gifts the Corinthians prided themselves with would cease when the perfect succeeds the imperfect. Unlike our gifts, the triad of faith, hope, and love remain exalted and purified in the next life. When Paul said that the greatest of the three is *love*, he did not suggest that this grace alone would remain and that faith and hope are no longer necessary. Ellicott said that the contrast was not "between love which is imperishable and faith and hope as being perishable, but between ephemeral gifts and enduring graces." The following lines are *opposite* of what Paul wrote:

> Faith will vanish into sight,
> Hope be emptied in delight,
> Love in heaven will shine more bright,
> Therefore give us love.

What three closely bound virtues! Here we have another threefold cord that cannot be broken.

FAITH

Although faith is mentioned first in the triad, *love* has the preeminence, as the *greatest* of the three. Perhaps faith is mentioned first because it is where we begin our spiritual pilgrimage—"*Whosoever believeth in Him should not perish*" (John 3:16). We are to walk in Him after we receive Him into our hearts. Saved by grace through faith, we go on living by faith. When we finally see the Savior we first trusted, our faith will glow even brighter, as it reaches perfection. A key word in Paul's summary on the graces is *abideth*, a word signifying eternity. In addition, its singular form binds "these three" together into one entity. Prophecies and tongues will vanish with time, but faith, hope, and love are not like the gifts granted to the early church. They will abide forever, beautifying heaven. Thus, it is only partially true to speak of faith being lost in sight, and hope in full fruition. Heaven would not be heaven if faith were absent.

A saint of old asks,

What is faith but a childlike trust in one wiser than ourselves? Even the holiest archangel must live by faith in whatever the all-wise God may say; and a continued trustful dependence on Christ will be the unfailing feature of the whole great host of the redeemed.

Here and now, faith plays a crucial role in the life of a sinner seeking salvation; it is the connecting link between a Holy God and a sinner desiring mercy—the essential condition of a spiritual blessing and the door into every new experience with God. Faith usually starts as a mental fact to the truths of the Gospel, and then develops into trust and obedience to the Lord Jesus in all He commands. Raymond Edmond said that this is "faith making the uplook good, the outlook bright, the inlook favorable, and the future glorious."

Augustine reminded us that "faith is secure in danger, but endangered by security." Paul made it clear that the climax of the faith life will be when we see Jesus and are as His body, made perfect through faith. (See Ephesians 4:12–13.) In the meantime, may we be strong in faith, giving glory to God. Nicolaus Zinzendorf taught us to sing,

> If the way be drear,
> If the foe be near,
> Let not faithless fears o'ertake us,
> Let not faith and hope forsake us;
> For through many a foe
> To our home we go.[60]

HOPE

This abiding grace is a major theme throughout Scripture, which is essentially a book of hope—bright with future prospects. *Hope* is one of the dominant words in the New Testament. The word itself implies the idea of cherishing something beneficial without actually obtaining it. It has also been described as "desiring with expectation" or "belief in the hope of obtaining." Therefore, the elements of *hope* are desire, expectation, and patience. Hope is not merely desire, for we may desire what we do not expect. For instance, we may desire to be rich, yet never expect to be. Furthermore, hope is not expectation only, for we may expect what we do not desire. A person expects to die from a dread disease from which he suffers, yet does not desire to die. Hope, then, is the combination of desire and expectation, exercised with patient endurance that can wait for the full realization.

---

60. Nicolaus Zinzendorf, "Jesus, Still Lead On," 1778.

What Paul calls *"the blessed hope"* is the appearance of Him who is *"our hope"* (1 Timothy 1:1). For the true believer, hope is not merely an event or advent, but a *person*. The Lord Jesus is *"the hope of* [our] *salvation"* (1 Thessalonians 5:8). It is *"through the Spirit wait for the hope of righteousness by faith"* (Galatians 5:5). But what is *the* hope of the righteousness we wait for? It is the crown of righteousness. (See 2 Timothy 4:8.) The apostle says that *"the hope of glory"* (Colossians 1:27) is the joy of seeing the indwelling Christ, who is the fulfillment of such a hope. Now there is not only *"the hope of glory,"* but hope *in* glory, seeing that it is an immortal grace. Hope will never cease if our lives with Christ in glory are progressive. Bishop Moule once said, "If hope lives by feeding on the present as the promise of the future, surely it will have a most abundant sustenance in that life as in this."

There must be room for hope in heaven, says G. H. Knight,

> ...not merely the hope of an enlarging insight into what are, at present, mysteries, but the hope of an enlarging experience of the "riches in glory," which are reserved for "the blessed of the Father." Heaven cannot possibly be merely the stereotyping of what has been given us, and wrought within us here. If, in the nobler life, God will have much to teach me which only faith can receive, He will also have much to give me which my eager hope will keep looking for with wonder and joy.

Comparing this abiding virtue with the previous one, we can say: Faith looks *backward*, while hope looks *onward* and *upward*. Faith is concerned with the *person* who promises and hope is concerned with the *one* and the *things* promised. Faith *accepts*; hope *expects*. Faith *appropriates*; hope *anticipates*. Faith *believes* and *takes*; hope *desires* and *waits*. Faith comes by *hearing*; hope comes by *experience*. Faith is the *root*; hope is the *fruit*.

As we await the culmination of all heavenly expectations, may we crave…

> Faith, patience imperturbable in Thee,
> Hope's patience till the long-drawn shadows flee.[61]

When the King was signaled in, the appeal to the enslaved was, *"Turn ye to the stronghold, ye prisoners of hope"* (Zechariah 9:12). The cell where the incarceration of political prisoners occurred at Field Castle was called "Hope Cell." The prisoners were sent there by the rulers of England and kept for as long as the king desired. What hope, then, could accompany the sorry plight of the prisoners? The prisoners obtained their release when the king died. Likewise, the King of Glory died and His regal title was nailed to His cross. Now eternal freedom is at the disposal of all sinners. And although our bonds are broken and we have received glorious liberty, we are still imprisoned. We are confined in the "Hope Cell" of this world, sighing for emancipation from the trammeling influence of flesh in the world. But when our crucified, risen, glorified King returns, we will respond with alacrity to His call: *"Rise up, my love, my fair one, and come away"* (Song of Solomon 2:10).

> "Upheld by hope," in darkest days
> Faith can the light descry:
> The deepening glory in the East
> Proclaims deliverance nigh!

---

61. Christina Rossetti, *Lord, It Is Good for Us to Be Here*.

"Upheld by hope," how glad the heart!
My soul is on the wing!
E'en now His hand is on the door,
He comes—my glorious King.[62]

LOVE

This Christian grace is supreme among the graces, sustaining its sisters—faith and hope. Having praised the superiority of love as the queen of graces, Paul urges us to pursue it wholeheartedly. The word *follow* means to "pursue without hostility." A word of explanation is required concerning the term *charity* as given in the Authorized Version, but translated as *love* in the Revised Version and all modern translations. The Greek word *agape*, or "love," is peculiar to the New Testament. *Charity* is an insufficient rendering of the original. Furthermore, the word signifies tolerance or almsgiving, which implies our sacrifice to feed the poor. Paul says that this, if unaccompanied by love, is worthless. (See 1 Corinthians 13:3.)

Love is a grace that will undoubtedly abide, for without it, heaven could not be a loving Father's home. We will not love Him as we ought until we enter that place. Once we are with our blessed Savior, love will continue to grow, both in range and intensity. Because *"God is love"* (1 John 4:8), it is the most godlike of the three graces. It will always remain true that *"the greatest of these is love"* (1 Corinthians 13:13). Why is it the greatest? For one, it was manifested by God on Calvary. This love also satisfies the demands of a loving God, seals us as His redeemed children, marks us as a true disciple, and secures our glorious eternity with God.

---

62. E. May Grimes Crawford, "Upheld by Hope," 1902.

> Beloved, let us love:
> Love is of God;
> In God alone hath love
> Its true abode.[63]

As a whole, these three virtues bind our heart to God, making our fellowship with Him more precious. They will continue to do so, making us more and more appreciative of His graces through the eternal ages. Presently, this triad of graces is the inspiration of all our efforts for the spiritual and material good of our fellowmen and a necessity for the sustenance and perfection of our inner life. Only faith can show us what God's will is—His will to purify inner mind and motives. Love makes us unselfish enough to serve God and others in any way, at any cost. Hope is indispensable to keep us patiently expecting results that have not yet appeared. As Christ's followers, we not only follow His bright example of faith, hope, and love, but yield to Him so that he can manifest the trinity of graces in and through our own lives. Will He remember at the close of life's day our work of faith, our labor of love, our patient hope?

These foundation virtues have been expressed in several combined forms by Mary Bazeley:

> We have access to God by *faith*; we rejoice in *hope*; we are filled with *love*, as the Spirit spreads it abroad in our hearts.
>
> *Faith* ever depends upon the supreme sacrifice of the Savior. *Hope* always builds on the solid foundation of divine righteousness. *Love* unceasingly rejoices in union with Christ as our never-failing treasury, filled with boundless stores of grace.

---

63. Horatius Bonar, "Beloved, Let Us Love," 1880.

Faith inspires us to *attempt* great things for God. *Hope* encourages us to *expect* great things from God. *Love* enables us to *accomplish* great things for God.

Faith trusts until the time of *full understanding*. *Hope* looks forward to the time of *full sight*. *Love* embraces the heavenly treasure even *now*.

Brother Lawrence, author of the spiritual classic *Practice of the Presence of God*, says of Paul's unique triad:

All things are possible to him who believes, they are less difficult to him who hopes, they are more easy to him who loves and still more easy to him who perseveres in all these virtues.

Hope unites these graces and lends inspiration as faith continues to mount high and love continues to stoop low in the interests of the kingdom of God. If faith wavers, hope withers and love weakens. Mary Bazeley concludes that of all our spiritual activity, faith is the driving force; hope is the incentive; and love is the expression of the heart's desire.

Faith is the *ear* always open to God; *hope* is the *eye* seeing Christ in every situation; *love* is the *heart* which stirs our work.

CHAPTER 24

THREE AVENUES OF TEMPTATION

The lust of the flesh, the lust of the eyes, and the pride of life.
—1 John 2:16

We must always remember that this trinity of evil appeared in John's exhortation to Christians not to love the world because it entices with lust and passes away into oblivion. We must yearn after the knowledge and accomplishment of the divine will if we want to live forever with God. (See 1 John 2:15.) The world makes a god out of this triad of sin; it worships it with the heart, soul, and mind. Regenerated though we are, we are still influenced by our Adamic nature, which revels in the unholy atmosphere of the world. Unless we are constantly on our guard, we will give into its lust. The three forms of evil John specifies are like Ana's three sons, which every true-hearted Caleb must drive out of Hebron before he receives the inheritance.

As we go back to the cradle of humanity, we see how our first parents fell to this threefold temptation. Standing beneath the Tree of the Knowledge of Good and Evil, they saw that "*it was good for food* [lust of the flesh]...*pleasant to the eyes* [lust of the eyes]...*to be desired to make one wise* [pride of life]" (Genesis 3:6).

Achan was another victim of this threefold temptation: "*I saw among the spoils* [lust of eyes]...*I coveted them* [lust of flesh],*and I took them* [pride of life]" (Joshua 7:21).

The devil also tried to entice Jesus in the same triple fashion, but there was no sin in Him for the enemy to appeal to. Tempted along the same three avenues we often are, Jesus did not sin, and the devil fled from him. James assured us that if we, too, resist the devil in the power of the victorious One, he will flee from us.

Later, John reduces the three categories to one—*"the lust of the world"* (1 John 2:17)—showing that whatever form this lust takes, it is still incompatible with the love of the Father. Paul said that *"All that is in the world is the lust of the flesh, the lust of the eyes, and the pride of life"* (1 John 2:16). Let us now consider these three harpies of the soul.

LUST OF THE FLESH

In his exposition on John's Epistles, Professor Findley says that...

> In this trinity of evil, there are two lusts and one vaunt, two forms of depravation arising from our needs and one from our possessions—unholy desire for things one has not, and unholy pride in this one has.

What exactly do we mean by the lust of "the flesh"? There are six main uses of this term in Scripture:

1. The material body—the skin, tissue, muscle, and blood covering the bones—*"well favoured...and fatfleshed"* (Genesis 41:2; etc.).

2. The quality of body: *"it was turned again as his other flesh"* (Exodus 4:7), a return from a leprous condition to normality.

3. The kinship of one to another by birth or marriage: *"flesh of my flesh"* (Genesis 2:24; etc.).

4. The contrast between the eternal God and man as an ephemeral creature: *"The Egyptians are men, and not God; and their horses flesh, and not spirit"* (Isaiah 31:3). All flesh is as grass in His sight. (See Psalm 90:5–6.)

5. The physical self—*"My flesh longeth for thee"* (Psalm 63:1). *"The flesh is weak"* (Matthew 26:41).

6. The element in human beings which is prone to sin. It has its own works, products, and characteristics. *"In my flesh dwelleth no good thing"* (Romans 7:18). *"The works of the flesh..."* (Galatians 5:19–21). This is what John had mind when he wrote of *"the lust of the flesh."* The original denotes the *nature* of the desire, not the *object* itself. It is the lust of a carnal sort, which the flesh prompts or occasions. It is the appetite of our sense in excess, out of order. The appetite of sense, however, is a gift from God, as is His provision to satisfy it.

It is the world's aim to pervert a gift of providence into lust, and to pander to them. Food is a legitimate and necessary expression of bodily need. We must gratify this need. But when the tempter told Jesus, *"Command that these stones be made bread"* (Matthew 4:3), his purpose was to swell desire into lust. As Ellicott expressed it,

> Lust of the flesh, is that proceeding from the earthly nature; all desire taking possession of the soul as a motive for thought and action which does not arise from principles in harmony with the will of God.

LUST OF THE EYES

Temptation and sin reach the heart through the eyes, for they are the windows of the soul. The *light* of the body is the eye, but it can also be the *lust* of the body. Our Lord declared that if *"thy right eye offend thee* [the Greek implies to cause another to stumble or fall into a snare], *pluck it out, and cast it from thee"* (Matthew 5:29). This phrase should not be interpreted literally. G. Campbell Morgan says,

> The seat of evil lies in the will, not in the organ of sense or action, and the removal of the instrument might leave the inward taint unpurified. What is meant is that any sense, when it ministers to sin is an evil and not a good, the loss of which would be the truest gain. This is a warning that taste, culture, aesthetic refinement may but make our guilt and our punishment more tremendous. It were better to be without them than "and for life's sake to lose life's noblest ends."

Distinct from *"the lust of the flesh"* and *"the lust of the eyes"* is lust or desire that has its seat in onlooking. This does not just mean that the flesh lusts through the eyes, or that the eyes minister to the lust of the flesh, but that the eyes themselves have their own lust, satisfied with mere sight. One of the sad burdens David speaks of in the Psalms was the temptation of jealousy when he looked at others' possessions. *"I was envious at the foolish, when I saw the prosperity of the wicked"* (Psalm 73:3). It is what we see in the corrupt world around us that, like Job, we have to make a covenant with our eyes. (See Job 31:1.) May we cultivate the pure eye Jesus had: *"Beholding him* [He] *loved him"* (Mark 10:21).

Sight is gift from God, but can be prostituted to evil, giving way to bewitching perils and glamorous corruption. When Eve *saw* that *"the tree was pleasant to the eyes"* (Genesis 3:6), she gave expression to the sense of beauty and glory in her soul. There are so many temptations reserved for the eye alone. The problem is when we start craving things for themselves alone. As an end in themselves, these things have no part in the maintenance of fellowship with the Father. If what we see stains the soul, then it is *"not of the Father,"* but *"of the world"* (Proverbs 27:20).

THE PRIDE OF LIFE

The New English Bible translates this phrase, *"The glamour of its life, springs not from the Father but from the godless world"* (1 John 2:16 NEB). There are many things in our lives of which we are justly proud, but the *pride* John speaks of is not to be admired. The Greek word he used is only found in one other place in the New Testament—in the admonition of James, *"Ye rejoice in your boastings"* (4:16). It is tantamount to the *"vain glory"* Paul spoke of in Galatians 5:26 and Philippians 2:3. Bishop Moule once said that the phrase "pride of life" represents,

> ...a boastful, ostentatious attitude in regard to the good things of this life allotted by God to be spent in His service. All living up to a supposed social position instead of as the responsible steward of undeserved bounties, is hereby condemned.

God hates the sin of false pride; it is perhaps the most subtle and devastating form of satanic temptation we have to guard against. Pride and ambition of intellect was the temptation Eve succumbed to when Satan promised her that she would become like a god, with the knowledge of good and evil. Jesus also experienced this temptation when the tempter chided Him, *"If thou be the Son of God, cast thyself down"* (Matthew 4:6). But Christ refused to parade His deity and supernatural powers before the multitude. Surely cultivating and maintaining a proud life for its own sake, as well as striving after a superficial ostentation to be correct and commendable, knowing full well it covers a jealous, envious heart, lead to the destruction of the soul. The only glory Paul prided himself in was the glory of the Lord he so dearly loved. He had learned how to "lay in dust life's glory dead."[64] What of ourselves?

The lust of the flesh may be mortified, crucified and nailed to the cross. The lust of the eyes may be overcome by the mighty power of love, the love which *"envieth not"* (1 Corinthians 13:4).

The pride of life, however, may continue to cling to us. It is not easy to rid ourselves completely of this worldly weakness. The world's vain pomp and pride is most appealing, but as John declares, *"it is not of the Father but of the world"* (1 John 2:16)—avoided by His children at all costs. The only way we can conquer these subtle foes is to ask ourselves, as we face the sharp line of demarcation between the allowed and forbidden, "Is this of the Father? Does it meet with His approval, and tend to His glory? Can we engage in this and still meet unabashed the Father's eye?" If an inner voice replies "no," then we know they must be defeated. We triumph when we make our physical, mental, and spiritual selves *"servants of righteousness"* (Romans 6:18).

---

64. George Matheson, "O Love that Wilt Not Let Me Go," 1882.

Related to the three avenues of temptation are the three greatest enemies of man: the *world*, the *flesh*, and the *devil*. The significance of this relationship is so obvious that no further exposition is necessary, except to say that such a trinity of hell is in contrast to the Trinity of heaven. The *world* is set against the Father. (See 1 John 2:15, 16.) The *flesh* is set against the Holy Spirit. (See Galatians 5:17.) The *devil* is set against the Son as the living Word and the written Word. (See Matthew 4:1; 1 John 3:8; John 8:44.)

CHAPTER 25

THREE DREAD WORDS

The transgression…sins…iniquity…
—Daniel 9:24

What a fearful triad this is! An impressive fact about the prayer of confession is that although Daniel bore, in the words of Tennyson, "the white flower of a blameless life," he still identified himself with the sins of the people. Plural pronouns, like *we* and *our*, are prominent in his cry for mercy. Daniel prayed in his confession, *"We have sinned, and committed iniquity"* (Daniel 9:5), but there is no record of the prophet associating with the nation's rebellion against God. King Darius admitted that Daniel was an obedient servant of the Lord, and spoke of him as *"thy [Daniel's] God"* (Daniel 6:20).

The prophet's penitential sorrow regarding his country's transgressions reveals his deep concern for the people's guilt. He interceded for them before the Lord, pleading because of His righteousness, His own sake, and His mercies. (See Daniel 9:16–18.) F. B. Meyer expressed it this way:

> Here was the secret of Daniel's strength; he was concerned most of all for the name of his God and for His interests in His sanctuary, His city and His people. He has not one single thing to ask for himself or even for his companions in captivity; but his whole heart goes out in supplication for the honour of the

name of his God, and for the interests of God upon the earth.

No wonder his passionate heart-plea found an immediate response in the divine heart.

Our immediate concern is to understand the three terms Daniel used to describe the evil of the people as he came into the presence of *"the great and terrible God"* (Nehemiah 1:5). We will look at them in the order that they appear in his petition.

SIN

Scripture gives us many definitions of sin. Paul summarizes them all Romans 3:23, saying that all who sin *"come short of the glory of God."* The statement from the Westminster Catechism cannot be improved on: *"Sin is any want of conformity unto, or transgression of, the law of God."* The term *sin* means "missing the mark, wandering from a marked out path of uprightness and honor, doing or going wrong." And with the exception of Jesus Christ, all from Adam on have sadly missed the mark and wandered far from righteousness. The Bible is not the only source that testifies universal sin, but also conscience, experience, and observation.

We can describe man's sin in a twofold way. First and foremost, he has a sinful nature. As a sinner from birth, he has an inherited disposition to sin, which affects every part of his being; he is by nature a child of wrath. This is what is known as "original sin." Because the federal head of all humanity sinned, so did the rest of the human race. *"In Adam all die"* (1 Corinthians 15:22). The fall of our first parents subjected all to sorrow, suffering, and death. The principle of heredity affects the whole human race.

But man is a sinner by practice as well as by birth. It was not long before original sin revealed itself in a child. Then original sin became committed sin. Although we are not held responsible for our inherited sinful nature, God does hold us responsible for our personal sins against Him and His commands. If there is any distinction between *sin* and *sins*, it is that *sin* is the root, referring to the Adamic depraved nature, and *sins* are the fruit. All have sinned, and all *do* sin. Actual sin is the act of a free moral agent violating divine commands. A man may appear outwardly moral and honest, even *good* in the eyes of the world, but he is lost in the sight of God as the worst, depraved sinner alive if he does not have a regenerated heart:

> By nature and by practice far—
> How very far from God!
> Yet now by grace brought nigh to Him,
> Through faith in Jesus' blood.[65]

It was because all men were lost in sin that the Lord Jesus assumed a human nature, and in *our* flesh destroyed the works of the devil, taking away our sins. "*Him who knew no sin he made to be sin* [not a "sinner"] *on our behalf; that we might become the righteousness of God in him*" (2 Corinthians 5:21 RV). The works of the devil produce ignorance, sin, and death. The Mediator Jesus, in His threefold office as prophet, priest, and king, defeated Satan's works! The glory of the gospel is that the precious blood shed at Calvary can make the vilest clean.

> My sin—oh, the bliss of this glorious thought—
> My sin, not in part, but the whole

---

65. Catesby Page, "A Mind at Perfect Peace."

Is nailed to His Cross, and I bear it no more;
Praise the Lord, praise the Lord, O my soul![66]

TRANSGRESSION

Any form of transgression is sin against law. The word itself means "passing beyond the limit." We often see the sign *Trespassers Will Be Prosecuted*. This means that if a person goes beyond the limit prescribed, he will be taken to court and either fined or sent to prison. God gave us rules in His Word that both respect human belief and behavior but also warn of the punishment if these broken rules. "*The soul that sinneth* [goes beyond divine limits] *it shall die*" (Ezekiel 18:20). A distinctive character of sin is the transgression of God's law, man doing his own will instead of God's will. This is what Jeremiah spoke of when he said, "*Thus saith the LORD...return ye now every one from his evil way, and make your ways and your days good. And they said, There is no hope: but we walk after our own devices, and we will every one do the imagination of his evil heart*" (Jeremiah 18:11–12).

We live in a society where man is "*not subject to the law of God, neither indeed can be*" (Romans 8:7). A lot is said about our permissive society, but there is too much that passes beyond the divine limits, breaking God's moral law.

Transgression, then, is a violation of law. Where there is no law, there is no transgression; however, Paul teaches that there is still sin. (See Romans 4:15; 5:14.) God gave Moses the Law on Mount Sinai, and although, there was no transgression from Adam to Moses, there was still death, the penalty of sin. Adam received and transgressed an exclusive law, resulting in a sinful, depraved nature he passed onto his

66. Horatio G. Spafford, "It Is Well with My Soul," 1873.

descendants. (See 1 Corinthians 15:22.) *"The tree of the knowledge of good and evil, thou shalt not eat of it"* (Genesis 2:17).

There is no relief or pardon for transgressors apart from the Savior, who made intercession for all sinners. Greater still, although He always lived within the orbit of God's will and never strayed, He was still numbered with transgressors. (See Isaiah 53:12; Mark 15:28.) Redemption was secured for our transgressions at Calvary and through faith, we can be sure that our transgressions have been blotted out. (See Hebrews 9:15; Psalm 51:1; Isaiah 44:22.)

INIQUITY

This commonly used word for evil further illustrates how a sinner willingly departs from the right way, for it means "a turning aside from the straight path," and conveys the same thought in the prophet's metaphor of sinners as being like sheep that have *"gone astray"* (Isaiah 53:6). Sin is not simply a defect in man's nature, but an evil will, a tendency toward his own way in preference to Him who is *the Way*. Because it resides in the domain of the will, sin affects the whole nature. "Crookedness" as opposed to "straightness" and "uprightness," wrong as opposed to that which is right—this is implied by the term *iniquity*, which in the New Testament is represented by two Greek words. *One*, used eleven times, means "lawlessness, contempt, violation of law"; the other word means "unrighteousness" and is translated "iniquity" six times and "unrighteousness" sixteen times. When, describing the characteristic features of the end of the Gentile age, Jesus said, "Iniquity shall abound," the word here implies "the mystery of lawlessness" which Paul mentions.

The broad path that man chooses ends in death; but the narrow path which Jesus calls us to journey over is life. The message of the Cross is that the Lord willingly bore the *iniquity* of us all. *"We have turned every one to his own way; but the Lord hath laid on Him the iniquity of us all"* (Isaiah 53:6). The psalmist, also dealing with this three-headed cerebus we have considered, said, *"I acknowledge my sin unto thee, and mine iniquity have I not hid. I said, I will confess my transgressions unto the Lord; and thou forgavest the iniquity of my sin"* (Psalm 32:5).

As a pardoned penitent, David knew what it was to have the three burdens of *sin*, *iniquity*, and *transgressions* rolled into one, and then to know what it was to be relieved of his great evil. He knew how helpless he was to shake off his load of guilt, but he learned that there was forgiveness with God that He might be feared. Afterward he exhorted others to cast their burden upon the Lord. The psalmist's confession was full and deep, and he realized that God's pardoning grace as whole-hearted as was his confession. His *sin*, his constant failure to measure up to divine requirements, was blotted out. As a helpless sinner he came to see that all he could do was to fling himself and his sin upon the mercy of God. His *iniquity*, his perverse leaving of the will of God for a crooked path of his own, was a real weight upon his soul, and David did not try to hide it from God. (See Psalm 32:5.) Then God forgave him the iniquity of his sin (see Psalm 32:2), and he purposed never to regard it in his heart again (see Psalm 66:18). His *transgressions*—his rebellious breaking through the fence of God's restraining law—these he confessed unto the Lord (see Psalm 32:5), and this enabled him to sing about his transgressions being removed from him as far as the east is from the west (see Psalm 103:12)—a distance no man can measure. *Sin*, whatever its phase, was dealt with once and for all at the cross, and as a consequence we can have the joy which comes from knowing our sins are forgiven.

CHAPTER 26

THREE AREAS OF UNCHANGEABLENESS

Jesus Christ, the same yesterday, and to-day, and for ever.
—Hebrews 13:8

Among the attributes of deity is *immutability*—"*I am the Lord, I change not*" (Malachi 3:6). Barbarians change their minds (see Acts 28:6)—we all do, often to our cost—but "unalterableness" is the mark of the Eternal One. God's commands are unalterable, just as His being is invariable. Because of all that He is in Himself, He cannot be anything but stable and permanent. All that He was in past eternity He is in time, and will be throughout the coming eternity. Past, present, and future all testify to His unchangeableness. This is *His* glory and *our* consolation. Such are the sentiments of Anna Shipton:

There is light for me on the trackless wild
As the wonders of old I trace,
When the God of the whole earth went before
To search me a resting place.
Has He changed for me? Nay, He changes not.
He will bring me by some new way,
Through fire and flood and each crafty foe,
As safely as yesterday.
Alas! we are creatures of change,

and we live in a changing world—
Change and decay in all around I see;
O Thou who changest not, abide with me.

Circumstances, friends, health, desires—all of these change as we live out our lives amid the changing seasons of each new year. We need a Friend who changes not, One who is ever the same; and this One we have in Christ.

All may change, but Jesus never,
Glory to His name.

YESTERDAY

Evidently the writer had the story of our Lord's gracious earthly life in mind when he wrote of His "yesterday." What a wonderful portrait the Gospels present of His life and labor among men! He is depicted in all His love, compassion, patience, understanding, mercy, forgiveness, authority, and power. It is legitimate enough to stretch the application of the past to include the "yesterday" of the Old Testament, which concealed the Lord revealed in the New Testament. All the glorious virtues associated with Jehovah in the Law and the prophetic books adorned the Lord's life in the Gospels, for He is ever the same. If it were not so, the value of the gospel for us would be almost totally lost. The Greek word for "same" is *autos*, meaning "Himself; and the word order in the original text—*Jesus Christ yesterday and today the same* [He Himself] *and for ever*" (Hebrews 13:8). His inherent constancy promises that His love, sympathy, and power toward us will never change. He is eternally stable, never varying in His dealings with men.

TODAY

The Master, who was all to the disciples in the days of His flesh, has remained near to the saints since He ascended on high. The promise for His saints in all succeeding, changing ages is: *"I will never leave nor forsake thee"* (Hebrews 13:5). Just as He walked with His chosen ones on earth, He still walks with us, our best companion on life's highway. It is striking to see that Hebrews 13:8 is surrounded by verses with contrasting ideas—that like a great mountain in the midst of the sea, Jesus Christ stands forever the same. His claim to always be the same is quite remarkable, seeing that it has been almost two millenniums since He walked here on earth. No one but God could make such a claim. The rock foundation of our lives, then, is that the Christ of our yesterday is the Christ of our today. Having been mindful of us, He will continue to bless us. F. B. Meyer said, "The memoir of this Christ is not a memoir of the dead, but of the living Lord, who is with me, for me, in me always, and in every place; His love and sympathy and power are the same as they ever were."

FOREVER

This word not only changes our future here below, but also the eternal ages beyond our life span. Heaven, in all its glory, cannot change the Savior's heart of love. "His earthly robe of human tenderness did not, like Elijah's mantle, drop off as He passed into the skies." How much comfort the disciples must have experienced when the heavenly messengers appeared to them and assured them that when He returned, it would be *"this same Jesus"* (Acts 1:11). How blessed we are to know that when we meet Him in glory, He will be the same unchanging Jesus! Although He is wearing a nobler form than He did here on earth, the same loving heart beats inside His glorified body.

> Yesterday, today, forever,
> Jesus is the same.
> All may change, but Jesus never!
> Glory to His name.[67]

What a great rock of immutability this is for our wave-tossed hearts! We can be safe there. There may be times when we find ourselves trembling on that Rock, but the Rock will never tremble under us. Whatever changes life brings, we can be sure that He who promised to be with us always will prove Himself faithful like He has always been. He is *"the Lord God Almighty, which was, and is, and is to come"* (Revelation 4:8). How apt and expressive are the words of S. Trevor Francis:

> My yesterday was Christ upon the tree,
> Who bore the condemnation due to me.
> Today I journey on and He shall lead,
> He knows my pathway, and He knows the need.
> Tomorrow is not: but His wisdom plans,
> I leave my future in His loving hands.

---

67. Albert B. Simpson, "Yesterday, Today, Forever," 1890.

CHAPTER 27

THREE GOD-CONTROLLED PATRIARCHS

I am the God of Abraham, and the God of Isaac, and the God of Jacob...this is my name for ever.
—Exodus 3:15

This trio of Old Testament worthies is associated with the eternal name of God. So why include the names of these three Jewish leaders with the august divine name? Commissioned by God to deliver His people from Egyptian bondage, Moses asked how he was to identify the one sending him with the message of emancipation for the slaves: *"When I come unto the children of Israel, and shall say unto them, The GOD of your fathers hath sent me unto you; and they shall say to me, What is his name? what shall I say unto them?"* (Exodus 3:13).

God replied, *"I AM THAT I AM; and he said, Thus shalt thou say unto the children of Israel, I AM hath sent me unto you"* (verse 14).

Then, expanding such a mysterious name, God continued in His commission to Moses: *"Thus shalt thou say unto the children of Israel, The LORD God of your fathers, the God of Abraham, the God of Isaac, and the God of Jacob, hath sent me unto you: this is my name for ever, and this is my memorial unto all generations"* (verse 15).

Having lived among the Egyptians for so long, the Jews became accustomed to every heathen god having a specific name. Up to this time, they called God by the following titles: *Elohim, Shaddai,* and *Jehovah.* Yet none of these passed into a proper name. This explains Moses' question and God's reply. It seems as though "*I Am that I Am*" is not a proper name, but rather a deep and mysterious statement of the divine nature which could not be described with human words or conceived by human thought. It was as if God said, "I exist in such a way that My whole inscrutable nature is implied in My existence. I exist, as nothing else does—necessarily and eternally. If I am to give Myself a name that expresses My nature, so far as language can do, let Me be called I Am. Tell them I Am has sent me to you."

As we know, Jesus used this name to describe His preexistence, deity, and divine authority: "*I Am the way*" (John 14:6). The prophet Isaiah also used this name: "*I Am and there is none beside me*" (Isaiah 45:6). As Ellicott states, this implies,

1. An existence different from all other existence.

2. An existence out of time, with which time has nothing to do. (See John 8:58.)

3. An existence that is real, all others shadowy.

4. An independent and unconditioned existence, from which all others derive and depend on.

Then, the *I Am* becomes *Jehovah* and *God of your fathers,* all three specifically named Abraham, Isaac, and Jacob. *Jehovah* is the predominant name of God used in the Old Testament, while Lord takes its place in the New Testament.

This trinity of Jewish fathers appears three times in the New Testament, each in a different connection.

A PROOF OF IMMORTALITY

Jesus said that those who inherit the kingdom of heaven will be true believers from the four corners of the earth and have the opportunity to sit with Abraham, Isaac, and Jacob. (See Matthew 8:11; Luke 13:29.) Surely this implies that these men were already in the kingdom. The very language suggests the immortality of these conspicuous Old Testament figures. It is untenable to think of the *living* associating with the *dead*.

We find stronger evidence of unending existence in Matthew 22:23–33. The Lord refers to these men in His discourse on resurrection to the Sadducees, who rejected this doctrine. Jesus said, *"Have ye not read that which was spoken unto you* [as representative of the Jewish nation] *by God, saying, I am the God of Abraham, and the God of Isaac, and the God of Jacob? God is not the God of the dead, but of the living"* (Matthew 22:31–32).

No wonder the people were astonished with this evidence of life beyond the grave. When Jesus said, *"I am the God of Abraham,"* He was not referring merely to the past, but the actual time he spoke them. They meant more than, "I am the God whom Abraham, Isaac, and Jacob worshiped in the past." Their relation to God remained permanent. The fact that these names were associated with God proved that they were living and not dead. The *dead*, or mortal, cannot possess the living God. Only the *living*, or immortal, can have the Lord in whom we never die.

REFERRED TO BY PETER (ACTS 3:1–18)

We see that when Peter restored the lame man, he discounted any power of his own. Instead, he gave all the glory to the Lord's resurrection power. Echoing the Lord's teaching, he said, "*The God of Abraham, and of Isaac, and of Jacob, the God of our fathers, hath glorified his Son Jesus; whom ye delivered up...whom God raised from the dead*" (Acts 3:13). It might have been the same precincts of the temple where Jesus used the three names as proof of the resurrection and Peter witnessed that Jesus rose from the dead.

MENTIONED BY STEPHEN (ACTS 7:2–53)

The first martyr of the early church may have been present when Jesus linked Abraham, Isaac, and Jacob together as a proof of His immortality. He used these same words in his masterly defense proclaiming that He who was speaking had Himself been raised from the dead and was now exalted at the right hand of God.

GOD OF PEOPLES AND PERSONS

But there are other lessons we can learn from this triad of Jewish fathers. It is true that God is often referred to as "*the God of Israel*," yet the three ancestors are described as having Him as their *personal* God. From this fact, we gather that He is the God of both generations and individuals.

THE GOD OF SUCCEEDING GENERATIONS

Moses declared in his psalm that the Lord had been the dwelling place for His people throughout all generations. From everlasting to everlasting, He is God; therefore, He is

God to all who inhabit the earth between eternity past and eternity future. (See Psalm 90:1–2.) He establishes the work of His hands on them in each generation. (See verse 17.) Abraham, Isaac, and Jacob represent successive generations, showing that each experienced God in his own way in his own generation. We have only to study the lives of these three outstanding personalities in early Old Testament history to realize how divine grace and power was vouchsafed to each one in his own age and generation and peculiar circumstances.

Abraham's encounter with God was unique in the fact that he was divinely chosen to be the father of the Jewish people. In Scripture, He is the first one to be called a *Hebrew*. At God's call, this intrepid pioneer of faith *"went forth not knowing whither he went"* (Hebrews 11:8), and proved that *his* God was the God of promise and power. How astounding the prophecy must have seemed to him, that *all* the families of the earth would be blessed through him! (See Genesis 12:1–3.) Abraham was ninety-nine years old when Jehovah visited him, telling him that his God was the *Almighty God* and *"the God of Abraham praise."* Throughout the seventy-five years of his generation, Abraham witnessed many signs of God's almightiness.

Isaac was a miracle child, having been born to old parents; at the time, Sarah was almost one hundred years old. He came as the son of promise, the one in whom the line of Christ would run. (See Genesis 17:17; 22.) In his generation, Isaac did not have to endure the trials, hardship, and sorrows of his aged father; nevertheless, he was assured that the God of Abraham would be his God throughout all his days—*"I am the God of Abraham thy father: fear not, for I am with thee, and will bless thee"* (Genesis 26:24). Without a doubt, Isaac influenced his generation with the faith and godly influence his father exercised in his own generation. Isaac's God was the one of confirmation and blessing.

Jacob has his own niche in the annals of Jewish history, for he became the father of twelve sons who represented the twelve tribes of Israel. This *"prince of God"* (Genesis 32:28) recognized that the God who led his father and grandfather in their respective generations would also lead him, even if not more so, in his generation. Listen to him in his confrontation with Laban over his unjust treatment: *"Except the God of my father, the God of Abraham, and the fear of Isaac, had been with me, surely thou hadst sent me away now empty"* (Genesis 31:42).

What rich experiences Jacob had of divine dealings! It is no wonder that Scripture says that *"God loved Jacob,"* and that He is referred to as *"the God [or mighty God] of Jacob"* almost thirty times. The psalmist reckoned that saints in any generation are privileged to have *"the God of Jacob as their help"* (Psalm 146:5). In fact, the spiritual and moral values Abraham, Isaac, and Jacob upheld in their own generations influenced succeeding generations. In our time, it is encouraging to know that their God is our God; that although civilization has changed and become more advanced in a highly scientific age, God is the same and He is still willing to fight for us like He did for those of old.

> Our vows, our prayers we now present
> Before Thy throne of grace;
> God of our fathers, be the God
> Of their succeeding race.[68]

---

68. Philip Doddridge, "O God of Bethel, by Whose Hand," 1737.

GOD OF PERSONS

Another thought to emphasize in the combination of these three figures is that, in each case, Jehovah is referred to as the God *of* Abraham, the God *of* Isaac, and the God *of* Jacob. From this we can conclude that He is not only the God of the ages or generations, but also of individuals.

THE GOD OF INDIVIDUALS

It is uplifting for saints to meditate on all that God has accomplished throughout the centuries and then say, *"This God is our God"* (Psalm 48:14). However, this generalization does not have near the same impact as when it is personalized and the redeemed can say, *"Thou art my God"* (Isaiah 25:1). Even in His anguish, Jesus cried, *"My God, my God"* (Matthew 27:36). David was very fond of the personal pronoun, *"Jehovah is my shepherd"* (Psalm 23:1). The three names we are considering also stand for three different types of character, all identifiable by the divine name.

THE GOD OF ABRAHAM

This figure of the ancient world is known as one of the noblest examples of faith and unquestioning obedience in the Bible. Certainly, there were times he failed when greatly trialed; but he was honored above most by God and by men. There was a close intimacy between the Almighty and Abraham.

THE GOD OF ISAAC

Isaac had a very different temperament from his father. He experienced none of the hardships Abraham saw on his pilgrimage into the unknown. Isaac's life was not remembered for any great deeds like his father was. His life was more placid and peaceful—almost obscure and undistinguished. Although he dealt with little embarrassments or struggles, the God of his father was *his* God as well.

THE GOD OF JACOB

Here we have one of the most conspicuous and lovable characters of the Old Testament—a man whose sons bore the names of the twelve tribes of Israel. Jacob was very different from Abraham and Isaac, suffering many trials. He was plagued by infirmities, weaknesses, and trials and stooped to deceit to gain his end and suffering for his wrongs under God's rod. Although Jacob was a great sinner, he was also a great penitent and, becoming *"a prince of God"* (Genesis 32:28), found great power in Him. It is comforting to know that the God of Abraham and the God of Isaac could also call Himself the God of a man like Jacob.

We can rejoice in a God who honors courageous faith, a God who blesses lowly service, and at the same time, pardons sinners' iniquity. He hears and responds to the penitent's cry and transforms a reckless transgressor into a praising saint. *"Who is a God like unto thee, that pardoneth iniquity?"* (Micah 7:18). We bow in adoration before the God of Abraham. We walk in quiet trust and meditate at eventide before the God of Isaac. But we shout for joy before the God of Jacob because here we see Him as one who wants to burn the evil out of our souls. There were times when Jacob's faith was very feeble, but God revived it and brought him into a deeper experience with Himself. *"The angel redeemed him from all evil"* (Genesis 48:16). When we are conscious of our failures and sorrow, God receives us and assures us that as *"the God of Jacob, he is our refuge"* (Psalm 46:7).

No two of us are exactly alike. Our natures, tempera-ments, outlooks, temptations, positions, and environments differ. But no matter *who* or *what* we are, the adaptable one, the God of Abraham, the God of Isaac, and the God of Jacob waits to be our God. In spite of our personal idiosyncra-sies and infirmities, He makes our lives the platform upon on which He displays His grace to a sinful and adulterous generation.

> My God, my Father, let me rest
> In the calm sun-glow of Thy face,
> Until Thy love in me expressed
> Draws others to Thy throne of grace.[69]

---

69. Charlotte Elliott, "My God, My Father, while I Stray," 1834.

CHAPTER 28

THREE DEGREES OF PRAYER

Ask, and it shall be given you; seek, and ye shall find; knock,
and it shall be opened unto you.
—Matthew 7:7

If you take the first letter of each of these key words in the Lord's teaching on prayer, you end up with A-S-K. This reminds us that the essence of true prayer is asking God for what we desire. We must, of course, remember the condition John lays down: *"This is the confidence that we have in him, that, if we ask any thing according to His will, He heareth us"* (1 John 5:14). In the Lord's threefold exhortation, we do not have three kinds of prayers, but three degrees of fervency in the praying heart—a fervency that grows more intense when we continue praying in delay.

The first prayer secret as we approach the throne of grace is the realization that we come into God's presence by invitation alone, for He always makes the first move. He bids us come and *ask*. Prayer, then, is not forcing yourself into His presence; it is not an intrusion, but a willing response to His call to seek His face. So then why do we hesitate to accept this royal invitation to meet the King in His appointed way? Too often we fail to keep tryst with Him who, to prevent any possibility of mistake, makes us bold to *ask, seek,* and *knock*. These three laws govern our prayer-life and are three doors into the very heart of God.

These three teachings suggest that prayer is of increasing urgency and reveal the privilege we have of drawing near to God. In his *Commentary on Matthew*, Richard Glover presents an appealing analogy of a child asking anything of his parent:

ASK—If mother is near and visible, he simply asks for what he needs.

SEEK—If she is not near and visible, he seeks her, and having found her, he then asks.

KNOCK—If, finding her, he finds her inaccessible, within her chamber, unwilling to be disturbed, he knocks, till he gains her attention and consent.

All suppliants at the throne of grace know something of all these three experiences. Sometimes when you need God's help, He is there, and you need only to lift up your eyes and *ask* in childlike simplicity. But sometimes surrounded by darkness you must cry out, *"Oh, that I knew where I might find Him"* (Job 23:3–9), and in such circumstances you *seek* Him. Then there are other times when, like Jeremiah, we say, *"He shutteth out my prayer"* (Lamentations 3:8), and God seems to say, *"I cannot rise and give thee"* (Luke 11:7). When this happens, Jesus says not to despair but to *knock*, or as the original present tense suggests, *"keep on knocking"* (Matthew 7:7).

Our failure is in the realm of patience—a little delay in answer and we grow weary and disappointed and cease to pray. Yet, if the three words—*ask, seek,* and *knock*—mean anything, it is that the response does not always come at once. Jesus is not only inviting us to pray but to persevere in prayer with diligence, never taking silence as refusal. Thus, as the Greek tense suggests, we must *keep on asking, keep on seeking,* and *keep on knocking.*

We can glean more from these commands if we consider them separately.

ASK, AND IT SHALL BE GIVEN THEE

Here we have the *humility* of prayer—we are so poor that we cannot buy. All of us rely on divine bounty. We are beggars in dire need of help, and our rich and bountiful Lord tells us to simply *"ask and it shall be given"* (Matthew 7:7). The rich He will send empty away. (See Luke 1:53.) He reminds us that we are *"wretched, miserable, poor, blind, and naked"* (Revelation 3:17, 18), and that if we only pray, He will make us rich. Furthermore, He promises that He will not fool us if I come as a suppliant. He does not invite me to *ask* in order to mock me by turning a deaf ear to my request. If I ask Him for bread, He will not give me a stone. (See Luke 11:11.) Bless His name, he gives us cake instead of bread; He gives us wine and milk when we ask for water. (See Isaiah 55:1.) No petition is as simple as *"asking."*

Then He responds with certainty, *"It shall be given thee."* It will be *given* to us, not lent; given to us, not sold to us. And what is freer than a gift? Ask—and have! But we *"receive not, because ye ask amiss, that ye may consume it upon your lusts"* (James 4:3). What is not worth the asking is not worth the having, which is worth nothing at all.

> Thou art coming to a King!
> Large petitions with thee bring!
> For His grace and power are such
> None can ever ask too much.[70]

---

70. John Newton, "Thou Art Coming to a King."

SEEK, AND YE SHALL FIND

True seekers exhibit eagerness in prayer. We covet treasure that is beyond our grasp or hidden from us. When the Lord seems so far away that we cannot speak of Him as we would, then we remember His second royal command, *"Seek, and ye shall find"* (Matthew 7:7). We begin searching for Him so that we might find Him as the gracious and sufficient Helper we need. In order to find Him, however, we must seek Him with a proper spirit characterized with humility and sincerity. The Bible has much to say about "seeking the Lord;" it assures us that He will be found by those who seek Him with the right spirit.

Our Lord was most positive in His declaration, *"Seek, and ye shall find."* He does not leave room for disappointment. It makes no difference whether we come as beggars asking alms or as searchers asking for the riches His grace; we receive whatever we approach Him for. Inspired by the Holy Spirit, Azariah said to Asa, *"If ye seek him, he will be found of you; but if ye forsake him, he will forsake you"* (2 Chronicles 15:2). Then we read, *"They sought him, and he was found of them"* (verse 4). Their search was rewarded because *"they sought him with their whole desire"* (verse 15). Perhaps this is why we fail? Do we seek Him with our whole desire?

> Seek this first. His promise trying;
> It is sure, all need supplying.
> Heavenly things, on Him relying,
> Seek ye first.[71]

---

71. Georgiana M. Taylor, "Seek Ye First, Not Earthly Pleasure."

KNOCK, AND IT SHALL BE OPENED UNTO YOU

The last strand of this threefold cord reminds us of the necessity of *perseverance* in prayer. When help and hope seem gone, we must continue knocking. Importunity is necessary when the door appears shut. The word *knock* refers to the act of knocking on a door for admittance. Jesus answered the question about few being saved as follows: *"When once the master…is risen up, and hath shut to the door, and ye begin to stand without, and to knock at the door, saying, Lord, Lord, open unto us; and He shall answer and say unto you, I know you not whence ye are"* (Luke 13:25).

But He never says *"I know you not"* (Luke 13:27) to the redeemed who knock persistently on the door of prayer. If the door does not open immediately, we must *"continue instant in prayer"* (Romans 12:12). Though He seems to tarry, we must wait patiently for Him to open the door. He did the same for man and waited patiently at the closed door of his heart, knocking and knocking for admission. (See Revelation 3:20.) The promise *"It shall be opened unto you"* (Luke 11:9), is sure and inviolable. Delay teaches us patience and persistence in prayer until the door is opened and the Master appears with His answer to our petition. May we never forget that Jesus knocked three times on the door of prayer and, *"being in an agony he prayed more earnestly"* (Luke 22:44). How He practiced His own precept: *"Men ought always to pray and not to faint"* (Luke 18:1).

> When we disclose our wants in prayer,
> May we our wills resign;
> And not a thought our bosoms share
> Which is not wholly Thine.[72]

---

72. Joseph D. Carlyle, "Lord, When We Bend before Thy Throne," 1802.

CHAPTER 29

THREE PERIODS OF PRAYER

Evening, and morning, and at noon will I pray.
—Psalm 55:17

This is yet another triad related to prayer, another trinity in unity. This command to pray three different periods of the day seems to contradict the command to pray always, without ceasing. However, the thought of frequency is the same. As John Perowne reminds us in his work on the Psalms,

> I can no more believe him to be frequent and spiritual in ejaculatory prayer, who neglects the season of solemn prayer, than I can believe that he keeps everyday in the week as a Sabbath, who neglects to keep that one which God hath appointed.

It is encouraging to remember that there is no limited time in the court of heaven for hearing petitions, that God's ears are always open to hear our supplications, His heart always open to understand and undertake our prayers. Whenever we call, He is ready to answer. *"He shall hear my voice"* (Psalm 55:17). Therefore, the psalmist had constancy of prayer in mind when he wrote of the three most fitting periods of the day for prayer. His intention was to, *"run a line of prayer right along the day, and track the sun with his petitions"* (Psalm 55:17). He knew his enemies were active day and night, so he met their activity through continuous prayer.

(See Psalm 55:10.) He kept his window toward heaven open all day long.

The Benedictine Rule was introduced to England when Augustine and his companions landed there chanting psalms and litanies. Novices were admitted into the order with a song. In fact, the order's canonical hours were regulated by verses like, *"Evening, and morning, and at noonday, will I pray"* (Psalm 55:17), and *"Seven times a day do I praise thee because of thy righteous judgments"* (Psalm 119:164).

As for the threefold distribution of time for prayer, we know that pious Jews were accustomed to kneel down three times a day in prayer to God. (See Daniel 6:10.) They felt a threefold need to converse with heaven. Furthermore, *noon* was one of Peter's hours of prayer. (See Acts 10:9.) Matthew Henry comments,

> Those that think three meals a day little enough for the body ought much more to think three solemn prayers a day little enough for the soul, and to count it a pleasure, not a task.

Hebrews began their day in the evening according to Jewish tradition. The ancient rabbis said that men should pray three times a day because the day changes three times. This occurred in the primitive church; although the times varied depending on the location. Our Lord did not seem to have an allotted time for prayer. He often spent whole nights in communion with the Father. He *"offered up prayers and supplications with strong crying and tears"* (Hebrews 5:7). How many of our prayers are saturated with tears? Since our day begins with the morning, let us reverse the psalmist's prescribed order.

MORNING PRAYER

David turned to God at the opening of the day: *"O God, thou art my God; early will I seek thee"* (Psalm 63:1). The chariot wheels of the day drag heavily if it does not begin in fellowship with Him. We should open our hearts to receive his mercies every morning, since they are new every day. *"My voice shalt thou hear in the morning, O LORD. In the morning will I direct my prayer unto thee"* (Psalm 5:3; See 88:13). Isaiah reminds us that it is the Lord God who wakes us *"morning by morning,"* and seeks to wake our ears as well, *"to hear as the learned"* (Isaiah 50:4). Our load will seem much lighter if we make the Lord our *"arm every morning"* (Isaiah 33:2).

We should not go forth without prayer when a fresh morning comes round again, knowing that we will face the same temptations and trials. Conscious of our failures the day before, we must make a morning supplication for guidance and strength to resist and overcome. Just as the Bible opens with, *"In the beginning God"* (Genesis 1:1), so our lives should do the same every day.

> Every morning lean thine arms awhile
> Upon the window sill of heaven
> And gaze upon thy Lord.
> Then, with the vision in thy heart,
> Turn strong to meet the day.[73]

NOONDAY PRAYER

Noontide signified more to those who lived in the East in Bible times than it now does to us in the West. Behind the

---

73. Thomas Blake, "The Windowsill of Heaven,"

question, *"Tell me where thou makest thy flock to rest at noon"* (Song of Solomon 1:7), is an allusion to the custom of shepherds in hot countries, who, in the head of the day, led their flock to shadowy places to rest in the shade. To the ancients, *noon* was the time of clear light between midday and night, a most fitting time to pray: *"At noon will I pray...and he shall hear"* (Psalm 55:17). It was about *noon* when a great light shone around Saul of Tarsus, and the night of his spiritual darkness vanished forever. (See Acts 22:6.)

One of the most suggestive features of *noon* is that when the hands of the clock reach twelve, they appear as one and point upward. Isn't this symbolic of the noontide praying the psalmist practiced? It may be impossible to pause and pray in our modern, complex, industrial world, to point our hands and hearts heavenwards. Yet despite our location, despite the occupation that claims our time and attention, we can lift up our inner thoughts to Him for grace and strength throughout the rest of our day.

The haze and heat of the noon veils the far horizon in the East. Likewise, the burning noon of the home and business tend to make us lose sight of *"the land that is very far off"* (Isaiah 33:17). But if we desire to keep right with God, we must silently and inwardly seek the Lord in the very midst of our daily tasks, diligent in prayer as the fight ensues. C. H. Spurgeon observed,

> The brilliance of the present veils the higher and nobler things that are beyond. It is difficult to keep in touch with the Eternal, when the temporal is dazzling the eye; and it is just in the rush of noon that the voices of the Eternal are least heard, or welcomed, or obeyed. At noon, therefore, I must get aside with God.

We must not let earthly obligations make us forget Him who is with us all day long.

> I need not leave the jostling world,
>   Or wait till daily tasks are o'er,
> To fold my palms in secret prayer
> Within the close-shut closet door.
> There is a viewless, cloistered room,
>   As high as heaven, as fair as day,
> Where though my feet may join the throng,
>   My soul can enter in and pray.

EVENING PRAYER

Looking at the day as a whole, G. H. Knight describes the condition of our heart:

At evening, my heart looks sometimes as if it had been all day long in a trampled highway with the soil beaten down hard, so that the best seed dropped over it could not sink in, and was snatched away by the fowls of the air.

In the morning, it feels sometimes like the stony ground. The feeble plant had been watered by the dews of night, and sprung a little into greenness and life, but when the sun arose it was scorched and dried.

At noon, the thorns choke: "the cares of the world and the deceitfulness of riches," take up all the room there is, and I bring forth no fruit to perfection. More than ever then, I need to pray. My whole life, indeed, must be steeped in prayer. The hour when my heart-intercourse with God is interrupted, will prove the most dangerous hour of the day.

When the day with its toil is over and the shadows fall, we have more time to pray. As T.S. Eliot expressed,

> The evening is spread out against the sky,
> Like a patient etherized upon a table;

Like Isaac, we must meditate at evening tide. *"At evening… will I pray"* (Genesis 24:63). After the fever of an exciting day has cooled and the twilight darkens to gloom, then we can hear the still small voice. It is often drowned by the world's noise throughout the day and reveals to us the sins, failures, and mistakes we have committed from sunrise to sundown.

The majority of us labor until the evening, but are comforted to know that the same Jesus who came at eventide and stood in the midst of the disciples is still with us as the shadows fall: *"Abide with us, for it is toward evening"* (Luke 24:29). Then we can open our hearts to Him and plead His forgiving grace in penitence. It is always best to repent of the day's debts at night, so that we do not carry sin into another day. George Herbert reminds us,

> Who goes to bed and doth not pray,
> Maketh two nights of every day.

Morning, noon, and night we must *"watch unto prayer"* (1 Peter 4:7). When we cannot turn aside and assume the physical attitude of prayer, then we must remember what James Montgomery taught us,

> Prayer is the burden of a sigh,
> The falling of a tear

The upward glancing of an eye,
When none but God is near.[74]

Therefore, the psalmist's exhortation to pray evening, noon, and night are tantamount to the command to pray always, with all kinds of prayer and supplications to the Spirit. A life bathed with prayer is summarized in the following prayer:

Begin the day with God,
Kneel down to Him in prayer;
Lift up thy heart to His abode,
And seek His love to share.

Go through the day with God,
Whate'er thy work may be;
Where'er thou art, at home, abroad,
He still is near to thee.

Conclude thy day with God,
Thy sins to Him confess;
Trust in the Lord's atoning blood,
And plead His righteousness.

---

74. James Montgomery, "Prayer is the Soul's Sincere Desire," 1818.

CHAPTER 30

THREE EXCELLENCIES OF CHRISTIAN CHARACTER

That…we should live soberly, righteously, and godly,
in this present world.
—Titus 2:12

Ye are witnesses, and God also, how holily and justly and
unblameably we behaved ourselves among you that believe.
—1 Thessalonians 2:10

Paul was writing about the glorious return of our Lord in the texts above. In light of such a *"blessed hope,"* he describes, *"what manner of person [we] ought to be in all holy conversation and godliness"* (1 Peter 3:11), as Peter expresses it. Believing this marvelous truth of the second advent matters little unless it affects our behavior. While *"looking for that blessed hope"* (Titus 2:13), we must live as Paul prescribes in the triad of virtues. We will receive the crown of rejoicing when, *"in the presence of our Lord Jesus Christ at His coming"* (1 Thessalonians 2:19), we behave in the threefold way Paul did among the saints in Thessalonica.

We cannot read Paul's epistles without noticing his gift of clearly and concisely expressing a most comprehensive theme. He never wasted words, nor was he guilty of verbiage. He knew how to embody the maximum truth in minimum words, as we see in the above triads. In thirteen words, he instructed Titus of his threefold obligation toward himself, his fellowmen, and his God. Titus was not to be satisfied with a mere negation of evil, in *"denying ungodliness and worldly lusts"* (Titus 2:12). He was responsible for exhibiting positive attributes of Christian faith and character as he waited for Christ's return.

LIVE SOBERLY

Paul exhorted Titus to live *soberly* in relation to the world within. The word *soberly* refers to "self-control"; W. E. Vine said that in the original form, it suggests "the exercise of that self-restraint that governs all passions and desires, enabling the believer to be conformed to the mind of Christ." In addition, Archbishop Trench said that the apostolic word *sobriety* expressed the same thought, "It is that habitual inner self-government, with its constant rein on all the passions and desires, which would hinder the temptation to these from arising." As children of the King, our inner lives can only glorify Him if we allow Him to govern all our inner impulses and restrain our unruly passions.

Paul was determined to *"keep under his body"* (1 Corinthians 9:27), that is, bring his thoughts into subjection to God's Word. Romans 5–8 describes the necessity of mastering our lower nature by allowing the high impulses of the Holy Spirit to dominate it. By His power, we are to exercise self-discipline and self-control to bring *"every thought into captivity to the obedience of Christ"* (2 Corinthians 10:5).

Such sobriety also affects our worldly aims and ambitions, for self-willed ambitions are often dangerous.

Time and time again, we see that spiritual power decreases when material possessions increase. A man can lose in one day all he gained through years of restless striving. *"Seekest thou great things for thyself? Seek them not"* (Jeremiah 45:5). The divine call is to *"seek ye first the kingdom of God"* (Matthew 6:33). May we be determined to live not in the flesh, but according to God's will. (See 1 Peter 4:21.)

LIVE RIGHTEOUSLY

From our life *within*, we turn to our life in the world, *without* and *around*. Like Demetrius, we are to have a good report of all men. (See 3 John 12.) Ananias also shared this virtue. (See Acts 22:12.) Living righteously simply means "living right in all our relations with others." Having been made through faith, *"the righteousness of God in Him"* (2 Corinthians 5:21), we will display the natural product of a righteous life. We are to behave "justly," being straight and upright in all our transactions. In this way, positional righteousness is translated into practical righteousness. Our *standing* in the righteous one becomes our *state* before men.

It is interesting to observe that in connection with the sparkling consistency of Demetrius, John uses a triad to express the range of this early Christian's "good report." It was *"of all men, and of the truth itself; yea, and we also bear record"* (3 John 1:12). There are some who are saints abroad but demons at home. The testimony of our intimates is more reliable than the record from mere acquaintances. Not only did Demetrius have a public reputation, a good report of *all men*, but also truth itself, or the Scripture he loved. In addition his own fellow-saints, *"we also"* bore witness to a life that was real, destitute of false religiousness, which characterized walks like Diotrephes. (See 3 John 9–10.)

It is sad that we so often fail to live righteously toward our fellowmen. What we *are* speaks louder than what we *profess to be.*

We do not possess that precious jewel of consistency. We fail to manifest the most transparent honesty in business dealings, and are not free from sharp practices in certain transactions. We do not strive to live in such a way that the world has no evil thing to say of us.

I am not merely to be *substantially* right, but, like Daniel in Babylon, to be so *conspicuously* right, that of any desire to bring an accusation against me, they will find it only is what they call my too scrupulous obedience to the law of God.

This type of obedience will never be put to shame. Browning reminds us,

> It all amounts to this!—the sovereign proof
> That we devote ourselves to God, is seen.
> In living just as though no God there were![75]

LIVE GODLY

Having considered our *inward* and *outward* lives, we will now think of our *upward* aspirations. What we are *godward* determines what we are *inward* and *manward*. The original term for "godly" suggests a devout manner of life, a reverence manifested in actions, or godlike. Arising from a relationship with God, godliness implies an attitude in every phase of life, not merely an imitation of godlike ways. It is not that

75. Robert Browning, *Paracelsus.*

we must try to be godly; rather we must allow ourselves to be so controlled by God so His virtues are seen in our lives. It is through the power of the Spirit that we become godlike in our opinions, judgments, aims, and decisions, and like Him in righteousness, kindness, sympathy, and forbearance.

There are two other triads from Paul bearing the truth of the threefold cord he gave to Titus. The one that was already cited was when the apostle called upon God and the church at Thessalonica to witness his behavior. He proved himself "holily" in his life *godward*; "justly" in his life *manward*, standing the test of microscopic investigation; and "unblameably" in his inward life, for he knew nothing against himself. We can link this trinity with another one in Ephesians, *"The fruit of the Spirit is in all goodness, and righteousness and truth"* (5:9 RV). Perfect consistency in all realms comes as *"the fruit of the Spirit."* Evidence of this is "goodness" in disposition, talk, and act; "righteousness" or *scrupulous* honor and honesty in all things, however small; and "truth," or inner sincerity, manifesting blamelessness in all our dealings.

O my God,
Draw me still nearer, closer unto Thee,
Till all the hollow of these deep desires
May with Thyself be filled![76]

---

76. Felicia Dorothea Browne Hemans, *The Indian's Revenge.*

CHAPTER 31

THREE SECOND ADVENT KEY WORDS

How ye turned to God from idols to serve the living…God; and to wait for his Son from heaven.
—1 Thessalonians 1:9–10

The church of Thessalonica was founded in a time of revival. Paul spent about a month among the idolatrous people in Thessalonica during his second missionary tour. Many were stirred and saved through his Spirit-inspired preaching, spurring the formation of an assembly. (See Acts 17:19.) These two epistles instruct the converts in all of the fundamentals of faith, including the second coming of Christ.

After Paul left the city, now identified as the modern Salonika, many of the believers thought about their loved who died in the Lord and began wondering how they would fare when Christ returned for His church. The first letter to the Thessalonians had a threefold purpose: (1) to strengthen the believers in faith, (2) to inspire the saints to a fuller life of holiness, and (3), to instruct them about the rapture, in order to comfort the bereaved hearts.

In these two verses, Paul describes the twofold obligation of the converts now that they were saved. The trinity in unity he describes is *turn*, *serve*, and *wait*, the three bound together as one. Some *turn* or become converted, but fail to *serve* the one who saved them. There are others who *turned* and *serve*, but do not *wait* for the Savior to return from heaven. The ideal believer—the one after God's own heart—is the one who turns *and* serves *and* waits.

TURNED TO GOD FROM IDOLS

Like the Corinthians, the Thessalonians worshiped dumb idols. (See 1 Corinthians 8:4; 12:2; 1 Thessalonians 1:9.) But Paul knew how to adapt gospel truth for idolaters to understand. The precise language he used to describe the idolaters conversion is interesting to observe. They turned to God *from* idols, not from idols to God. Many have a false impression of this claim of Christ. They are troubled about what they will have to give up if they choose follow Him. But He does not ask sinners to surrender any idols they have worshiped. He calls them first to *take*, not give up. He pleads for the sinner to surrender himself; once this takes place, idols fall from his life just as dead leaves fall from a tree. When the Philistines brought the ark into the house of Dagon, this highly revered idol fell quickly.

It is likely that Paul said nothing about *idols* in his message to Thessalonian idolaters, because he never used the negative in preaching the truth. He presented the living God in all His love, grace, and power; those who listened were so enraptured with the vision of the mighty God that in receiving Him, they abandoned their idols. God fashioned the heart in such a way that it can only worship one god at a time, and the Thessalonians found a home in God.

Moreover, God meant the heart of man to be His own shrine. Augustine's dictum is true: "Thou hast made us for Thyself, and our hearts are restless, till they find their rest in

Thee." A Sunday school teacher asked a class of boys the question, "How many Gods are there?" A bright lad answered, "Only one." "How do you know?" the teacher questioned. The little boy answered, "Because there is only room for one." We read of those of old who, *chose new gods: then was war in their gates*" (Judges 5:8). This is true of both nations and individuals. There is always strife and conflict in the hearts of those who serve strange gods; peace is unattainable.

However, the Thessalonians *turned* to God. This term implies a deliberate break with idolatrous ways. They repented and had faith, recognizing God as the only object of their worship. Such a marvelous conversion was a spiritual fulfillment of Isaiah's prophecy, *"In that day a man shall cast [out] his idols of silver, and his idols of gold, which they made each one for himself to worship…[and bow to] the glory of His majesty"* (Isaiah 2:20–21). An idol is anything or anyone that comes between our heart and God. Idolatry robs God of His rightful place in His temple.

> Is there a thing beneath the sun
> That strives with Thee my heart to share?
> Ah, tear it thence, and reign alone,
> The Lord of every motion there:
> Then shall my heart from earth be free,
> When it hath found repose in Thee.[77]

SERVE THE LIVING AND TRUE GOD

We are saved to serve. There are those who feel that they must serve God in order to be saved. But He does not ask

77. Gerhard Tersteegen, "Thou Hidden Love of God," 1729.

anything from a sinner other than repentance, faith, and surrender. Once born anew in the Spirit, however, then He claims our time, talents, and treasures. This idea of serving God as a slave was new to the heathen mind. Freed from idolatry, the Thessalonians learned how to live as the slaves of God who had freed them. (See Romans 6.) Now the serving comes between the turning and waiting; this is because God-inspired and God-directed service is the evidence and expression of salvation and anticipation.

Paul emphasized two aspects of the immortal and invisible God.

HE IS THE LIVING GOD

The Israelites knew that God was the living God because He drove out the Canaanites and other heathen forces from the promised land—something a dead, dumb idol could not do (See Joshua 3:10; Psalm 135.) How striking is the apostle's affirmation, *"We know that an idol is nothing in the world, and that there is none other God but one"* (1 Corinthians 8:4). Paul reminded the Galatians that *"when ye knew not God, ye did service unto them which by nature are no gods"* (Galatians 4:8). This truth dawned on the deluded priests of Baal when Elijah mocked them in their desperation to get the dead gods to act on their behalf. As the source of all life, what else could God be but the *living* God—able to hear, see, speak, provide, save, and keep us through all our seasons? The transformation of the Thessalonians was a striking display of the living, active God's power.

HE IS THE TRUE GOD

All man-made gods are *false* in that they usurp the place of the one and only God. There are no other gods before

Him alone who is the Lord God Almighty. Those that Paul preached to eventually realized that the gods they worshiped were fictitious; that, being lifeless, they were destitute of power to deliver from sin's thralldom, as well as the ability to guide and direct, console and satisfy. There is a story of a Roman Catholic priest who lay dying, and a brother priest who visited him in consolation. He held a crucifix before the dying man's eyes, urging him to look at it. But he replied, "That cannot help me, I made it myself." How can inanimate gods, fashioned by human hands, assist those who bow down to them?

> Thou art the true, the living God,
> Who hearest when we call,
> And grantest liberally food,
> While watching over all.

WAITING FOR HIS SON FROM HEAVEN

The three links of this golden chain cannot be broken. Those who do not *wait* lack a mighty incentive to fruitful service. Nothing can inspire us to serve the Lord without reserve like the thought of the Master appearing at any moment to try our work, of what sort it is! The life and work of those who have turned from sin to God would be revolutionized if they kept in mind the judgment seat of Christ. Paul loved expressing his trinities of truth in various forms, often linking one triad to another. For example, link 1 Thessalonians 1:3, 9, and 10, and what do you find? Why, triplets that explain one another!

"[Turning] *to God from idols*" (1 Thessalonians 1:9) is equivalent to "*your work of faith*" (verse 3), for this is the only kind of *work* God expects from a sinner. *"This is the work of God, that ye believe on him whom he hath sent"* (John 6:29). This is exactly what the Thessalonians did when they *turned* to God.

"Serving the living and true God" (1 Thessalonians 1:9) was *"their labour of love"* (verse 3). They did not serve because they felt they had to, seeing God had saved them; but because they loved Him. They labored joyfully and sacrificially for all He had accomplished for them.

"Waiting for his Son from heaven" (verse 10) is matched by *"your patience of hope"* (vcrse 3). In a different language, the same threefold cord is stated in our previous triad: *"Denying ungodliness and worldly lusts"* (Titus 2:12)—turning; *"[living] soberly, righteously and godly"* (verse 12)—serving; and *"[looking] for that blessed hope"* (verse 13)—watching.

Paul's epistles are drenched with the truth of Christ's return. Without a doubt, he is the apostle of the second advent. He always proclaimed that God's glorious appearing would be the consummation of His redemptive work. In every chapter of First Thessalonians, Paul deals with this advent, approaching it from different angles.

Chapter 1, as the inspiring hope for the young convert.

Chapter 2, as the encouraging hope for the faithful servant.

Chapter 3, as the purifying hope for the believer.

Chapter 4, as the comforting hope for the bereaved.

Chapter 5, as the rousing hope for the sleepy Christian.

The phrase *to wait* means to remain constant in waiting, like those who watch for the morning. (See Psalm 130:6.) Do we share this attitude? Is ours not only an operative, appropriating faith, but an expectant faith as well? Having turned, and while serving, are we also watching?

> Call to each waking band,
> Watch, brethren, watch!
> Clear is our Lord's command,
> Watch, brethren, watch!
>
> Be ye as men that wait
> Ready at the Master's gate,
> E'en though He tarry late:
> Watch, brethren, watch![78]

---

78. Horatius Bonar, "Hark, 'Tis the Watchman's Cry."

CHAPTER 32

THREE MEMORABLE DAYS

[The first day, John] said, I am the voice of one crying
in the wilderness.
—John 1:23

The next day John seeth Jesus coming unto him,
and saith, Behold the Lamb of God,
which taketh away the sin of the world.
—John 1:29

The next day after...two disciples heard him speak,
and they followed Jesus.
—John 1:35, 37

Both the Bible and history record many remarkable, conspicuous, and unforgettable days that changed the destinies of nations and men. What a stupendous day in the annals of the world when man conquered space, reached the moon over a quarter of a million miles from earth, and walked on its untrodden dust. How thrilled millions of people were when they watched this daring episode occur! But wasn't the fourth day of creation more wonderful, when God made the glorious moon, sun, and countless stars? In fact, each day of that first week was momentous for something in particular, ending with God's final masterpiece on the sixth day—man created in His image.

One of the most tragic days in modern times was when the fearful tidal wave swept over East Pakistan, killing thousands in a matter of hours and devastating much of the countryside. Horrified, the whole world joined forces to relieve the hungry, homeless, and diseased. But what about the day Noah entered the ark, and the world was destroyed by the universal flood? Wasn't that more catastrophic than the tidal wave? How precious is the rainbow, the divine promise that universal flooding would never plague the world again.

One of the most auspicious days in American history was when Abraham Lincoln signed the Declaration of Emancipation, freeing slaves from their bondage once and for all. What a jubilant day that must have been for thousands of slaves! But there was an even greater day for the human race, when the ultimate emancipator signed the proclamation of freedom with His blood. It enabled us to preach deliverance for the captives and freedom for the bruised. (See Luke 4:18.)

We could continue comparing and contrasting these truths with significant days; however, our immediate purpose is to consider the three days between the end of John the Baptist's mission and the beginning of the Messiah's ministry. (See John 1:15–37.) The apostle John probably experienced a life crisis during these three days and was, therefore, well qualified to write about them. The Baptist was John's earliest teacher, but Jesus Christ's tutelage perfected his spiritual education.

FIRST DAY: SELF-ABNEGATION (JOHN 1:19–28)

It is not surprising that the teachings of the dynamic, revival-preaching John the Baptist spread like wildfire. The

Sanhedrin authorities could not quench his growing influence; no one could ignore this rugged man of the desert, with unshorn locks, rough garments, flashing eye, and austere manner. His thrilling voice and blistering messages pierced the listeners' hearts. No wonder the crowds surrounded him near the Jordan, spell-bound and stricken by his words. His popularity forced the Sanhedrin to take action; they commissioned some Pharisees to go to the Jordan to gather all the information they could about this unorthodox revivalist.

This was the day of confrontation F. B. Meyer referred to as "the day of self-abnegation." Imagine the scene, the forerunner of Jesus encountering the ritualists of the day, who would one day plot His death. Dr. Meyer said,

> Imagine a vast circle. On one side stands the herald of the new age, surrounded by the chivalry of a noble youth; on the other the grey-beards, representing an order of things old and ready to vanish away. How breathless was the silence which followed the first inquiry, "Who art thou? Art thou the Christ?"

The jealous, disturbed Pharisees did not wait long for the answer, for without a moment's hesitation, the Baptist humbly confessed, "*I am not the Christ*" (John 1:20). This was followed by another question: "*What then? Art thou Elias?*" Had the religious inquisitors asked him if he was the one Malachi and Isaiah prophesied about, who would precede the Messiah in the spirit and power of Elijah, John would have replied, "Yes! I am he." But to answer their blind question, he said, "*No! I am not*" (John 1:21). Knowing the letter of the law, the inquisitors asked amiss again: "*For Moses truly said unto the fathers, A prophet shall the Lord your God raise up unto you of your brethren, like unto me"* (Acts 3:22)? Bishop Westcott says that, "the abruptness of the question is remarkable." But amid hushed suspense, with increasing brevity, the Baptist answered, "No."

At this point, with the Pharisees began to force the issue, *"Who art thou? That we may give an answer to them that sent us. What sayest thou of thyself"* (John 1:22). Then came a confession—sublime in humility and Christ-honoring in is content. The three days the Baptist gave this testimony have been called the "three golden days." Therefore, perhaps we can describe John's three testimonies he gave these days as the "three golden testimonies," each given through astonishing humility. In the first testimony to the jealous Pharisees, he denied any claim to the messiahship.

"I am not the Christ" (John 1:20). Yet he did claim to be the herald of His coming. In a most emphatic way, he declared that he came to prepare the way for Christ (see verse 23), to bear witness concerning Christ (see verse 7), to speak of Christ (see verse 30), and to make Christ known through the ordinance of baptism (see verse 31). Just as a road sign indicates the way, but is not the way itself, so John pointed the way to Christ, but was not the Christ himself. The Baptist was not *"the Light,"* but a witness to it; not *"the Sun,"* but a star announcing the dawn; not *"the Bridegroom"* (John 3:27–30), but his friend; not *"the Shepherd"* (John 10:3), but the porter opening the door into the fold; not *"the Prophet"* Moses spoke of, but a prophet who led Jesus to say, *"Among those that are born of women there is not a greater prophet than John the Baptist"* (Luke 7:28).

Furthermore, John showed true self-abnegation by declaring that he was not *"the Word of God,"* but the voice of God through which the incarnate Word was, "*made manifest to Israel.*" "*I am the voice*" (John 1:23). The I here was not an utterance of self-assertion; rather, in the Greek, it was implying the speaker's unworthiness. It was an apologetic, John speaking of himself in self-abasement and deep humility. John sanctified this degraded pronoun when he confessed that he was only a *voice.* Jesus was the Word; John was the voice through which the Word found its early utterance; and all who listened to his preaching heard the voice of God. The figure John used to refer to himself was most apt, for everything about him spoke of God. He had one of the "lives that speak."

Here was the *divine voice*—"*The voice of One*" (John 1:23). Which One? God's name is omitted, but only that it is not used with undue familiarity. The deep reverence of this expression suggests that he was aware of the great privilege he had as God's spokesman.

Here was an *earnest voice*, for the original word for "crying" means "to cry," or "to shout." As the Lord's voice, John vibrated tones of compassion and love.

Here was a *far-reaching voice*, for from his stance in the wilderness it reached "*all* [of] *Jerusalem*" (Matthew 3:5), and other regions; furthermore, it ultimately reached the ears of Herod the king (see Mark 6:20), at whose hands John was beheaded.

Here was a *warning voice*. The Baptist quoted from Isaiah 40:3 when describing himself, speaking of what Jerusalem had to do (see Luke 3:7), and what his life's task was—to make a path over which the Messiah could ride with His chariot. (See Malachi 3:1.)

Here was a *Christ-honoring voice*. John had little to say of himself; His chief desire was to speak of his Lord. Many are slow to learn that we cannot make much of Christ *and* ourselves at the same time. This narrative shows more of Jesus, less John. Though the Pharisees did not realize, the Baptist knew Christ, and his recognition of Christ is unique. Christ came *after* John—a proof of His humanity. Christ was *before* John—an intimation of His deity. Christ was *superior* to John, who felt un-worthy to perform services usually rendered by a slave, such as loosening His shoe laces.

SECOND DAY: CHRIST-DESIGNATION (JOHN 1:29–34)

John dealt with the religious hierarchy on the previous day in no uncertain terms; yet the next day, his message was addressed to the great congregation attracted by his powerful preaching—*"Saying unto them all"* (Luke 3:16). After delivering his soul to the official, a religious representative of the people, John now faced the people themselves. Although he was not recognized, unordained as far as the Sanhedrin was concerned, he was still the divinely ordained minister for his time. In the history of the church, many God-sent men are found outside duly recognized channels, and have been impelled to break through conventional regulations to accomplish God's will.

The spur to the Baptist's message to the crowd before him is found in the phrase *"John seeth Jesus"* (John 1:29). Old Testament prophets saw His day before He came, but John saw Him after He came as the *man* Christ Jesus who came to save; and as *Christ*—the one sent of God. Now he invites his audience to behold what he had seen. His eyes inspired his tongue. (See 1 John 1:3.) How tragic and ineffective for a preacher to describe the Savior who has never even experienced His saving grace for himself!

While we continue examining John's message, we come across two striking features.

First, there was his use of the well-known symbol of the lamb. John's Jewish audience was very familiar with the figure of a *lamb*, seeing that lambs were sacrificed daily in the temple. These lambs on "Jewish altars slain"[79] were only types, however, of Christ who was now in their midst, *"the Lamb of God"* (John 1:36). Because most of the people knew of Isaiah's prediction of the Lamb led to slaughter (see Isaiah 53:7), they would appreciate John's assertion that the Lamb before them in flesh was to take away the sins of the world. As Dr. Meyer expresses it, "The gospel glistens in it [this verse] as the whole sun in a single dewdrop." This statement of the sin-bearing Lamb could be regarded as the first clear presentation of the cross in New Testament times.

Second, there were the Baptist's intimations regarding Christ. Pertinent phrases stood out in his messages when he called on the congregation to, *"behold, the Lamb of God"* (John 1:29 esv). The first phrases concern his relationship with Christ. The Bible teaches that John and Jesus were related and their mothers knew each other very well. (See Luke 1:39–56.) Therefore, John must have known Christ, yet he said, *"I knew Him not"* (John 1:33). At first, John only knew Him as his cousin, not as the Messiah. The spiritual aspect of the relationship came later. As a result, when he presented Him as the Lamb, he no longer saw Him as the Jesus he had known after the flesh.

---

79. Isaac Watts, "Not All the Blood of Beasts," 1709.

In honor of Christ he said, "[He was] *preferred before me*" (John 1:30). John rendered to Jesus what was due to Him, implying no personal slight whatsoever. No greater person had been born of a woman than John. Jesus was born of a woman, and John gives Him the preeminence over the best of men. "*That in all things He might have the preeminence*" (Colossians 1:18). The exalted one was now being made known in Israel.

Still bearing witness of Christ, John testified to the anointing Christ received for the beginning of His ministry, "*I saw the Spirit descending from heaven like a dove, and it abode upon him*" (John 1:32). Was this the moment John saw Jesus as the Messiah instead of his cousin, divinely anointed for the work He would accomplish? (See Luke 4:18.) There followed an unequivocal testimony to Christ's deity—"*I saw, and bare record that this is the Son of God*" (John 1:34). God had said that same thing about Himself. (See Matthew 3:17.) John denied that he was Christ, but he fearlessly confessed that Jesus was the Christ.

THIRD DAY: MISSION FULFILLED (JOHN 1:35–37)

The Baptist now directs his attention to a narrower circle of believers who had become his disciples; he had the same message for them that he proclaimed the day before. (See John 1:29, 35, 36.) Yet there is something sad about this third day as John looked wistfully and eagerly on Jesus walking away. Perhaps this was the last time his eyes would behold the man he so greatly esteemed. For the second time he designated the one he labored for as, "*the Lamb of God*" (John 1:36).

There must have been something especially striking in the way John uttered this tremendous truth, for as, *"two disciples heard him speak, and they followed Jesus"* (John 1:37).

Now the Voice somehow implied that those who had followed the Baptist must now transfer their allegiance to Christ. Now that the King had arrived, the forerunner's task was finished. Do you ever wonder how that rugged desert preacher felt as he watched his disciples leave to follow Jesus, knowing that his work was done? Did he have any jealousy or regret as he watched the crowds ebb away, or did he experience a momentary sense of desolation and loneliness? No, for the satisfaction of a completed mission is apparent in his matchless words, *"This my joy…is fulfilled"* (John 3:29).

One of John's disciples was Andrew, who led his brother Peter to Christ; the other was probably John, who became Jesus' beloved disciple. These disciples, along with others, did not sit at the Baptist's feet in vain; for they went on to do great things for the Lord because of his godly example and influence. The Baptist had fulfilled his course in them. (See Acts 13:25.) He triumphed when he could exclaim, *"Behold the Lamb of God,"* not, "Behold the forerunner!" Dr. Meyer comments on the consummation of John's mission:

> It is sad to see the crowds depart; to note the drying of the brook whose waters were so sweet, the ebbing of the tide, the waning of the day, the falling of the leaves; but, where the soul has learnt to live in Jesus and for Him, it is not so hard to die to all these things, because the Lord has become its light and its salvation, the strength of its life and its everlasting joy.

For a while, it was profitable for the disciples to spend time with someone who was greater than a prophet. But they were even more blessed to follow Jesus, "The Fairest of all the earth besides."[80] There is a poem by John Keble in the *Christian Year* called "St. John Baptist's Day," that is truly appealing:

> Where is the lore the Baptist taught,
> The soul unswerving and the fearless tongue?
> The much-enduring wisdom, sought
> By lonely prayer the haunted rocks among?
> Who counts it gain
> His light should wane
> So the whole world to Jesus throng?

> So glorious let Thy Pastors shine,
> That by their speaking lives the world may learn
> First filial duty, then divine
> That sons to parents, all to Thee may turn;
> And ready prove
> In fires of love,
> At sight of Thee, for aye to burn.

---

80. Manie P. Ferguson, "That Man of Calvary."

CHAPTER 33

THREE ESSENTIAL MUSTS

Ye must be born again.
—John 3:7

Even so must the Son of man be lifted up.
—John 3:14

He must increase.
—John 3:30

It is impossible, of course, to have a book without words. The total number of words in the greatest book in the world—the Bible—comes to approximately seven hundred seventy-three or six hundred ninety-two. The Authorized Version was printed in 1611, instigated and authorized by King James I. It was published in a time when the English language was at its zenith of beauty, and laid the foundation for other literary works in later generations. The Bible's prose and poetic language are incomparable. Furthermore, reading the King James Version not only enriches one's vocabulary, but also one's entire life. It is true that much longer works have been written, but God's infallible Word still outweighs the entire realm of literature.

One of the most striking features of the Bible is that there are vast numbers of short, simple words that any schoolchild could read and easily understand. It does not suffer from "a barren superfluity of words." Samuel T. Coleridge wrote in *Table Talk*, "I wish our clever young poets would remember my homely definitions of prose and poetry; that is, prose = words in their best order; poetry = the *best* words in the best order." One virtue of the Bible is that it always gives "the *best* words in the best order." Quoting James Boswell, the greatest advice of Samuel Johnson was, "Don't, Sir, accustom yourself to use big words for little matters"—advice the Bible strictly adheres to. It avoids "words of learned length."[81] In the *Letter to a Young Clergyman*, Jonathan Smith urged him to remember that "proper words in proper places, make the true definition of a style." This is why the Bible is a supreme work of literature. When the divine author inspired men to write it, He was "in all His words most wonderful."[82]

We will now consider one of the simplest words which is used quite a lot, and closely associated with the life and labors of Jesus. It is the four-letter word *must*. One of the most compelling words of Scripture, it occurs some seventy times in the New Testament, including this current triad. It was often on Jesus' lips, revealing how He was constantly carrying out His Father's will. The first time He used it was when He was twelve years old. After being rebuked by His parents for tarrying in the temple, He answered, *"Wist ye not that I must be about my Father's business?"* (Luke 2:49). From then on He acted on an inner, divine compulsion, as His frequent *musts* reveal. Even as He died, He uttered the same divine constraint, *"The Son of man must be delivered"* (Luke 24:7).

In one of the most outstanding and well-known chapters of the New Testament, John gives a unique trinity of *musts*, forming another threefold cord that is not easily broken:

81. Oliver Goldsmith, "The Village Schoolmaster."
82. John H. Newman, "Praise to the Holiest in the Height," 1865.

(1) the *must* of salvation—*"Ye must be born again"* (John 3:7); (2) the *must* of sacrifice—*"Even so must the Son of man be lifted up"* (3:14); and (3), the *must* of sanctification—*"He must increase, but I must decrease"* (3:30). We will at the second *must* first, because the other two spring out of it. As our redemption, Christ became our righteousness and sanctification.

SAVIOR AND SACRIFICE (JOHN 3:14)

It is interesting to observe that John repeats the phrase *lifted up* three times, and that taken together, they emphasize a triad of spiritual truth: (1) the reason of the cross—*"Even so must the Son of man be lifted up"* (John 3:14); (2) the revelation of the cross—*"When ye have lifted up the Son of man then shall ye know that I am he"* (John 8:28); and (3), the reign of the cross—*"And I, if I be lifted up from the earth, will draw all men unto me"* (John 12:32). The first reference is associated with the prophecy of Scripture, the second indicates the ministry of the Holy Spirit, and the third depicts the perpetual ministry and power of the Crucified One.

But why the *must* of Calvary? Why did Jesus have to die as a felon on a wooden gibbet? Was there no other way God could save the lost? No, it was willed in the divine counsels that Jesus would bear our sins on the tree! He must be lifted up for several reasons.

His death was a *predestined* one. In the past eternity, "love…drew salvation's plan"[83]; so it was, that Jesus came as the Lamb slain *before* the foundation of the world. God provided the remedy before the disease. The plan of Jesus provid-

---

83. William R. Newell, "At Calvary," 1895.

ing redemption through His blood was predestinated. (See Ephesians 1:5–7.)

His death was a *predicted* one. Having been promised and prophesied as the One who would destroy the works of the devil; the One whose pierced hands and feet would be stricken for those who had turned their own way. Jesus had to die, according to the Scriptures. (See Genesis 3:15; Psalm 22; Isaiah 53.)

His death was a *prefigured* one. The Lord Himself used the image of Moses lifting up a brazen serpent on a pole to illustrate His own sacrifice. The sacrifice of the lambs on Jewish altars and Abraham's sacrifice of Isaac also prefigured God's sacrifice. His son would become the sin-bearing Lamb.

His death was a *prepared* one. Jesus could wholeheartedly say, "*A body hast Thou prepared for me*" (Hebrews 10:5). His incarnation was necessary for the fulfillment of God's salvation, conceived in the dateless past. We were born to live— Jesus was born to die. He came to the world to obtain our redemption. He often spoke of His decease, as He did with Nicodemus. He was lifted up to die, but His death was also *voluntary*, in that He had power to lay it down. As a result, He walked the path of a lamb to the slaughter.

His death was a *vicarious* one. He was sinless and had no sin of His own to atone for. "*The soul that sinneth, it shall die*" (Ezekiel 18:4), yet Jesus never sinned; yet He died for sinners who had fell short of divine glory—"*He died for our sins*" (1 Corinthians 15:1–3).

Finally, His death was a *victorious* one. Christ did not remain dead, but rose triumphantly over the grave. "*I...was dead; and, behold, I am alive for evermore*" (Revelation 1:18).

Lifted up was He to die;
"It is finished!" was His cry;
Now in heav'n exalted high.
Hallelujah! What a Savior![84]

SINNER AND SALVATION (JOHN 3:7)

During that midnight talk with the ruler of the Jews, Jesus made it clear that the basis of regeneration is redemption. He said that when He was lifted up on the cross, He would then be able to raise the spiritually dead to a new and higher life. This accounts for His authoritative command, "*Ye must be born again*" (John 3:7). But why must He be born again? Surely a man like Nicodemus—religious, cultured, and influential as he was—did not require such a drastic change. After all, he was the master of Israel. Yet Jesus pointed out in His reply— "*Ye* [yes, even you, Nicodemus] *must be born again*," or "*born from above*." It seems as though there are two characteristics that create the need for redemption—seeing that *all* have sinned and there is not one who can save himself. No, not one.

THE NATURE OF THE HEART

According to the flesh, Nicodemus was a child of Abraham because he was a partaker of Abraham's physical and sinful nature. This is why a new birth was absolutely necessary if he wanted to become a child of God. Through Abraham, he was a member of the Jewish family, yet Jesus had to say to him, "*Except a man be born again, he cannot see the kingdom of God*" (John 3:3). Nicodemus was religious, but not regenerated. This necessitated the *must* of Jesus for

---

84. Philip P. Bliss, "Hallelujah! What a Savior!" 1875.

redemption. Because he was born in sin, he needed to be born anew by the Spirit—the only one who could make the believing sinner a partaker of the divine nature.

THE NATURE OF HEAVEN

Heaven was a prepared place for a prepared people, and the only way we can prepare to enter this blissful abode is to repent of our sin and experience a changed heart that comes from the regeneration of the Holy Spirit. We are brought into a human family at physical birth, but we are brought into a heavenly family at spiritual birth. It is the Spirit who imparts in us the heavenly nature with which to go to heaven and teaches us how to appreciate this gift. If unregenerate persons could go to heaven, they would be the most unhappy people there, simply because they would not have the heavenly life needed to enjoy a heavenly environment. In the same way, if a saved person went to hell, he would be utterly miserable with nothing in the caverns of the lost to satisfy his new nature. Thus, the nature of the human heart and heaven necessitates that every sinner be born again through the power of God.

O ye who would enter the glorious rest,
And sing with the ransomed the song of the blest,
The life everlasting if ye would obtain,
"Ye must be born again."[85]

SAINT AND SANCTIFICATION (JOHN 3:20)

We touched on the background of this third *must* in the preceding triad. John the Baptist had successfully fulfilled

85. William T. Sleeper, "Ye Must Be Born Again," 1877.

his mission as the forerunner of Jesus, and he harbored no hard feelings as he watched the crowd turn to follow Christ, saying, "It is quite all right. I have had my day. Now it is His!" *Jesus must increase, I must decrease.* The Greek word equivalent to "forerunner" is *paranymph,* or the one who is obligated to bring the bride and bridegroom together. This was the Baptist's mission. Jesus spoke of John as *"the friend of the bridegroom"* (John 3:29). The consummation of his task as a *paranymph* helped prepare the spiritual bride for the heavenly Bridegroom.

Notice that the second *must* in the verse we are considering is in *italics.* This means that it is not part of the original text, but was added later on to enforce it. Phillips translates it, *"He must grow greater and greater, and I less and less"* (John 3:30 PHILLIPS). Another translation has it, *"He must become more important, but I must become less important"* (NIV). Here we see true holiness, growing in sanctification—increase of Christ and decrease of self. But are our hearts daily freed from sin and moving closer to Him? Have we a greater and more magnificent conception of our Lord now than when we first came to know Him? Is it "Some of self and some of Thee," or "None of self and all of Thee"?[86] The will of the Holy Spirit is that we grow into the full stature of Christ.

> Make this poor self grow less and less,
> Be Thou my life and aim;
> Oh, make me daily through Thy grace
> More meet to bear Thy name.[87]

---

86. Theodore Monod, "None of Self and All of Thee."

87. Johann C. Lavater, "O Jesus Christ, Grow Thou in Me," 1780.

CHAPTER 34

THREE DIVISIONS OF THE HUMAN RACE

Give none offence, neither to the Jews, nor to the Gentiles,
nor to the church of God.
—1 Corinthians 10:32

The Bible is the only authentic record of the early identification of the nations for those who are interested in studying the *ethnic* division of mankind. Walter Scott wrote in the *Bible Handbook,*

> The oldest document for the Chronologist is Genesis 5, and for the Historian, Genesis 10. In these chapters we have divine sources to draw from, and a divine basis to work upon. The instructions, therefore, upon those useful branches of study, chronology and history, is authoritative and invaluable. All conclusions drawn from other sources ever prove misleading, and are generally overturned by others better taught. The moment we leave the sure pages of inspiration we are off the ground of authority, and all is mere theory and guess work.

Scripture says that Adam is the head of the human family—the parent root or source of mankind. But ethnology says there are three origins of nations and tongues which trace back to Noah's three sons, found in Genesis 10. As individuals of the race, Adam was our progenitor; however, they stand in a peculiar and distinct relation to the world when viewed as heads and sources of families and nations. Moses was instructed to give an account of the rise of nations, peoples, and tongues. He also recorded the dispersion of mankind, God's plan to people the earth into families to speak a common language, and their dwelling together in amity. (See Genesis 9:1.)

God replenished the earth after the flood and allowed Noah's three sons to repopulate the earth, producing three streams flowing into the broad river of humanity. These streams consisted of the eldest *Japheth*; the second *Shem*; and the youngest *Ham*. However, Shem is named first in the order of grace (See Genesis 9:26), and Japeth is named first in the order of *birth* or *nature*. (See Genesis 10:2). Ethnically, descendants of the three sons are as follows:

From *Japheth*—the Medians, Greeks, Romans, Russians, Gauls, and the Britons.

From *Shem*—the Hebrews, Persians, Assyrians, and many Arabian tribes.

From *Ham*—the Egyptians, Africans, Babylonians, Philistines, and the Canaanites.

The nations from Adam to Abraham were referred to as the *Gentiles* (see Genesis 10:5), but there emerged a new nation with the call of the first *Hebrew* Abraham, chosen as a medium to bless all other nations—namely, *Israel*. (See Genesis 12:1–3.) Furthermore, a different segment of humanity emerged as a result of Christ's death, resurrection, and ascension, which He called, *"my church"* (Matthew 16:7, 18). This church consists of regenerated Jews and Gentiles. This brings us to Paul's threefold classification of the whole human race. In order to divide the peoples of the Word of God correctly, we must preserve the distinction between Jew, Gentile, and the church of God. Let us consider these in the apostolic order.

THE JEW

Approximately one-half of the Bible is concerned with the people of Israel. What a romantic history for the amazing, indestructible Jews! The Jew has been a conspicuous figure throughout all history, whether we are thinking of his honored, yet tragic past, his perilous present, or his glorious future. If we had no other evidence that Christ was near, the establishment of the Jew in his own land—a gift and a right—would be sufficient. Yet his tenure of the land is not permanent; both Ezekiel and John predicted his expulsion to the wilderness. (See Ezekiel 38; Revelation 12.) But they will return to the land after the upheaval. Then, the Messiah will say from His throne in Jerusalem, *"Israel, my glory"* (Isaiah 46:13).

Presently, armies surround Jerusalem and the Arab world's hatred threatens its peace. Israel's predicted anguish, called *"the time of Jacob's anguish,"* will be the worst hour before her matchless dawn. The return of Christ is the hope of all humanity; in particular, Christ is mentioned as, *"the hope of Israel"* (Jeremiah 17:13; Acts 28:20). The Jews will look upon the Christ whom they pierced and mourn for Him. (See Zechariah 12:10.) The Jews rejected Him as their Messiah when He came almost two millenniums ago as their King. Orthodox Jews are still awaiting the return of the one the prophets proclaimed. What a day it will be when He manifests Himself as the one born of a Jewish mother! Our present obligation is to pray and labor for the salvation of the people who gave us the Bible and our Savior.

> Father bless and save them,
> Israel's sons, we pray;
> Turn to joy their bondage,
> Turn their night to day.

THE GENTILE

The Gentiles are those that were not elected by God as His chosen people. They are of the Jewish faith and race and are descendants of Jacob. (See Genesis 10:5; Acts 13:46.) Out of the nearly 7 billion people who make up the present population of the world, only around thirteen million are Jews, making the great majority Gentiles. The Bible has much to say regarding the rulers, government, and destiny of the Gentile world.

All nations today, with the exception of the newly formed Israel, are Gentile. The Bible says that we live in *"the times of the Gentiles"* (Luke 21:24). Nevertheless, Gentile domination will reach its climax and consummation when Christ returns as King of Gentile kings and Lord of Gentile lords, transforming the nations into His own world kingdom and reigning without rival. (See Revelation 11:15.) Haggai's prophecy teaches us that Christ is the hope of both the Jew and the Gentile, *"I will shake all nations, and the desire [hope] of all nations shall come"* (Haggai 2:7). When baby Jesus was presented in the temple, Simon declared that He came not only as, *"the glory of [His] people Israel,"* but as, *"a light to lighten the*

Gentiles" (Luke 2:32). Since then, millions of Gentiles have come to know Him as their Light.

Presently, all nations are baffled by the problems of our time. Distress with perplexity is their portion. If only a superman could emerge with the strength and wisdom to catch the tangled threads of civilization and restore peace to this troubled world. What our disordered world needs is not a superman, but a *supernatural* man. The only man that can do this is the one who is already on His way to clean up the mess of mankind and cover him with peace and righteousness. Our obligation living in this devil-driven world—for Satan is described as *"the god of this world"* (2 Corinthians 4:4)—is to intercede for a mighty ingathering of the millions of lost Gentiles.

> Ye Gentile sinners, ne'er forget
> The wormwood and the gall;
> Go, spread your trophies at His feet,
> And crown Him Lord of all.[88]

THE CHURCH OF GOD

While the Old Testament has much to say about Jews and Gentiles, it has no direct reference to *"the church of God"* (1 Corinthians 1:2), as Paul speaks of within the human race. The mystic fabric of the church of God, which Jesus referred to as, *"my church"* (Matthew 16:18), is specifically a New Testament revelation. Paul speaks of the church as a mystery hid from previous ages, but revealed to the apostles by the Holy Spirit. (See Ephesians 3:2–5.) In Old Testament times, it was no mystery that Jews and Gentiles would be saved.

88. Edward Perronett, "All Hail the Power of Jesus' Name," 1780.

The mystery was that regenerated Jews and Gentiles would be fused into one spiritual body—Jews and Gentiles as the, *"fellow-heirs, and of the same body"* (Ephesians 3:6). Christ broke down the wall of partition between Israel and her enemies through His death and resurrection, thereby making redeemed Jews and Gentiles, *"both one in Christ Jesus...the household of God"* (Ephesians 2:11–22).

The true church is composed of far more Gentiles than Jews, partly because of the vast disparity between the number of Gentiles and Jews. Orthodox Judaism still rejects Christ as the Savior-Messiah. But it is still wrong to refer to the church as "the Gentile bride of Christ," a theory based on the symbolic significance of Joseph marrying a Gentile bride. If this were true, then all regenerated Jews, including the apostles and thousands of early believers, would be excluded from the church of Christ. There is, *"neither Jew nor Gentile"* (Galatians 3:28) in Christ, but only, *"a holy temple in the Lord"* (Ephesians 2:21).

The church is precious to the heart of Jesus, for He bought her with His own blood. Soon she will be presented to Him without spot or blemish. This is why His return for her is called *"the blessed hope"* (Titus 2:13). This is also why some of the old divines spoke of the rapture as "the polestar of the church." She will never live in darkness if she directs her course with his light: *"the bright and morning star"* (Revelation 22:16). What a glorious hour for the church when she hears the musical voice of her Lord saying, *"Arise, my love, my fair one, and come away"* (Song of Solomon 2:13)! How suitable are Dean Alford's lines in *The Coming One*:

They tell me
That some have heard the mighty chariot wheels

Roar in the distance! That the world's salt tears
Are cleaving their last furrows in their cheeks.
It may be so. I know not. Oft the ear,
Attent, and eager for some coming friend,
Construes each breeze among the vocal boughs
Into tokens of His wished approval.
But this I know; He liveth, and shall stand
Upon this earth; and round Him, thick as waves
That laugh at noon with light, uncounted hosts of
His redeemed.
O dawn, millennial day! Come blessed morn!
Appear, desire of nations! Rend Thy heavens,
And stand revealed upon Thy chosen hill.

CHAPTER 35

THREE
MAGNIFICENT ADVERBS

My servant Caleb who hath faithfully followed me.
—Numbers 14:24

Caleb...wholly [fully] followed the Lord his God.
—Joshua 14:14

A profitable series of Bible studies for preachers and teachers of the Word are those with characters who are cast in pairs, so that when we think of one, we most instinctively think of the other. For instance, we may think of Cain and Abel, David and Jonathan, Andrew and Peter, or Martha and Mary. Usually, the pairs portray contrasting characters. For example, the Israelites were terrified to march into the Promise Land before Joshua and Caleb's conquest, due to the unfavorable report of the other spies. Joshua, who stood with firmness and courage, was joined by Caleb, equally brave, in opposing the Israelites' perverse spirit. These two valiant hearts found that conquering the country was not only practicable, but easy with faith in the Lord Jesus Christ!

Three magnificent adverbs are used to describe Caleb's consecration to the Lord's service—*faithfully, wholly,* and *fully.* We are guilty of compromising far too often. We shape our lives around the world's rules. We lower our standards to accommodate carnal society and suit our religion to its taste. However, Caleb's character was of a different texture. He was woven of one piece throughout, just like Jesus' garment. His strong faith endured until he received his divine pledges of love. God crowned his wholeheartedness with reward. By the grace of God, Caleb, like Paul, carried on. While the others perished along the way, these Old Testament warriors lived on with the joy and honor of being the only two from the original multitude to leave Egypt and cross into Canaan.

HE FOLLOWED FAITHFULLY

God called the Israelites an *"evil congregation"* (Numbers 14:27) because they rejected His will and purpose. Their bitter murmurings upset Him; they were unfaithful followers. But amid the nation's faithlessness, Caleb stands out as a living monument in loyalty to the divine command. He followed the Lord faithfully until the end of the road, despite whether the road was rough or smooth. He was no fair-weather follower. Someone said of Caleb, "Beginning well, he continued and ended well." His fellow-countrymen gave into lust in the wilderness, yielding to their fleshly desires and were guilty of disobedience and idolatry. As a punishment, they perished before they reached the Promise Land.

Joshua and Caleb, on the other hand, both knew the mind of the Lord and were loyal to fulfill His requirements. The other pilgrims from Egypt were fickle and spasmodic in their allegiance to God. For this reason, God did not bring them into the land flowing with milk and honey.

Day in and day out over forty years, Caleb did not deviate from the path of faithfulness. Therefore, when the final challenge came to rise and possess the land, he was not found wanting. When we face the Master in the land beyond, may His benediction be, "*Well done, good and faithful servant…enter thou into the joy of thy Lord*" (Matthew 25:21). The reward He will give when we see Him is not determined by our fame but our fidelity!

Give me a faithful heart,
Likeness to Thee.[89]

HE FOLLOWED WHOLLY

We are told three times in one chapter that Caleb wholly followed the Lord his God. (See Joshua 14:8–9, 14.) The word *wholly* literally means "whole-complete" or "through and through." This courageous, loyal man was no half-follower, but proved his full allegiance to God. What a fine picture Caleb presents—expelling giants and claiming his inheritance. Well might I pray, "Lord, give me such a life, one which starts in youth with Thee; one which, amid the burdens of manhood, knows whom it has believed; one which, though autumn winds blow and there are premonitions of snow, brings forth fruit in its old age though others fail!"

Returning to the days when Caleb was a spy, we see how he told Moses about his discovery. True, the report of Joshua and Caleb was the minority, but majority decisions are not always correct. In this case, it was the majority report that melted the hearts of the people as they heard of the fearful giants that awaited them in the Promise Land.

Caleb knew all about these giants, for he saw them with his own eyes. But he also saw the mighty Lord, who was fully

---

89. Sylvanus D. Phelps, "Savior, Thy Dying Love," 1862.

capable of overcoming the obstacles, enabling the Israelites to possess the land. Alas! The giants scare us, and we fail to follow the Lord "through and through" as did the warrior of old. We are guilty of following in fits and starts. We are in and out followers—more often out than in. Like the rich young ruler, we too want to follow the Lord...but keep our great possessions. We lack the Caleb's determination to wholly abandon ourselves to God's will.

> Breathe on me, Breath of God,
> Till I am wholly Thine:
> Until this earthly part of me
> Glows with Thy fire divine.[90]

HE FOLLOWED FULLY

This aspect of Caleb's character in the triad intimates completeness. If a glass is *full* of water, then it can hold no more. The whole of its capacity has been realized. And so it was with Caleb, impossible for us to follow the Lord more closely than he did. He never ran before nor lagged behind; he maintained an unbroken, harmonious walk with God and, with his eye on the goal, never halted till the inheritance was won. The tragedy is that the majority of us have hearts *fully* set on evil. (See Ecclesiastes 8:11.)

Perhaps the most obvious feature of Caleb's wholeness is that he *followed*. Following implies a leader, someone who is able to inspire trust and confidence. Caleb leaves no doubt to who he claims allegiance: "I...*followed the Lord my God*" (Joshua 14:8). Jesus said that His sheep hear His voice and follow Him. He knows all about the perils and needs

---

90. Edwin Hatch, "Breathe on Me, Breath of God," 1878.

his followers will meet along the way and makes provisions accordingly. It is easy to sing about our willingness to follow Him anywhere and everywhere, but to follow *faithfully*, *wholly*, and *fully* means to walk many thorny roads in a land full of giants. God, however, is mightier than all our foes and will be our Guide and Protector until we cross into Canaan.

After Joshua entered the Promise Land and controlled most of it, Caleb and his tribe met him at Gilgal. This is where the partitioning of the land was carried out. Caleb asked to acquire the part of the country inhabited by giants, and Joshua granted his request. *"Joshua blessed him and gave Caleb...an inheritance"* (Joshua 14:13). If we prove ourselves faithful followers of our heavenly Joshua, then He will bless us when we meet Him at the judgment seat, and grant us even more of an inheritance than Caleb received.

His faithful follower I would be,
For by His hand He leadeth me.[91]

---

91. Joseph H. Gilmore, "He Leadeth Me," 1862.

CHAPTER 36

THREE SETS OF TRIADS IN THE LORD'S PRAYER

Hallowed be thy name. Thy kingdom come.
Thy will be done in earth, as it is in heaven.
—Matthew 6:9–10

Give us...forgive us...deliver us.
—Matthew 6:11–13

Thine is the kingdom,
and the power, and the glory, for ever. Amen.
—Matthew 6:13

Christ gave this oft-repeated model prayer to His disciples when they asked, *"Lord, teach us to pray"* (Luke 11:1). The prayer is so simple that a child could use it—and multitudes of children do—yet so profound that the most experienced saint could exhaust it. Then there are those that thoughtlessly utter the prayer, who live contrary to the spirit of this pearl of prayers. To *live* the prayer is a hard task even for the strongest saint. It is only when we begin practicing it that we see how far-reaching and penetrating it is, how it embraces all our needs.

Before we examine the three distinct triads of constitute this prayer, we will first look at who has the right to use it. Countless people would never think of tumbling into bed at night without rattling off the Lord's Prayer, even though they have no relationship with the Lord Himself. The prayer begins with, *"Our Father which art in heaven"* (Matthew 6:9), marking it as a family prayer. Inspired by seeing Jesus in prayer, one of His disciples asked, *"Lord, teach us to pray"* (Luke 11:1). He responded with, *"When ye pray, say, 'Our Father…'"* Thus, this prayer is a child's petition to an all-wise, all-loving, and all-powerful Father-God. Jesus, then, builds the foundation of prayer on relationship. Furthermore, He freely charges Himself with all the responsibilities, as His heart glows with affection for all who believe in His name. (See Matthew 6:25–32; 7:9–11; Luke 11:1–4.)

We cannot know God or approach Him as *Father* without the work of His beloved Son—*"No man cometh unto the Father but by me"* (John 14:6). All men *are not* God's children, for He is not the Father of all men. We hear much about the fatherhood of God and the brotherhood of man, but what is missing is the Saviorhood of Christ by which God becomes our Father and all else who accept him. So the relationship referenced at the onset of this comprehensive prayer is based on redemption, reserved only for His *disciples*. The constitution of this prayer involves three trinities, the first concerning the honor and glory of God—the *invocation*; the second concerning our personal need—*petition*; and the third concerning God's sovereignty whereby He fulfills His will—*doxology*.

FIRST TRIAD—THE VOICE OF REVERENCE

At the onset, Christ taught His disciples to put the most important things first, also in prayer. The middle part of the

Lord's Prayer is concerned with human need, but this must never take precedence over God's rights. Too often we come to God as beggars, pleading with Him to give us this and that material thing. But when instructing His disciples to pray, Jesus said that they must first approach God as worshipers. So in the first three phrases of His prayer, we are taught to seek the glory of God the Father—"*Hallowed be thy name*" (Matthew 6:9); the glory of God the Son—"*Thy kingdom come*" (Matthew 6:10); and the glory of God the Spirit—"*Thy will be done*" (Matthew 6:10).

Today, the divine name is blasphemed more than imagined, but also reverenced by multitudes. Sacred names, such as *God* and *Jesus Christ*, are used as swear words. How common it has become to take the Lord God's name in vain!

HALLOWED BE THY NAME

This portion of the prayer naturally rises first, for if we do not approach God with fear, we are not qualified to use the rest of the prayer. There is a lack of fear and hallowing of God's name today. *To hallow* means "kept holy." The term *name* not only designates a person, but also infers all that a person stands for. Applied to God, it represents the whole of His being and character. As a result, this first phrase means something like, "Help us to revere Thy Father-name; to trust it; to behave as Thy revered children." If "*Our Father*"—the most tender of all names—is spoken by a *son*, then "*Hallowed be Thy name*" is spoken by a saint.

THY KINGDOM COME

The present tense is used later in the prayer, "Thine is the kingdom," but here we have the future tense. It instructs us to pray for the coming of God's kingdom. This reminds us of the missionary and millennial aspect of the prayer Jesus gave His disciples as a model. Jesus was born a King, but His kingdom was rejected by those who cried, "*We will not have this man to reign over us*" (Luke 19:14). The King was crucified at Calvary, and His visible kingdom is in abeyance until He returns again as the rightful King and Lord, ushering in this universal reign. He is not presently building His kingdom, but gathering a group of people to call His own, namely, his church. An earthly people will form His kingdom when He comes. The habitation of God through the Spirit is composed of a heavenly people.

Yet there is a spiritual request of His kingdom rule for those delivered from "*the power of darkness, and translated into the kingdom of His dear Son*" (Colossians 1:13). Just as our sorrows spring from rebellion, so our blessings spring from obedience to the Lord. Therefore we pray for the Kingdom to reside in our hearts: "Come and rule in our hearts; subdue the pride that makes submission partial; take our hearts, for we cannot give them to Thee, and keep them when we cannot keep them for Thee; subdue our hearts to Thy sway!" "*Thy kingdom come*" (Matthew 6:10), is said with the voice of a *subject*. It means that my home, personal habits, social intercourse, and public life must bear witness to my walk with God, molded by divine authority and law.

THY WILL BE DONE IN EARTH, AS IT IS IN HEAVEN.

Once we have a correct understanding of God and His claims, He becomes our chief desire and we surrender our plans to His. Our plans are often foolish and malicious; but His plans always enrich our lives. In heaven, the angelic hosts do not resign themselves to God's will because it is hard and irksome. Doing God's will is the perfect bliss of purity, gladness, and service; as a result, the saints below should joyfully acquiesce with the good and acceptable will of God. With the help of the Holy Spirit, we must joyfully obey all God's commanding will, and willingly obey His disposing will. Our ambitions are sobered and our grievances are sanctified when our submissive spirit prays, "*Not my will but Thine be done*" (Luke 22:42). The only way we can discern the divine will is through sincere prayer; we grow wise quickly upon our knees. We discern in prayer that the heavenly Father's desire must be fulfilled above our own. If we truly know God as our Father in heaven, there will never be any doubt as to His will for our lives. "*Thy will be done,*" says the voice of the servant.

> May Thy will, not mine, be done;
> May Thy will and mine be one;
> Chase these doubtings from my heart,
> Now Thy perfect peace impart.[92]

SECOND TRIAD—THE VOICE OF REQUEST

After *invocation* comes *petition*. This is as it should be in the Spirit-inspired prayer. God's honor and will are paramount and our needs follow second.

What a trinity of need these three phrases proclaim! As G. H. Knight says,

> From the throne on high this prayer leads me down,
> by successive steps, to my work as a loyal servant of

---

92. Marry Ann Serrett Barber, "Prince of Peace, Control My Will," 1858.

the heavenly King; and after that, climbs up again on its returning way through supplication, first for bodily sustenance, next, for spiritual healing, and then, for victory over foes that would hinder me from reaching the holy heaven at last.

GIVE US

The Prodigal's "give me" request was disastrous for his happiness, for he squandered all he received own lustful desires. (See Luke 15:12.) The request Jesus taught His disciples to use, however, not only suggested the family aspect of the prayer with the plural pronoun, but also suggested divine interest in our material and physical needs. From the first phrase in the middle triad, we observe that (1) our wishes are to be moderate—for "*bread*" or the necessities of life; (2) limited to one immediate need—we ask daily for that day's portion; and (3), asked in kindly prayer—we bring others' needs to God as well as our own, and ask for theirs as much as ours.

Our first earthly need is daily bread. Jesus teaches us to acknowledge our absolute dependence on Him for it. The effort and skill we use to produce bread are His *gifts* to us, and they can be removed at any moment. Our God, who, because of His fatherly care, "*feeds the young ravens when they cry*" (Psalm 149:7), does not allow His obedient children to starve.

> The raven He feedeth, then why should I fear?
> To the heart of the Father, His children are dear.[93]

"*Give us this day our daily bread*" (Matthew 6:11) constitutes the voice of the *suppliant*; after asking the Father

---

93. Lewis E. Jones, "In Tender Compassion and Wonderful Love."

for bread, we must not turn to sinful methods to obtain it. Martin Luther's exposition on this phrase is enlightening,

> I mean by it everything belonging to the want and supply of our life; that is, meat, drink, clothes, dwelling, gardens, lands, flocks, money, happy marriage, virtuous children, faithful servants, upright and just magistrates, peaceful government, wholesome air, quietness, health, modesty, honour, true friends, faithful neighbours, and other things of like kind.

It is interesting to note that this is the only clause in the petition that mentions our material need. All the rest of the prayer is spiritual in nature. One of the early fathers, feeling that *all* supplication should be spiritual, suggested that as the bread He refers to here is symbolical in nature, and God's children appropriate His Son as their daily portion. *This* day, and *every* day, we deeply need the bruised and broken Bread from above.

> Thou bruised and broken Bread,
> My lifelong wants supply;
> As living souls are fed,
> O feed me, or I die.[94]

FORGIVE US

More than daily *bread*, we need daily *pardon*, for we are full of sin along with good natural desires. Although I was saved and brought into a relationship with God, whereby He became my gracious heavenly Father, I have been pardoned often and still need fresh pardon every day. Why should I ask for daily bread if the life and strength I receive from it

94. John S. B. Monsell, "I Hunger and I Thirst," 1873.

only satisfies my own fleshly desires? Yesterday's bread must be used to make me more fit to live for God's glory today. While the first need of the body may be bread, the first need of the soul is forgiveness. In that God might be feared, there is an abundance of it.

"Forgive…as we forgive" (Matthew 6:11). From this petition, we arrive at several truths: (1) it is imperative to acknowledge our debts to God, as well as our needs; (2) we must put ourselves on the same level as others who require pardon; and (3), we must seek forgiveness for those we condemn along with ourselves. Are we more proud than penitent when we say, *"as we forgive"*? Or, if God forgives us like we forgive our debtors, would very little pardon come our way? Shun the truth as we may, it remains: we have not repented of our own sin until we forgive others, and God cannot forgive us if we do not repent. Of course, we recognize that under grace, divine forgiveness is not dependent on human forgiveness.

"God for Christ's sake hath forgiven you" (Ephesians 4:32). But, being forgiven is our solemn obligation to emulate such divine virtue. To forgive is godlike. It was Tennyson who wrote of "little hearts that know not how to forgive."

Furthermore, when we ask for forgiveness, we must have no secret delight in the sins we confess or a desire to return to them when the past is blotted out. How grievous and dishonoring to the Father when His child continues sinning and repenting! We are far too often guilty of trading His abundant grace and mercy. It is true, and will always remain so, that if we confess our sins He will forgive us; but how pleasing it would be to hear less confession of sin and more praise for victory! The words of F. W. Faber are fitting:

And is the duty hard to do?
No one, dear Lord, hath done to me
Such wrong as I have done to Thee.
Why should not all men go to Heaven?
They who forgive will be forgiven.

DELIVER US

We not only have need of *food* and of *forgiveness*, but also *deliverance* from our foes. Fresh pardon is not enough; we need *daily victory* as well. The three petitions in the middle of this prayer make a complete circle of requests for deliverance from the *guilt of sin*, the *solicitation to sin*, and the *fountain of sin* within. We have a twofold supplication in the double phrase, "*Lead us not into temptation, but deliver us from evil.*" The supplication is the (1) protection from everything *outward* leading us astray; and (2), protection from everything *inward* moving us astray.

It is useless to pray not to be led into temptation if we carelessly put ourselves in temptation's way, or run into it.

The Greek word for *temptation* includes two thoughts the English represents with the word *trials*, or "sufferings which test or try," and *temptations*, or "allurements on the side of pleasure which tend to lead us into evil." It is the former we will discuss here, namely, trials of persecution, spiritual conflicts, and the agony of body or spirit which test our faith. We should not shrink from these, but accept them in faith, believing that God's grace is sufficient as we face these trials. However, conscious of our weakness, we cannot be blind to the fact that we might fail. That calls for this cry which acknowledges our weakness, "*Lead us not into such trials.*" Jesus Himself prayed, "*If it be possible, let this cup pass from me*" (Matthew 26:39).

"Temptation" is when lust meets opportunity; God never leads us into temptation: *"God cannot be tempted with evil, neither tempteth he any man* [with evil]" (James 1:3). God may *permit* confrontation with the evil one, as He did with His beloved Son who was tempted in all points that we are; but God never *provides* such temptation. He permits it in order that we resist it, and praise Him through faith for the victory He has provided over the tempter himself. Thus we pray, "Deliver us from the power of him who is our enemy and thine." Temptation is not a sin in itself. We only sin when we yield to the tempter's voice.

> Yield not to temptation,
> For yielding is sin.
> Each victory will help you,
> Some other to win.[95]

The bravest of all prayers is the one that asks for freedom from evil and all machinations of the evil one, whatever the cost. There is nothing like a believing, humble, and pleading prayer. Either persistent prayer will stop my sinning, or persistent sinning will put an end to my praying. I cannot live in both. Note that all the petitions are in the plural form. This prevents selfishness in our prayers. *"Deliver us"*—and the *best* of us are in need of daily deliverance. Each one of us needs to turn to Him daily to ask Him to arrange the circumstances of our life so that we may be freed from temptations that we would be too weak to resist. We must also pray to be invigorated in faith so that we can say to the evil one, *"Get thee hence"* (Matthew 4:10). How fitting is this prayer *Temptation* by Cardinal Newman:

---

95. Horatio R. Palmer, "Yield Not to Temptation," 1868.

O Holy Lord, who with the children three
Didst walk the piercing flame,
Help, in those trial-hours, which, save to Thee,
I dare not name;
Nor let these quivering eyes and sickening heart
Crumble to dust beneath the Tempter's dart!

THIRD TRIAD—THE VOICE OF RECOGNITION

This whole doxology is not found in the best of ancient manuscripts or in earlier versions of the New Testament. The early fathers, who comment on the rest of the Lord's Prayer, do not recognize it. Additionally, both the Revised Version and modern translations omit it; yet its presence in the Authorized Version gives a most fitting conclusion to the prayer. Jewish prayers usually ended with a proper recognition of God. Scholars tell us that early transcribers of the text added the doxology for liturgical use of the prayer. So what we can say is that this simplest and most profound prayer is not complete without a revelation of who God is and the honor due Him. God always says *Amen* to a prayer that fully recognizes Him as the Lord God Almighty.

Those who consider the doxology spurious affirm that the request *"Deliver us from evil,"* should be followed with *"Amen!"* to seal the contents of the prayer. But it is encouraging to know that because the kingdom and the power are the Lord's, He is able to fulfill all of our supplications. In support of the omission of the doxology, one commentator says that...

We may give up the pleasing and familiar words with regret, but surely it is more important to know what the Bible really contains and really means, than to cling to something not really in the Bible merely because it gratifies our taste, or even because it has for us some precious associations.

Well, this may be so, but seeing that God's kingdom, power, and glory are prominent throughout the Bible, we value the praise of the Godhead and His wonderful characteristics. Just so, the sixteenth-century translators deemed fit to include the doxology.

THINE IS THE KINGDOM

In the first triad of the prayer, *"Thy kingdom come"* refers to the future aspect of divine reign. Here its present aspect is emphasized by the present tense, *"Thine is the kingdom."* The kingdom has always been His. At the onset of the prayer, we are instructed to look on God as our loving Father, who is willing and waiting to bless us. At the end of the prayer, we are reminded that He is the King whose kingdom is boundless, and who rules over all men, angelic host, and all things. Therefore, He is able to make *"all things work together for good to them that love God"* (Romans 8:28). As the King, *"none can stay His hand, or say unto him, What doest thou?"* (Daniel 4:35). In these days of apostasy and anarchy, when men blatantly defy His rule, let us encourage our hearts with the truth of His sovereignty. *"The* LORD *reigneth,*[here and now] *let the people tremble"* (Psalm 99:1).

Furthermore, no matter how vast or varied our needs are, they can never exhaust the resources of Him whose kingdom rules over all. As the King immortal, invisible, and eternal, He always has *"enough and to spare"* (Luke 15:17). However perplexing our emergencies appear to be, there is power to deal with it where the word of the King resides. John Newton taught us to sing—

> Thou art coming to a King,
> Large petitions with thee bring;
> For His grace and power are such
> None can ever ask too much.[96]

THINE IS THE POWER

It is because of His omnipotence that God plans to establish His kingdom on earth; that He presently rules in the destinies of men and nations; and that He is able to meet all our needs. He is more than capable of delivering us from all our sin. God never says what Elijah said to Elisha, *"Thou hast asked a hard thing"* (2 Kings 2:10), because there is nothing too hard for Him to deal with. When confronted with a great and hostile army, King Asa looked up to heaven and prayed, *"Lord, it is nothing with thee to help, whether with many, or with them that have no power"* (2 Chronicles 14:11). When Jesus sent His disciples out to preach the gospel, He assured them that all power was His in heaven and on earth. (See Matthew 28:18.) Why, then, should we burden our souls with care when there is infinite power at our disposal?

The fear of asking too much of our heavenly Father vanishes when we remember that *"He is able to do exceeding abundantly above all that I ask or think"* (Ephesians 3:20). The depth of this revelation does not overwhelm us as it should! Shakespeare reminds us that...

> A greater power than we can contradict
> Hath thwarted our intents.[97]

---

96. John Newton, "Thou Art Coming to a King."
97. William Shakespeare, *Romeo and Juliet*, Act 5, Scene 3.

This "greater power" always works in the interests of those who honor Him, and always against those who intend to thwart His plans. *"Will he plead against me with his great power"* (Job 23:6)? Let us adore Him and sing of His wondrous grace!

> There is none beside Thee,
> Perfect in power, in love, and purity.[98]

THINE IS THE GLORY

The Scottish Catechism asks the question, "What is man's chief end?" and replies, "Man's chief end is to glorify God and to enjoy Him forever." The nature of the glory, coupled with the kingdom and the power, can be interpreted in two ways. First, there is God's own eternal glory—His inherent glory displayed in His created works. Second, there is the glory He receives from His children—the praise, honor, and adoration we ascribe to Him for His transcendent attributes and qualities. Herod died a terrible death because he glorified himself instead of God. (See Acts 12:23.) God will not share His glory with another.

We give Him the glory for all the blessings we receive in answer to our prayers. We magnify Him as the prayer-hearing and prayer-answering God. For every prayer fulfilled, we say with a grateful heart, *"Thine is the glory."*

> Give us, at last, the house of Thy preparing,
> That, face to face Thy heavenly glory sharing,
> We may praise Thee, our love for e'er declaring:
> We worship Thee, O God![99]

---

98. Reginald Heber, "Holy, Holy, Holy," 1826.
99. Henry W. Frost, *We Worship Thee.*

As we begin this simple yet sublime prayer, we rise above on the wings of faith to our loving heavenly Father. Then we will look down on all the perplexing trials and needs of life with un-perplexed hearts. Then, as we come to the end of the prayer, our hearts fill with praise and adoration for all that God is in Himself, and for all He has showered upon us. The more we pray as Jesus taught us to pray, the more delighted we will be to pray. We will also experience serenity and strength through this divine communion with Him.

> My God, is any hour so sweet,
> From blush of morn to evening star,
> As that which calls me to Thy feet,
> The hour of prayer.

> Then is my strength by Thee renewed;
> Then are my sins by Thee forgiven;
> Then dost Thou cheer my solitude
> With hopes of heaven.[100]

---

100. Charlotte Elliott, "My God, Is Any Hour so Sweet?" 1836.

CHAPTER 37

THREE COMMENDABLE VIRTUES

Be ye stedfast, unmoveable,
always abounding in the work of the Lord.
—1 Corinthians 15:58

The word *therefore* that introduces this most practical triad is "like the nail on which hang three companion photographs." This threefold cord comes at the end of Paul's "Magna Carta of Resurrection," signifying that these are the highest hopes affecting our work here below. *Vision* enables us to achieve the utmost in our *vocation*. Paul never divorced position from practice, or doctrine from duty, or our lives in Christ from our lives on earth. Ellicott commented on this last verse, dealing exclusively with the doctrine of the resurrection,

> It is very striking and very expressive of the real spirit of the Gospel that a chapter which leads us step-by-step through the calm process of logic, and through glowing passages of resistless eloquence to the sublimest thoughts of immortality, should at last thus close with words of plain and practical duty.

Christianity never separates, in precept or in promise, "the life that now is" and "that which is to come."

The apostle introduced his exhortation with "therefore," implying that we should live our present lives worthy of what lays ahead, knowing that our resurrection will come in the near future. Therefore, we must not grow weak and faint-hearted in our work for God as we await our participation in the resurrection from the dead. *Because* our labor is "in the Lord," it cannot be "in vain." Much of our religious life *is* in vain, simply because we live in the flesh and not in the Lord. We speak a great deal about *our* work for God. But the only fruitful labor is the Lord working in and through us. We are not to function as creators of service, but simply as channels through which He expresses His desire to bless the souls of men.

Is your life a channel of blessing?
Is the love of God flowing through you?
Are you telling the lost of the Saviour?
Are you ready His service to do?[101]

BE STEADFAST

Although Paul did have visions and revelations, he was no mere visionary. For instance, he speaks here of the glorious hope that awaits those who have victory over the grave. He never meant such a blessed future to foster a dreamy joy, but to translate instead into a strong working force. As Alexander Smellie put it,

From gazing on the celestial heights where they die no more, I am bidden to look on the dusty plain beneath, so full of misery and sin and death, and see

101. Harper G. Smyth, "Make Me a Channel of Blessing," 1903.

that to be my appointed sphere of courageous and consecrated service at the present hour.

The apostle begins here with an exhortation to steadfastness, or a firm establishment in the faith forever settled in heaven.

The English term *"stedfast,"* which occurs twenty times in the Bible, is represented by several Hebrew and Greek words. Here, it is the original *hedra*, meaning "a seat," and denotes one who is seated or settled, metaphorically speaking of moral and spiritual fixity or stability. Paul commended the Colossians for their steadfastness, or the fixity of their faith in Christ. (See Colossians 2:5.) Some scholars think that the word *stedfast* is used in a military sense to indicate a "solid front," or having no gap in the ranks when marching to battle. The Bible also has some profitable things to say about this quality in our witness and warfare.

GOD IS THE PERFECTION OF STABILITY

Daniel declared Him to be *"the living God, and stedfast for ever, and His kingdom that which shall not be destroyed"* (Daniel 6:26). What an assuring truth—*"stedfast for ever"*! What a wonderful example we have to follow!

JESUS MANIFESTED THIS DIVINE QUALITY

We read that He *"stedfastly"* set His face toward Jerusalem to die for the sins of the world. There was always a look of fixed determination on His benign countenance, suggesting that neither devil nor man could deter Him from accomplishing His divine mission. (See Luke 9:31.)

THE INFALLIBLE WORD ALSO IS "STEDFAST"

The truth communicated *"by angels was stedfast"* (Hebrews 2:2). This means that it was fixed in heaven. The Word, like the world, is established and cannot be moved. (See Psalm 96:10.)

THE SAINTS ARE EXHORTED TO BE "STEDFAST"

Following the Savior as our guide, we should hold confidence in Him *"stedfast unto the end"* (Hebrews 3:14). Peter urged us to resist the devil steadfastly in the faith (See 1 Peter 5:9), and to be found in the last hour looking steadfastly into heaven. (See Acts 7:55.) We must be steadfast and not fear amid the trials of life. (See Job 11:15.) We are more than conquerors if our hearts stand steadfast. (See 1 Corinthians 7:37.)

We are also warned against retreating from a fixed position. Some fail to be steadfast in faith because they allow room for error. (See 2 Peter 3:17.) The Israelites were condemned because their spirit was not steadfast with God, nor His covenant. (See Psalm 78:8, 37.) The Word teaches that the glorious hope set before us is an anchor for the soul, both sure and steadfast. (See Hebrews 6:19). May we cling to such an anchor *"which entereth into that within the veil"*! John Bunyan reminds Christians of the hope we have in the Gospels, "Set your faces like a flint: you have all power in heaven and earth on your side." Later on, the Dreamer in *Pilgrim's Progress* recalls a pilgrim named Mr. Standfast who was always on his knees on the Enchanted Ground. How triumphant Standfast finished his course! "Tell them," he said, "of my happy arrival at this place, and of the blessed condition in which I am." After entering the river, there was a great calm. Not a breath disturbed the air, not a ripple curled the water. Beyond the water, Standfast heard a sweet voice and looking upon a more desirable face than the sun itself, was filled with joy over the welcome given to pilgrims. May we be found a very good pilgrim just like Standfast, remaining true to God and His Word until we reach the river too.

Browning would have me "hold a steadfast course till I arrive, at my fit destination." But because of the dangers within myself, I must first of all be *steadfast*. I am in danger of growing cold, conventional, listless in my spiritual life; of becoming so engrossed with earthly things that I lose my relish for heavenly things; of being so self-indulgent that I lose my once fervent enthusiasm for the Christ who saved me. I need to emulate Paul's gift of endurance, given by the grace of God. Joseph Addison teaches us to hold fast unto the end:

> Though in the paths of death I tread
> With gloomy horrors overspread,
> My stedfast heart shall fear no ill,
> For Thou, O Lord, art with me still!
> Thy rod and staff shall give me aid,
> And guide me through the dreadful shade![102]

BE UNMOVEABLE

Marcus Aurelius is credited with having said, "Stand firm like a rock against which the waves batter, yet it stands unmoved, till they fall to rest at last." This is something of the sort Paul had in mind when he urged the saints at Corinth to remain "*unmoveable*," a term indicating establishment in the faith as related to assault from temptation or persecution. This English word occurs only one other place in Scripture,

---

102. Joseph Addison, "The Lord My Pastor Shall Prepare," 1712.

in connection with the shipwreck Paul experienced on the way to Rome—*"they ran the ship aground, and the fore-part stuck fast, and remained unmoveable"* (Acts 27:41). This position was parabolic of Paul's firm witness for the truth. The psalmist could say, *"I have stuck unto thy testimonies"* (Psalm 119:31), and the apostle *"stuck fast"* to the Word, remaining *"unmoveable"* living out and defending the Word. Nothing could shake the ship out of its fixed place in the sea. How reassuring it is to know that we are part of a kingdom that cannot be shaken! (See Hebrews 12:28 RV.)

Alas! The tragedy is that far too many people in the church are unmovable in a wrong sense. It breaks pastors' hearts to see their flock so content with spiritual progress and aggressive service. Rock-like, they resist spiritual influences that could greatly enrich their lives, if only they would respond to them. They say in their hearts, *"I shall not be moved"* (Psalm 10:6). But there is a necessary unmovability for those who go about doing well like the Master.

Coupled with dangers within that threaten steadfastness, there are foes without that attack as well. The worldly atmosphere is a corroding influence. We are surrounded by false teachings of God, life, and eternity, along with the deception of that which calls itself "newer truth," yet is only falsity under a new name; all this seeks to corrupt me from *"the simplicity that is in Christ"* (2 Corinthians 11:3), till I become *"unstable as water"* (Galatians 49:4) or like *"a reed shaken with the wind"* (Matthew 11:7). Paul would have us put on the whole armor of God, that we would be able to withstand the evil day and having done all we could do, *"to stand"* (Ephesians 6:13). If our eyes are constantly on the Lord, He will not allow our foot to be moved (see Psalm 121:3), just as He promised His ancient church,

"She shall not be moved" (Psalm 46:5). David also wrote, *"I have set the LORD always before me: because He is at my right hand, I shall not be moved"* (Psalm 16:8). David made it clear that if we follow the divine plan laid out for us, then we shall never be moved. (See Psalm 15:5.) When Martin Luther nailed the ninety-five theses to the church door, it was accompanied by the courageous outburst, "Here I stand; I can do no other. God help me!" Greatly influenced by Paul's teachings, this mighty reformer certainly knew how to be unmovable in defending the faith. His determination to stand fast in the faith is expressed in the hymn, "A Mighty Fortress Is Our God"

> And through this world,
> With devils filled,
> Should threaten to undo us,
> We will not fear,
> For God hath willed
> His truth to triumph though us.

> Let goods and kindred go,
> This mortal life also;
> The body they may kill:
> God's truth abideth still,
> His kingdom is forever.[103]

> Stir me, O stir me, Lord, Thy heart was stirred
> By love's intensest fire, till Thou didst give
> Thine only Son, Thy best beloved one,
> E'en to the dreadful cross, that I might live.
> Stir me to give myself so back to Thee,
> That Thou canst give Thyself again through me.[104]

---

103. Martin Luther, "A Mighty Fortress Is Our God," 1517.
104. Helen Roseveare, *Stir Me*.

CHAPTER 38

THREE BIBLE BLESSINGS

When thou goest, it shall lead thee;
when thou sleepest, it shall keep thee;
when thou awakest, it shall talk with thee.
—Proverbs 6:22

Solomon, who had experienced a godly upbringing under parental law, speaks here of the influence of a higher law, the Law of God. His father David, who hid the Law within his heart, often told his son that if he loved, honored, obeyed, and remembered the Law, he would live a blessed life. This was one reason Solomon shares this triad of blessing with us, so that we might love God's Word as well.

IT SHALL LEAD THEE

All the guidance we need is found in the Bible, safe and secure. The phrase *"When thou goest"* means that when we set out each day, the light of the Word shines on our pathway and the inner voice says, *"This is the way, walk ye in it"* (Isaiah 30:21). Obedience to the Bible leads us *away* from the path of sin and *through* the difficulties ahead. Then it takes us *into* the joyous peace of everlasting rest.

IT SHALL KEEP THEE

What a precious truth Solomon adds here to the promise—*"when thou sleepest."* The Word is our guard through the night as well as our guide during the day. If His promises dwell in us richly in all wisdom, then our dreams at night will be pure and good. "The soul that is guided by its precepts in the day will be kept by its promises in the dark." If we cannot sleep through the night, the precious truths of Scripture will steady the heart and keep it calm.

IT SHALL TALK WITH THEE

"When thou awakest, it shall talk with thee" (Proverbs 6:22). There is no better way to start the day then with a few moments in the Bible, praying that God will give us a message to take throughout the day. Although we might not know what difficulties and crossroads lie ahead, God does, and he promises in His Word that he will strengthen us to meet any trials and temptations, duties and difficulties the day may bring.

May grace ours to be as the Raratonga Christians called themselves—"Sons of the Word." Let us make the Bible the map by which we walk, the sundial by which we set our life, and the balance by which we weigh our acts. The Word is the clear light that shines across the sea, undimmed in neither storm nor calm. May we never forget the couplet D. L. Moody wrote on the flyleaf of his Bible,

> This Book will keep you from sin,
> Sin will keep you from this Book.

CHAPTER 39

THREE FRAGRANT ODORS

Myrrh…aloes…cassia…
—Psalm 45:8

Among the other Christ-exalting Psalms, this messianic Psalm occupies a prominent position. As C. I. Scofield expresses, "This great Psalm of the King obviously looks forward to the advent in glory." The psalm is full of the King of Glory. No other can claim the honor and holiness, the glory and grace, and the fame and fragrance described in this psalm. His kingly presence, power, and possessions dominate this beautiful delineation of our blessed Lord. Notice the use of the pronoun *thy.* "*Thy lips,*" "*Thy thigh,*" "*Thy sword,*" "*Thy glory,*" "*Thy majesty,*" "*Thy right hand,*" "*Thy throne,*" "*Thy kingdom,*" "*Thy fellows,*" "*Thy garments.*" Everything is His.

God's garments in the triad of fragrance indicate all that He is and has. Clothes speak of character. "Clothes make the man," we often say. We can understand the Father's house above by the "ivory palace." If only we had the silver tongue of Gabriel to declare all the glory and magnificence of heaven!

MYRRH

In Old Testament times, the king's robes were often fragranced with aromatic plants that were kept in ivory perfume boxes. Three distinct fragrances gladdened the king's heart. The *myrrh* usually represented the love of the heart. Mary poured the precious contents of her alabaster box on her Savior, the sweet savor of the ointment gladdening the King. It was sweet because it was a symbol of Mary's love. Does our love for Jesus take practical shape, like Mary's love with her fragrant oil?

ALOES

Aloes represent the holiness of our lives, which is ever pleasing to the Lord. Israel's burnt-offerings symbolized the sinner's complete surrender to the Lord, which was called *"a sweet savour unto the Lord"* (Leviticus 1:9). Nothing gladdens the heart of the Redeemer like a sinner yielding himself as *"a living sacrifice"* (Romans 12:1). How sad then, that although we are equally redeemed, we do not equally gladden the Redeemer. Some of His children bring him more pleasure than others.

CASSIA

This fragrant herb often symbolizes the service of our hands. Paul called the monetary help he received from the Philippians for his gospel work as, *"An odour of a sweet smell, a sacrifice acceptable, wellpleasing to God"* (Philippians 4:18). How it gladdens the Master to see practical service from those that love Him! If only our labor for Him could be as limitless as His love to us! His service for us is constant and unending. Is the cassia of our loving, ungrudging labor gladdening the King? What a privilege it is not only to provide fruits for His table, but to contribute perfumes for His refreshment and joy. May the wind of the Spirit awake and blow on your garden and mine, so that its spices may flow forth. (See Song of Solomon 4:16.)

> Like a watered garden
> Full of fragrance rare,
> Lingering in His presence,
> May our life appear![105]

---

105. E. May Grimes, "The Quiet Hours," 1920.

CHAPTER 40

THREE GRADES OF TALENTS

To one he gave five talents, to another, two, and to another, one;
each according to his own ability; and he went on his journey.
—Matthew 25:15 NASV

The parable of the talents is full of spiritual instruction to do the work of the Lord. First of all, the parable teaches us that all God's servants are not equally endowed.

When Christ ascended on high, He gave gifts to men, but these gifts differ in number and measure as do the stars in the heavens. (See Ephesians 4:7–13; 1 Corinthians 12:8–28.) The second truth gleaned from this parable is that the absent Master expects equal diligence in the use of unequal gifts, and such diligence results in an equal reward. Thirdly, those who receive talents will be charged with unfaithfulness if they do not use those gifts for the purpose they were given.

A key phrase in the parable is *"according to his own ability."* The Master does not require for more than we can give. He does, however, expect us to serve Him to the capacity of our gifts. Although we are not expected to do more than we can achieve, we are also not expected to do less. The Lord does not look for the two-talented man to produce what the five-talented man is equipped to produce. Neither does He demand from the one-talented man what the two-talented one can give.

There are many varieties of service, just as there are various qualifications for service. He calls us to the special service He qualified us for. The question is, have we discovered what our gifts are—or our gift is—and are they being used to the fullest capacity for Him? I may not be squandering my talent in sin, but laziness and indifference to the Master's desire to use the gift is just as sinful. If we are faithful and wise stewards, the Lord will say of us when He returns, *"Blessed is that servant, whom his lord when He cometh shall find his doing"* (Luke 12:43).

Faithfulness is the basis of reward at the judgment seat of Christ. It makes no difference how many talents we have. Unlike as they may be, the same reward will be given to those who are faithful with what the Lord gave them. The servant with five talents will receive the same benediction as the servant with one talent, *"Well done, good and faithful servant… enter thou into the joy of thy Lord"* (Matthew 25:21). The Judge will not reward our fame, but our fidelity; not our apparent success, but our sincerity; not how much we have done or given but what our motivations were. This principle rebukes all arrogance in the highly-gifted, or all despondency and negligence in the less-gifted.

CHAPTER 41

THREE NOTES OF
THE NEW SONG

Worthy art thou to take the book, and to open the seals thereof:
for thou wast slain, and didst purchase unto God with thy blood
men...and madest [us] to be unto our God a kingdom and
priests; and they reign upon the earth.
—Revelation 5:9–10 RV

The songs of the Bible form a profitable study. Conspicuous praise graces its sacred pages. The *"new song"* John writes about in Revelation has three distinct notes: redemption, dominion, and consecration and intercession.

REDEMPTION

He *"didst purchase* [us] *unto God with thy* blood" (Revelation 5:9). Here is the beautiful note of redemption. Those that are glorified in heaven sing, *"Worthy art thou to open the book,"* rejoicing in the matchless salvation of the Lamb that made heaven a reality for them. *"Worthy is the Lamb that hath been slain."* Christ, through breaking the alabaster vase of His unblemished body and pouring forth *"the costly spikenard of His blood,"* delivered me from the guilt and despair of sin. For this reason, His blood-bought emancipation will be the subject of our praise throughout all of eternity. May we not forget that there is a song we must learn to sing now if we want to sing in the choir of the redeemed above.

DOMINION

"Thou madest [us] *to be unto our God a kingdom."* Here is the note of dominion. We are made "kings" to Him through grace. Royalty and true nobility become ours when we surrender our lives to the Lord. We are made rulers over the fear of men, the dread of death, and the darkness of our foes. Our position with the Redeemer on His own throne is assured through the cross. We can grab hold of the promise that He will share His great empire with us. The question is, does He presently reign over the empire of our lives? Are we His true, loyal, and obedient servants here and now? If so, it will be our honor to assist Him in His governmental control of all things when He returns to reign!

CONSECRATION AND INTERCESSION

"Priests thou madest us also." Here is the note of consecration and intercession. Only those who have been pardoned are priests. Apart from His perpetual priesthood, the only other effectual priesthood on earth is the priesthood of believers. Do we realize how sacred and sacramental our service is? We are so privileged to function as white-robed, white-souled ministrants, thanking and adoring our great High Priest with our lives! We have the opportunity of offering the incense of our prayers to Him, along with offering the continual sacrifice of our spirits, souls, and bodies! Like our

Advocate on high, we too can lift up holy hands in ceaseless intercession.

Worthy is the Lamb who will receive all of the power, riches, wisdom, might, honor, glory, and blessing for all He accomplished for sinners, lost and ruined by the fall.

CHAPTER 42

THREE STAGES OF SPIRITUAL GROWTH

First the blade, then the ear, after that the full grain in the ear.
—Mark 4:28

Fruit that sprang up and increased; and brought forth, some thirty, and some sixty, and some an hundred.
—Mark 4:8

Christian development is a gradual process. While a crisis makes a sinner a saint, there comes a process of maturity that follows accepting Christ. After we receive Christ, we must walk in Him to grow full in stature in Him. The divine Gardener expects to reap a full recompense for His toil: *"First the blade, then the ear, after that the full grain in the ear"* (Mark 4:28). These stages of growth are equivalent to what was expressed in the previous verse, *"Fruit that sprang up and increased; and brought forth, some thirty, and some sixty, and some an hundred"* (Mark 4:8).

STAGE ONE

"First the blade...some thirty." The one who is truly regenerated does not have a sign of coming fruit, but naturally bears it, although the cluster is small. The days when grace

begins should not be despised. God does not expect fully rip-ened fruit before its time. The peril is that many are satisfied with remaining blades like they were at the beginning, refus-ing to grow into fuller, healthier blades. Somehow they fail to grow in grace and the knowledge of the Lord. If the small, tender shoots fail to develop from lack of water or weeds of worldliness, it will be our fault, not the divine Gardener's.

STAGE TWO

"Then the ear...some sixty." We do not look at our garden in early spring and expect to see the flowers that only come in summer. Just so, God does not despair when He does not see our Christian lives growing in all the wisdom, steadfastness, and fruit of spiritual maturity. He does expect, however, that the blade becomes an ear, and that the thirty multiple into sixty. He has a lot of patience for the fully ripened fruit, and does not harvest before its time. Is our spiritual development pleasing to the heart of the divine Gardener? Are we growing into the full stature of Christ?

STAGE THREE

"After that the full corn...some an hundred." While we cannot live a perfect life in the service of the Lord, we should register a maturity in spiritual things. Fellowship with Him should be more real and deep; our love for His Word more intense; our thirst for holiness more evident; and our fruit-fulness more marked. How sad it is to see an aging Christian barren and unfruitful! At whatever stage we are in the Christian walk, may we have the assurance that we are grow-ing at a healthy rate into spiritual maturity.

There is, of course, another way of approaching this triad. We must never criticize those who do not seem to be progressing as quickly as we are. We must not be uncharitable toward them if they do not appear to be growing as fast as we have. We must remember that their soil might be different in quality than ours; it might be more difficult for them to nourish the good seed of grace. For example, our surroundings may be conducive to spiritual growth. What we do know is that God accepts the difference. He does not look for "sixty" if only "thirty" is possible. He knows that the difference is not because of the seed or preventable causes. Disparity in results is partly due to the soil and partly to position. Some plants may have more water at the root and more sunshine overhead and more favorable surroundings in every way, enabling them to produce more fruit than others. Our responsibility is to see if there is anything *in ourselves* that is robbing the divine Gardner from receiving a full harvest.

CHAPTER 43

THREE FREE CORDIALS

Ho, every one that thirsteth, come ye to the waters, and he that hath no money; come ye, buy, and eat; yea, come, buy wine and milk without money and without price.
—Isaiah 55:1

We have what we need to sustain and satisfy us in God's cup of salvation. There is no deficiency or disappointment in what He provided for our needy hearts. The prophet Isaiah tells us that there are three cordials that cannot be bought; and even if they could be bought, there is not enough money in the world to buy them. Both the rich and poor must come to God's market to receive them as the gifts of love—water, milk, and wine.

WATER

One of the first things God offers to us is spiritual refreshment. He finds us in the desert of sin, dying of thirst, and offers us living water out of His deep well of grace. This living water revives us, whereas water from the earth leaves us dry and thirsty. What a joy it is when we discover the divine resources!

MILK

After the draught of water from the cup of salvation, we need spiritual nourishment in order to keep growing. So He provides nourishing milk—the sincere milk of the Word. Frail and powerless, we need strength to fight the many foes waiting to assail our new-found life. By drinking deeply of the divine promises, we are strengthened by His grace. Then as we wander through the rich pastureland of the Bible, we find ourselves in *a land which floweth with milk and honey* (Numbers 14:8). By partaking of both milk and honey, we exchange our weakness for God's strength.

WINE

How great a God we have, who not only provides water to liven and refresh, and milk that nourishes and sustains, but also the wine that cheers and gladdens! In exchange for our fruitless seedbeds of sorrow, proud dejectedness, and cheerless weariness, there is *all joy...in believing* (Romans 15:13). As wine gladdens the heart, so the sunshine of His love banishes fog and gloom. God does not want His children walking through life with lagging steps and hanging head, but with a buoyant heart and radiant face.

Yet there are many who do not receive this gift of wine. They drank deeply of the *water* and *milk*, but refused God's brimming cup of *wine*. As a result, they do not *rejoice in the Lord always*; they are justified by grace, but not joyful. C. H. Spurgeon used to speak of "sour saints and sweet sinners." How imperative it is for saints to be cheerful, not only for their own sake but for the sake of others also! Joyless Christians cannot attract the lost to the Savior, who seeks to impart infinite joy into their hearts.

CHAPTER 44

THREE FEATURES
OF THE PRIESTHOOD

And hath made us kings and priests unto God.
—Revelation 1:6

The doctrine of priesthood, whether that of Christ or of the believer, forms a subject of absorbing interest. Certain religious organizations set apart certain people to function as *priests*. But all true believers are ministering priests—kings *and* priests. (See Revelation 1:6).

In connection with our Lord Jesus Christ, different aspects of His priesthood are demonstrated by the three different services performed by Aaron, high priest of the Jews.

AT THE MERCY SEAT

Once a year, Aaron approached the mercy seat in the Holy of Holies with blood in hand. Sometimes it is said that he displayed his garments *"for glory and beauty"* (Exodus 28:2) that occurred when he stood under the wings of the cherubim on the Day of Atonement, the manifestation of Jehovah's presence. But it is more correct to say that Aaron was dressed in a linen coat, breeches, and girdle when he passed beyond the veil to make a sacrifice for our sins. (See Leviticus 16:4, 23.)

The fine linen, clean and white, symbolizes human righteousness. (See Revelation 19:8.) It speaks most plainly of Christ who was made in the likeness of men and made many men righteous through His obedience. He entered into heaven as our righteousness (see 1 Corinthians 1:30) and our advocate (see 1 John 2:1). If there was a single spot of sin *on* Him or *in* Him, He would not have appeared as our great High Priest before the throne. The act of sprinkling the blood on and before the mercy seat is typical of Christ's presentation of His blood to the Father.

AT THE ALTAR OF INCENSE

The second phase of the Aaronic priesthood is when, arrayed in *"garments for glory and beauty,"* Aaron ministered in the tabernacle. He ministered on a daily basis in the section of the temple where the golden incense, the golden candlestick, and the table of showbread were located. These lovely garments consisted of a blue robe; and an ephod of gold, blue, scarlet and purple and fine twined line with two onyx stones on the shoulder, each engraved with the names of six tribes of Israel; a breastplate of the same material jeweled with twelve costly stones, each engraved with the name of one of the tribes; an embroidered coat; a girdle; and a miter of pure gold engraved with *"Holiness to the Lord."*

Despite how wonderfully adorned he was, Aaron was still an imperfect sinner. He is only an example of the glory and beauty of our great High Priest, the Lord Jesus Christ, who appears on behalf of sinners every moment in the presence of God, bearing them on His *shoulders*—the place of strength; on His *breast*—the seat of His affections; and on

His *forehead*—the height of His own acceptance of us in the Father's view.

AS GOD'S REPRESENTATIVE

The third glimpse of Christ's priesthood is prefigured when the children of Israel were cleansed by the blood; when they gathered around their banners and stood in the person of their *"very high"* (meaning of *Aaron*) representative within the tabernacle. He was covered with the fragrant incense of the golden altar, radiant in the light of the golden candlestick, and having communion at the golden table that contained the bread from heaven. It was here that Aaron pronounced the priestly benediction: *"The LORD bless thee, and keep thee; the LORD make his face shine upon thee, and be gracious unto thee; the LORD lift up his countenance upon thee, and give thee peace"* (Numbers 6:24–26).

This priestly blessing, along with sending the people forth in the wilderness under the grace and keeping of God, is a wonderful example of what we have in Christ. The word of promise secured divine protection for a redeemed people. Through Aaron's offerings and services, they experienced the His shining face; the knowledge of His grace; the lifting up of His countenance; and the full enjoyment of His peace. In the same manner that Christ's last act symbolized His ministry for us—*"He lifted up his hands, and blessed them"* (Luke 24:50). In heaven, He is still lifting His pierced hands before the throne in priestly benediction over all who believe. (See Hebrews 7:25; 8:1.)

CHAPTER 45

THREE HARVEST FRUITS

*The fruit of the light is in
all goodness and righteousness and truth.*
—Ephesians 5:9 RV

Reading through the apostle Paul's writings, we find that if we sow the light, we will reap a golden harvest; that our Christian life should withstand the test of both telescopic observation and microscopic investigation.

GOODNESS

Our "goodness" is manifested in our disposition, talk, and deeds; the first fruit of our life manifested in our sympathy, generosity, and love. This if often lacking in an otherwise attractive fruit. A person may be saved—yet sour; respected—yet unloved. The "goodness" Paul speaks of is the embodiment of grace. The holy fire of divine love burns out selfishness, envy, malice, and temper. We develop warmth, tenderness, and generosity through the cross, becoming good like our Savior.

RIGHTEOUSNESS

Practical righteousness is the outworking of our *positional* righteousness. We do not produce this positional righteous, but merely bear its fruit. This is the sanctification of conscience—the distinct aroma of a character void of all that is crooked, unworthy, or doubtful. The fruits of God's light include high principle, scrupulous honor, and a stern fidelity to duty, even in the smallest things.

TRUTH

Paul would have all believers to be Nathanael's *"in whom is no guile"* (John 1:47). And when we walk in the light as Christ is in the light, we do not act in pretense but a transparent innocence. The Righteous One saves us from all inconsistency and affectation, whether false service or false allegiance. When the Light shines in us and through us, then we reflect all that He is to an unrighteous world.

CHAPTER 46

THREE AREAS
OF CONSECRATION

Right ear…right hand…great toe of his right foot…
—Leviticus 8:23

The consecration of the ancient, holy priesthood is expressively symbolic of the consecration of the believer, who is a priest to God through faith. Aaron was blood-marked in a threefold way when set apart for his sacred task. The priests were first cleansed through a threefold process from personal sin, then consecrated through a threefold blood mark for God's service.

THE RIGHT EAR

The act of putting sacrificial blood on the ears showed that they had to be open to the heavenly voices, but closed to earthly voices, which entice one away from truth and godliness. In a time like ours, when the worldly voices are more insistent than ever, we need to be sensitive to the quiet whispers of the Spirit. We need ears that alert to the cry of a lost world, desperately in need of God, as well as ears that instinctively close to all gossip, slander, and ungodly jokes.

THE THUMB OF
HIS RIGHT HAND

Consecrated ears inevitably lead to consecrated hands. Hands that are ready to help come with listening to the voice of God, which call us to service, and hearing the sinner's cry. Loving hands are stretched out to wrestlers in troubled waters. Furthermore, consecrated hands willingly surrender money to maintain the divine cause.

THE GREAT TOE OF
HIS RIGHT FOOT

When the ear, hand, and foot are marked by the blood, they seem to say, "You have been redeemed. Now every organ, every faculty, and every power must be surrendered to the Redeemer. You are God's from head to foot, and you must serve Him in body as well as in soul and mind."

Our great High Priest is the only one who was perfectly consecrated. In the days of His flesh, His ears always listening for His Father's voice and the cry of the needy; His hands active in the gracious task of relieving the distressed and diseased; His feet carrying Him over rough and rocky roads, weary *in* his work but never *of* it! The following poem suggests our proper response:

> Three things the Master hath to do;
> And we who serve Him here below,
> And love to see His kingdom grow,
> May pray or give or go.

He needs them all—the open hand,
The willing feet, the asking heart,
To work together and to weave
The threefold cord that shall not part.[106]

---

106. Annie Johnson Flint, "Pray–Give–Go."

CHAPTER 47

THREE PRECIOUS JEWELS

Fear not; for I have redeemed thee,
I have called thee by thy name; thou art mine.
—Isaiah 43:1

Have you ever tried to count the *fear nots* of the Bible? One writer said that there are three hundred sixty-five of them, one for every day of the year. Isaiah gives us one of the most precious *fears nots*, with a wonderful triad of divine love. It is a threefold cord no one can break, binding us tightly to the Lord.

I HAVE REDEEMED THEE

God's grace and love is shown in His perfect redemption for a sin-bound humanity. We were under the load of an incalculable debt. We could not say, *"Have patience with me and I will pay thee all"* (Matthew 18:26), for we were spiritually bankrupt. Then the liberating Redeemer came our way and said, "Transfer your debt to Me; My atoning death will be in settlement of every claim." He told us what Paul told Onesimus regarding his debt, *"Put that on mine account"* (Philemon 1:18). Jesus paid it all; and we know that when we accept His grace, our debt has been paid. Across our discharge from bankruptcy is written, "free, full, final."

I HAVE CALLED THEE BY THY NAME

Our despondent hearts are cheered by both God's redeeming love and His individualizing love. It is so wonderful to know that He does not deal with me as if I were just one of a great mass of humanity. God does not throw His blessings over a crowd, leaving everyone to fight for his own. He separates us, and deals with us as individuals. He knows our names, the number of the houses we live in, and all our personal cares. His has a particular and personal love for you and I individually. My name may not be known beyond relatives and friends; or if it is, be apt to be forgotten. But although may blot out my name from their remembrance, my dear Lord says, "I will never blot out thy name from the book of life. It is everlastingly inscribed in My book of remembrance for Me to see." If you have been tempted to doubt God's love and care for you, rest in the knowledge that He knows every one of His sheep by name. Along with Paul, we can say, *"The Son of God, who loveth me"* (Galatians 2:20).

THOU ART MINE

The everlasting love which God pours on us is a protecting love. Because we are His and redeemed by the blood, He promises to guard and guide us every hour of every day. God says to us just what the father said to the eldest son, *"My son thou art ever with me, and all that I have is thine"* (Luke 15:31). His love will never let go. He will preserve us until we are called into His presence above. "His forever, only His."[107]

107. George W. Robinson, "I Am His, and He Is Mine," 1876.

"*Thou art mine*" (Isaiah 43:1)! Ownership implies full possession. I own a few books, but I do not possess them. A friend borrowed them and forgot to return them. God must not only own us, seeing that He bought us, He must also possess us through and through. We have nothing on our own as His. His has the right to claim all we are and have. Thus, we do not surrender ourselves *in order to become* His, but *because* we *are* His.

CHAPTER 48

THREE PHASES OF THE SPIRIT'S WORK

And he, when he is come, will convict the world in respect of sin, and of righteousness, and of judgment: of sin, because they believe not on me; of righteousness, because I go to the Father, and ye behold me no more; of judgment, because the prince of this world hath been judged.
—John 16:8–11 ASV

Jesus said that when the Holy Spirit came to the world, He would, among other works, convict the world in respect of sin, righteousness, and judgment. We must have a deeper, clearer, and more practical view of these three aspects of the Spirit's operation. How guilty we are of misunderstanding and underestimating sin, righteousness, and judgment! It is only by the Holy Spirit that our eyes can be opened to the truth from the divine standpoint.

CONVICTS OF SIN

What a lamentable lack of conviction there is in the world today! This lack makes the evangelists' work exceptionally hard and discouraging. Sinners and Christians alike need more of an awareness of the malignity and loathsomeness of sin. There is a tendency to dress sin up and present it as a human weakness or failure. But the Spirit strips sin of all its specious disguises and calls it by its true name. He reveals its real essence—flat and flagrant opposition of the will of God. In its true character, sin is a rejection of divine authority and love; and it has a tendency to continue in this rebellion. Sin is the attempt to banish God from the world in which He reigns.

CONVICTS OF RIGHTEOUSNESS

The paltry effort of the unregenerated heart to weave its own righteousness proves that it needs the righteousness of Christ, who was righteousness in Himself. Man's garment of self-righteousness is as a filthy rag in God's sight. But through the light of the Holy Spirit, we can see that Jesus is the only righteous Man that ever lived. Though reviled as an impostor and crucified as a blasphemer, Jesus was vindicated and crowned for obedience by His Father. What counts is not what we are in ourselves, but what we are in him, whose imparted righteousness manifests in our own lives.

CONVICTS OF JUDGMENT

Jesus did not say, "judgment to come," but simply "*judgment.*" We need the Spirit's constant revelation that Christ overthrew Satan's reign when He died on the cross! The Devil's judgment and defeat at Calvary is a token of his failure at every attempt to hinder the ultimate victor of our blessed Lord. The sinner's hope is that his debt is already paid for by the Savior, and all condemnation is taken away through accepting Him. (See Romans 8:1.)

We should bless God for the saving and sanctifying work of the Spirit, who first shows us our need and then provides a *"righteous servant"* (Isaiah 53:11). Then He goes onto justify us by bearing our iniquities and setting us free. What a blessed assurance to know that we are forever secured through His timeless work! The Holy Spirit's work always includes conviction, salvation, and assurance.

CHAPTER 49

THREE NOTES OF THE ANGELS' SONG

Glory to God in the highest,
and on earth peace, good will to men.
—Luke 2:14

Luke tells us that the first song ever sung over Jesus was at His incarnation. The angels joined in chorus to produce the first Christmas carol. From Scripture, we glean that there were three notes in this glad song, and the loftiest was sounded first.

GLORY TO GOD IN THE HIGHEST

Although there was no visible sign of glory in the manger scene, farm animals surrounded baby Christ, the angels saw that His birth illuminated heaven. What does the picture of these sinless angels singing over Jesus suggest? It suggests that they knew what sin had done among themselves and in the world. They knew Lucifer prior to the fall, who was the highest of all angelic beings and who was cast out of heaven. They knew that there was no Redeemer promised at this time, and probably thought it would be the same for men.

But we see that the good angel understood the way of grace for sinning men with this song, singing glory to God for His infinite wisdom and holy love.

ON EARTH PEACE

Seeing Jehu, son of Nimshi, riding furiously across the Jezreel, King Joram sent out messengers to ask, "*Is it peace, Jehu?*" (2 Kings 9:22). Jehu answered each of them, "*What hast thou to do with peace? turn thee behind me*" (2 Kings 9:19). If it were possible for earthly messengers to meet Jesus on His way down to a sinful world asking, "Is it peace, Jesus?" He would have been justified replying, "*What hast thou to do with peace?*" Even so, the whole heavenly host of messengers forestalls the question, "Is it peace?" by singing, "*On earth peace, good will toward men*" (Luke 2:14). What can we do but bow our heads in wonder and adoration for all the newborn Child accomplished for a lost world. International strife and the threat of nuclear war make it seem that earth is far from "*on earth peace,*" but a day is coming when the Prince of Peace will indeed reign in peace.

GOOD WILL TOWARD MEN

In all its parts, the gospel is a message of "*goodwill to men.*" This message is even for the vilest, for the Lord has no pleasure in the death of the wicked. The warnings, as well as the provisions and promises of the gospel, are permeated with God's good will. His will is ever good. On the other hand, there is a lack of good will among men—in home-life, business life, and although sad to confess, even in the religious realm. What sad divisions exist between men! The kindness of God, however, is evident in all His works.

CHAPTER 50

THREE WITNESSES IN AGREEMENT

For there are three that bear record in heaven, the Father, the Word, and the Holy Ghost: and these three are one. And there are three that bear witness in earth, the Spirit, and the water, and the blood: and these three agree in one.
—1 John 5:7–8

Under ancient Jewish law, three witnesses were needed to confirm any matter, which acted as a safeguard against any false evidence or testimony. (See Deuteronomy 17:6; Matthew 18:16; Hebrews 10:28.) Scripture talks about occasions when false witnesses appeared against the testified, as in the Lord's trial when He was condemned on false evidence. But as Solomon reminds us, *"a faithful witness will not lie"* (Proverbs 14:5). The assessment of these two triads then cannot be anything but true and just.

One of Paul's favorite words was *witness*—one of the key words in the Gospels. In John 21:24, he uses it to induce and confirm people's faith in the incarnation, with an understanding that *"life in his name"* (John 20:31) goes along with victory in the world. It is not surprising then that there is in his first epistle, which proves the deity of Christ, a strong emphasis on the word *witness*. In one form or another, this word occurs nine times in five consecutive verses (in the Greek, the word occurs ten times). John asks the question, *"Who is he that overcometh the world?"* and then answers, *"He that believeth that Jesus is the Son of God"* (1 John 5:5). Afterwards, the apostle cites three witnesses in heaven and on earth, all in perfect agreement that Jesus is the Son of God.

The phrases *"these three are one"* (1 John 5:7) and *"these three agree in one"* (verse 8), imply that the double witness is for *"one end"*—namely, a confirmation of the deity of God's beloved Son. Wherever words, phrases, or verses are repeated in Scripture, the purpose of such repetition is to emphasize the truth. Thus, twice over John refers to water, blood, and the Spirit as being the witnesses on earth to the Godhead of Jesus.

> *This is He that came by water and blood, even Jesus Christ; not with the water only, but with the water and with the blood. And it is the Spirit that beareth witness, because the Spirit is truth. For there are three that bear witness, the spirit, and the water, and the blood: and the three agree in one.* (1 John 5:6–8)

In what sense were these three witnesses to the sonship of the Lord Jesus Christ? How did they cooperate to *"the one end"* in magnifying Him who came in the image of the Father? It is important to understand this threefold witness because our Christian faith is built on its strong foundation. Additionally, it is imperative to examine this threefold fact, seeing that our present hope, along with the hope of the world, rests on the fact that Jesus really was the promised divine Redeemer.

BY WATER

What exactly constituted the witness of the *water* to the deity of Jesus? Is it referring to the water of His baptism in

Jordan? After all, this is where He was consecrated for the redeeming work He came to accomplish; where He identified Himself with the sinful race He came to save; where a heavenly voice revealed He was the Son of God? The general consensus is that this agreement refers to Jesus' baptism, when He received His Father's confirmation that He was the Beloved Son in whom He was well pleased.

Furthermore, the apostle John records the Baptist's experience of the descending Spirit on that occasion: *"I have seen, and have borne witness that this is the Son of God"* (John 1:34). In this particular reference to the baptism of Jesus, John may have been thinking of the false teaching of Cerinthus. Distinguishing between Jesus *and* Christ, he taught that that the divine Christ descended upon the human Jesus at baptism, and left before the crucifixion; that is to say, He came *"by water,"* not *"by blood."* However, David Smith points out, "Thus redemption was excluded; all that was needed was spiritual illumination." At His birth, He was declared as the Savior—*"Christ the Lord"*; and in the narrative before us, John combats the radical heresy of Cerinthus, who did not believe in the virgin birth and declared that God was incarnate in the Savior all the days of His flesh.

BY BLOOD

Undoubtedly, the blood refers to Calvary and the marvelous deliverance accomplished there. We see the *blood* of Christ's atoning cross when He suffered as *"the just for the unjust"* (1 Peter 3:18), and as *"the Lamb of God, which taketh away the sin of the world"* (John 1:29). The modern, cultured mind may reject the witness of the blood, but we know that without the shedding of Christ's blood, there is no remission of sin. Without His blood "so red, for me was shed," a sinner is both helpless and hopeless. Calvary, then, bears witness to the sinner's need and God's ability to meet that need. Having come *"by blood"* in the sense of propitiatory atonement, Jesus now can make the vilest clean.

> Just as I am, without one plea,
> But that Thy blood was shed for me,
> And that Thou bidst me come to Thee,
> O Lamb of God, I come, I come![108]

Having both His blood and bidding, what more do we want if we are conscious of our need for deliverance from the slavery and dominion of sin? Expositors do not agree on whether John's mention of *water* and *blood* refers to the water and blood that flowed from the Savior's side on the cross. There are those who interpret the *water* as a symbol of the Spirit, and who, therefore, see a combination of Calvary and Pentecost in the water and the blood. This is the double cure for sin: the gift at Calvary delivers us from guilt and the gift of Pentecost emancipates us from its power.

BY THE SPIRIT

Jesus mentions this third witness before He shed His blood on the cross, *"He* [the Holy Spirit] *shall testify* [bear witness] *of me"* (John 15:26). This heavenly witness has authority and is reliable. John describes him as *"the truth,"* just as our Lord said that He Himself is *the truth.* (See John 14:6.) The Spirit not only leads us into truth, but is Himself truth personified. Furthermore, as *"the truth,"* His witness is through

108. Charlotte Elliott, "Just as I Am, Without One Plea," 1935.

keeping His character. Because of His godhead, He cannot act contrary to what He is.

If we want to understand this third testimony, then we must realize the significance of the *water*, that represents the Lord's life, and the *blood*, that represents his death.

Without the Spirit's enlightenment, the wonder and glory of the Son of God becoming human flesh and redeeming mankind is not only hidden from us, but also unintelligible. We lack the vital union with Christ without the third witness, which makes faith fruitful for life and service. Paul reminds us that *"the natural man receiveth not the things of the Spirit of God"* (1 Corinthians 2:14). But the redeemed have the witness of the Spirit, the interpreter, to enable them to understand the historic facts of their redemption.

The Spirit testifies that Jesus is the Savior through the written word, and His enlightening and convincing ministry within the soul. Within the passages that speak of the Spirit as a witness is also one of the strongest proofs of the Spirit's personality. Although the Greek word for *Spirit* is a neuter noun, it is linked with masculine terms. All three nouns used for the *Spirit, water,* and *blood* are neuter; but when they are referred to as *"the three,"* the expressions are masculine. This must be because of the personality of the only One who could be referred to in this way. Without the Spirit's divine teaching, the witness of the water and the blood is not understood. He is the one who makes all truth shine.

Although we have considered these three witnesses separately, they agree as one and indeed are one—a trinity in unity. One alone will not suffice. If we look only at the water, or see Jesus as the only one commissioned to preach the good news, becoming entranced by the beauty of His life and message, we are in danger of forgetting our need for the blood. In seeking to imitate His perfect pattern, we fail to see our need of His atoning sacrifice to free our guilty soul from the penalty and curse of God's broken law.

Furthermore, Benjamin Warfield says that it is possible to look at both the water and the blood, "believing them simply as undeniable historical facts, regarding the historical Christ, but without having them made living realities to us through the Spirit bringing them home to our hearts in such a way as to give me a personal experience of saving and sanctifying grace." None of these witnesses can be ignored if we are looking for full assurance and rest. They are a threefold cord that cannot be broken, binding us closer to the divine Master every day. When other cords break under the strain of fear and sorrow, the unbreakable cord of the water, blood, and Spirit draw us closer to the one Isaiah called *"the Mighty God"* (Isaiah 9:6), whom Paul spoke of as the one *"who loved me and gave himself for me"* (Galatians 2:20).

Some scholars impugn the legitimacy of the three heavenly witnesses John mentions in verse seven—the Father, the Word, and the Spirit. They claim that many Greek manuscripts omit it, as do the Revised Version and various modern translations of the New Testament. But what a wonderful trio of witness there is in the Father, the Word, and the Spirit! Matthew Henry comments on this trinity of heavenly witnesses, testifying the authority of Jesus Christ:

> The first that occurs in order is *the Father*; He set His seal to the commission of the Lord Christ all the while He was here. (See John 5:36.) The second witness is *the Word*, a mysterious name. He must bear witness to the human nature, or to *the man* Christ Jesus.

But could this stand for the written word, of which the original resides in heaven? *"Thy Word is settled in heaven"* (Psalm 119:89).

The third witness is the Holy Spirit. True and faithful must He be to whom the Spirit of holiness sets His seal.

The Spirit is the one who not only testifies to Christ's claims, but also glorifies Him. (See John 16:14.) Such are the witnesses in heaven, bearing record from heaven; they are one in their testimony to the godhead of Christ. To those of us who have experienced the cleansing efficacy of His blood and transforming power, there is no doubt to His deity.

His power, increasing, still shall spread;
His reign no end shall know:
Justice shall guard His throne above,
And peace abound below.

CHAPTER 51

THREE DISTINGUISHABLE MEN

The natural man...spiritual...carnal.
—1 Corinthians 2:14–15; 3:1–4

Paul not only divided the whole human family into the three groups—the Jew, the Gentile, the church of God—but also identified three different types of men—the natural man, the carnal man, and the spiritual man. A scriptural understanding of these distinguishable men saves us from confusion as to their identity. There are three preliminary thoughts to bear in mind as we consider these three men.

The first is that there is an obvious difference between the character and quality of people acknowledged and defined in the Bible, with its emphasis on human life and experience. Just as the range of Christian life was higher among the Ephesians than the Corinthians, so we can place those we meet in any of the three categories the apostle gives to us.

We must also bear in mind the improvement of the character and quality of those around us. While the bad are becoming worse—more devoted to idols, less God-honoring and God-fearing—the good are becoming better. (See Daniel 12:10.)

Earnest, spiritually-minded believers have a desire to line themselves up with the will of God. They long for richer service, along with a deeper holiness and more passionate love for God.

The third thought is that these three groups, as Paul classifies them, are identified by their attitude toward God's truths. People are grouped according to their ability to understand and receive certain aspects of scriptural truth. The natural and carnal men are not able to go into the deep mysteries of God. They cannot extend their respective spheres. But with the enlightening Holy Spirit within, the spiritual man is invited into the mysteries and communication of heavenly things.

Dr. A. T. Pierson reminds us that…

Man is a mirror, and it is an all-important matter which way the mirror is turned. If downward it can reflect only earthly things, the mire, the dirt, the filth of earth: if turned upward it may reflect the heavens with all their glory of sun, moon, and stars. The mirror turned downward is the carnal mind; the mirror turned upward is the spiritual mind. Sometimes in an instant of time, the inversion is accomplished, and he who before was of the earth, earthy, comes to discern and reflect the things of God and of heaven.

THE NATURAL MAN: LACKING THE SPIRIT (SEE 1 CORINTHIANS 2:14)

The natural man is under the influence of his unchanged and unchangeable Adamic nature. Not giving Christ any place in his life, he is spiritually unchanged. Jude describes him as "*having not the Spirit*" (Jude 1:19), making him utterly unable to appreciate and appropriate the truths revealed through the Spirit. Having only the spirit and wisdom of man, he cannot comprehend divine things. As Paul puts it, "*they are foolishness*" (1 Corinthians 2:14) to such a man.

The natural man may be cultured, learned, and religious, yet unable to discourse on moral precepts. He is nevertheless unable to grasp spiritual contents of Scripture, for they are discerned only through the Spirit. Although he may be educated in all the wisdom of this world, he cannot know the deep things of God without the Spirit, for the world by its wisdom cannot know Him. As far as he is concerned, the things of God may be dull and stupid. Measureless evil arises when people assume that when a man is well advanced in "*earthly wisdom*" (James 3:15), his opinions are valuable in spiritual matters as well. However, knowledge of the sciences can never replace the enlightenment of the Holy Spirit. Because there is no regeneration apart from the Holy Spirit, no unregenerate person can impart spiritual truth. How could he, since he has no relation with the embodiment of truth? As Paul expresses it, the natural man cannot *know* the truth, that is, he incapable of discerning its true nature. The fault comes not in his will, but in his lack of understanding without the Spirit.

What authority do we have to suppose that teachers and preachers, brilliant in certain departments of acquired human knowledge, are equally capable of spiritual discernment? Although one might be highly and sufficiently educated, he is incapable of receiving and understanding the simplest truths of Scripture if he is an unregenerate person. This discernment is not brought about by the exercise of human brains. All divine truth is revelation which is bestowed in response to childlike faith. Therefore, the *natural man* is one who has no contact with Christ and the Holy Spirit who is the Regenerator, Sanctifier, and Revealer.

THE CARNAL MAN: BORN OF THE SPIRIT (SEE 1 CORINTHIANS 3:1-4)

There are no divine classifications among the unsaved; all are *natural*. Whether good or bad, learned or ignorant, cultured or coarse, rich or poor, they are grouped under *natural man*. Yet Paul describes two classes of men among the saved—the *spiritual* and *the carnal*—both having crossed the border of the *natural*, despite the fact that "carnal" is sometimes used of the unregenerate. In one sense, the *carnal man* can be classified as spiritual because he received the gift of the Spirit. But although he has been regenerated, he lacks the Spirit's graces and is therefore unable to comprehend spiritual truths and relish spiritual things. Paul uses the word *carnal*, meaning fleshly, to describe the spiritually-retarded Corinthians. It implies a renewed man who walks after the flesh instead of the Spirit. He lives a self-life instead of a Christ-life. The apostle says that the carnal mind has three noticeable characteristics—death, enmity, and displeasure. (See Romans 8:6–8.) Furthermore, Paul indicates two inescapable features of the carnal man in Corinthians.

First, the carnally-minded is only a babe in Christ; therefore, he can only drink milk because he is unable to masticate strong meat. Although a *babe* is better than a *corpse*—the natural man who is spiritually dead—he is missing out on the abundant life of a spiritual adult. The *carnal* Christian then, no longer incapacitated like the natural man to understand spiritual truth, is only capable of understanding the simplest truths of Scripture, like a child knows little more than the ABCs. Those who are carnal must live on *milk* because they lack a strong spiritual constitution. They have little appetite for deep spiritual truth, little enthusiasm for the Word, little delight in the fellowship of the saints, and little interest in consecrated service for the Master.

Second, the carnally-minded yield to envy and strife. They walk as men of the world, guided by worldly principles instead of the Holy Spirit. Although they are saved by grace, they still walk according to the course of the world. Their objectives and inclinations are grounded in the unspiritual world of the natural man. Because they are carnal, their flesh dominates all they say, think, and do. All of this is in sharp contrast to the spiritual man who walks not after the flesh but in the Spirit. Paul describes how the carnality of the Corinthians gave birth to envy, strife, and sad divisions in the church. Truly, a loveless, carnal believer brings much damage to the life and service of a church. Our only safeguard from such an unsatisfactory, dishonoring life is to *"walk in the Spirit, and ye shall fulfil the lust of the flesh"* (Galatians 5:16). It would seem from Paul's epistles that issues of carnality are sevenfold: carnally minded (see Romans 8:5, 7); carnally limited (see 1 Corinthians 3:1); carnally weak (see 1 Corinthians 3:2); carnally bound and enslaved (see Romans 7:14); carnally disposed (see 1 Corinthians 3:3, 4); carnally opposed to God (see Romans 8:7); and carnally doomed (see Galatians 6:8).

THE SPIRITUAL MAN: FILLED BY THE SPIRIT (SEE CORINTHIANS 3:1–3)

If the natural man is gives no place to Christ in his life, and the carnal man gives *only* a place to Christ, then the spiritual man is the one who gives the preeminent place to Him. The latter is the divine ideal for every Christian—the life God desires for every believer in life and service. He is at peace with God and lives in unbroken fellowship with Him. While this word *spiritual* occurs only once in the Old Testament (see Hosea 9:7), it occurs at least twenty times in the New Testament. It designates those who live in obedience to the Spirit. The *spiritual man* is a man of the Spirit, implying a person who Spirit-filled and in communion with God. Paul referred to his bodily scars as *"the marks of the Lord Jesus"* (Galatians 6:17). The marks of the Spirit were also evident in his life, which was so fully controlled by the Spirit.

The spiritual are able to discern all things, with no limitation to their comprehension of the deepest truths of Scripture. Their spiritual condition, indwelt by the author of the Word, makes the revelation of these truths possible. They freely receive the divine revelation, while the natural man lacks understanding and the carnal man lacks appreciation. The spiritual Christian, then, is one who allows the Holy Spirit to fully control his tripartite being and, because of His unhindered ministry in heart and mind, receives a spiritual robust constitution so that they can eat strong meat.

In summary, the *spiritual man* is the one who is filled with the Holy Spirit. The unhindered Spirit manifests Christ in him and through him, producing a true Christian character.

He exercises true Christian service because of his distinct gift, or gifts, from the Holy Spirit; He yearns for a deeper acquaintance with the Word of God through the inspiration of the Spirit; and He strives after unbroken fellowship with the Spirit, in which he is empowered to pray, believe, and rejoice.

True spirituality is more than a cessation of worldly things; it consists of a divine output. It is characterized by what one *does*, not what he does *not* do. It is not suppression but expression. The biblical and practical cure for worldliness is to be filled with the Holy Spirit, so that our hearts and minds are joyously preoccupied with good things. (See Philippians 4:8.) Furthermore, spirituality is not a pious pose gained through struggling; nor is it an imitation of a divine ideal. Rather, it represents a life that is claimed with the impartation of divine power. Believers can only experience the fullness of Christ when they abandon rules and mere negations, when they learn to walk by the Spirit in God-ordained liberty.

The Christian walk is characterized by two great spiritual changes: the change from the natural to the regenerated and from the carnal to the spiritual. The change from the natural man to the regenerated man only occurs through the Spirit, when faith is exercised in all that Christ made possible by His death at Calvary. The adjustment to the Holy Spirit in life and service transforms the carnal man into a spiritual man. If he desires to be spiritual, the believer must grow in the grace and knowledge of the Savior. More often than not, those who repent and believe do not fully appreciate what is involved in fully surrendering to the Spirit, who brings salvation. As they journey on with the Lord, they become aware of the old, corrupt nature within and how the evil is always present with them when they try to do good. The discovery of the vast resources of the Spirit is overwhelming and almost equivalent to a second conversion to those who thirst for holiness and to live in the likeness of their Savior.

Natural, carnal, spiritual—to which class do we belong? This is a question each of us must answer alone with the triune God.

CHAPTER 52

THREE PREDICATIONS OF GOD

God is spirit.
—John 4:25 RV

Walk in the Spirit.
—Galatians 5:16

God is light.
—1 John 1:5

Walk as children of light.
—Ephesians 5:8

God is love.
—1 John 4:8, 16

And walk in love.
—Ephesians 5:2

There are, of course, other predications as to the nature or being of God. For instance, He is described as our refuge and strength (see Psalm 46:1), salvation (see Psalm 68:20; Isaiah 12:2), a consuming fire (see Hebrews 12:29), full of pardon (see Nehemiah 9:17), and patient and ready to console (see Romans 15:5). But the three descriptions Paul uses to describe Him—spirit, light, and love—are particularly rich in significance.

GOD IS SPIRIT

It is strange, then, that Jesus uttered immortal words to the disreputable woman at the well. It was to this sinful soul that the Master expounded the deep truths of God's being—of the necessity of spiritual worship. If the disciples fully knew His heart, they would not have wondered why he was speaking to this woman. (See John 4:27.) The Bible teaches that the Jews had *"no dealings with the Samaritans"* (verse 9)—but *Jesus* did. Did He not speak well of one (see Luke 10:30–37), heal another of leprosy (see Luke 17:16), and rebuke two of the disciples for wanting to destroy them with fire from heaven? (See Luke 9:52–56.) Here is a Samaritan woman who first marveled at Jesus' knowledge, was transformed by His power, and will probably marvel throughout all eternity at the riches of His grace. The Samaritans in her city came to confess Jesus as *"the Saviour of the world"* (John 4:22) through her testimony.

Our immediate concern is the designation Jesus gives to the women at the well, *"God is spirit"* (John 4:24). The disciples were scared when He appeared to them, thinking he was a spirit or a ghost like they did when they saw Him walking on water. (See Mark 6:49; Luke 24:37.) But calming their troubled hearts, Jesus said, "Don't be alarmed. It is really Me!" Then He invited the disciples to touch Him to see that He really was the Crucified One. Yet He explained that the Spirit does not have a corporeal substance, *"Handle me, and see; for a spirit hath not flesh and bones, as you behold me having"* (Luke 24:39).

Jesus probably had this in mind when He declared that "*God is spirit.*" The Samaritans had previously altered many passages in the Pentateuch, using language applicable to man to suggest that God had a human form and feelings. This became a special doctrine in Samaritan theology. Therefore, although the woman of Samaria was a worshipper, she was not cognizant of the object of her worship. But Jesus eventually led her into an understanding of God in whose essence is spirit, and therefore must be worshiped "*in spirit and in truth*" (John 4:24). God is symbolically described as having human faculties and emotions to make Him real to our hearts; however, he is essentially *spirit*.

WORSHIP IN SPIRIT

Ellicott said that "The link between human nature and the Divine is in the human spirit, which is the shrine of the Holy Spirit. (See 1 Corinthians 6:19.) All true approach to God must therefore be in spirit." But sadly, so much of modern day worship is external and fleshly.

WORSHIP IN TRUTH

Unless our worship is in harmony with God, we are not "*true worshippers*" (John 4:23). Worship must be in line with the truth we find in Scripture. God condemns those who profess Him with their lips, but whose hearts are far from Him. (See Matthew 15:8.) Matthew Henry's understanding of the phrase "*God is spirit*" is helpful:

It is easier to say what God is not than what He is. The spirituality of the divine nature is a very good reason for the spirituality of divine worship. If we do not worship God who is spirit, in the spirit, we miss the end of worship.

GOD IS LIGHT

Perhaps the most spiritually enlightened among the apostles, John loved to write about *light*. In fact, he uses it well over thirty times in the Gospels, the Epistles, and Revelation. How this disciple sought to walk in the light, not only as He is in the light but also as *"the light of the world"*! John believed that God should be represented as a pure and perfect Light to a dark world. Believing that to a dark world the great God should be represented as pure and perfect *Light*. God is all the beauty and perfection that can be represented to our minds by light. There is no defect or imperfection in Him— no darkness at all! John says that *"the light shineth in darkness; and the darkness comprehended it not"* (John 1:5). There is no darkness in Him who is the Light—even when shining in darkness that cannot comprehend Him. Light is always in opposition to darkness and always seeks to dispel it. *"The power of darkness"* (Colossians 1:13) came upon Jesus when He died for the sins of the world, wrapping His sin-laden spirit in a horror of thick night and hellish gloom. But on His resurrection day, He was robed with a more brilliant light than ever before.

In Scripture, this *light* is an expressive metaphor applied to God, Christ, the Holy Spirit, Satan, Scripture itself, and the saints. John used this figure of speech to reveal a world of varied analogies between the God's nature and light as a material element. Robert Candlish said that in 1 John,

Light is diffusive, penetrating, searching; spreading itself over all space, and entering into every hole and corner. It is quickening and enlivening; a minister of healthy vigour and growth to all living creatures, plants and animals alike, including man himself. It is pleasant also; a source of relief and gladness to those who bask in its bright and joyous rays.

How applicable this ministry of light is to Him who not only said, "*Let there be light: and there was light*" (Genesis 1:3), but who is the perfection of light in Himself! "*God is light*" (1 John 1:5).

Dr. E. Bullinger also recognized a threefold understanding of God as the light:

The *heat* ray (red), which is felt, not seen, witnesses of the Father, "*Whom no man hath seen…at any time*" (John 1:18; see 1 John 4:12).

The *Light* ray (yellow), which is seen, not felt, witnesses of Jesus, who hath "*declared Him* [the Father]" (John 1:18; see 12:45; 14:9; Colossians 1:15; Hebrews 1:3).

The *Actinic* ray or *chemical* ray (blue), which is neither seen nor felt, but whose presence is revealed by its effects in a chemical action…produces changes, as in photography. This witnesses…the Holy Spirit, who is known by His wondrous operations. (See John 3:8.)

And of the hymn, which said,

> O Light of light, shine in!
> Cast out this night of sin,

Create true day within:
O Light of light, shine in.[109]

GOD IS LOVE

As we have seen, repetition indicates divine emphasis and John uses a twofold *"God is love"* (1 John 4:8, 16) within nine verses to make a point. It is interesting to notice the similarities of John 3:16 and 1 John 3:16. They both declare the same glorious message: *"God so loved the world"* and *"Hereby perceive we the love of God, because He laid down His life for us."* The sacrificial nature of God's love is a prominent theme throughout John's writings.

Inscribed upon the cross, we see,
In shining letters, God is love![110]

Not only did God create man to love; not only does He manifest His love in everything He does; but He *is* love in Himself, the paragon of love. Where in Scripture can we find a triad of words comparable to the one before us now—*"God is love"* (1 John 4:8)? In the narrative dealing with the love life of the believer, John declares that such a life finds expression in the life of love. Because God so loved us, we ought to love one another (see 1 John 4:11)—yes, we *ought*, but do we? The root and fruit of love is found in the phrase, *"We love him, because he first loved us"* (1 John 4:19). God is love; therefore, true love is of God.

The purpose of the incarnation was to manifest God's love to a lost and sinning world. The beloved Son is a perfect

---

109. Horatius Bonar, "O Light of Light, Shine In," 1899.
110. Thomas Kelly, "We Sing the Praise of Him Who Died," 1815.

illustration of "the love which is of God." Dwelling from past eternity in the Father's bosom, Jesus was of one nature with the Father, so much so that He could say, *"He that hath seen me hath seen the Father"* (John 14:9). He and the Father were one in all things, especially in a love for a world of lost and ruined sinners. *"God is love"*—therefore, we do not know God if we do not love. To love with the love which is of God is to know God. Furthermore, if we profess to love God, then we will also share His passion and compassion for the lost world.

We return to the thought that love not only flows from God, but is the essence of His nature. Now because love is such a pivotal part of His nature, He cannot be anything else but perfect love; it be will never be absent from His being and His dealings with us. This love has never waited for the perfect occasion to come forth; instead, it has always been active, self-manifesting and self-communicating. It existed in the dateless past at Creation all the way through to Calvary, and since then, he has never ceased to show it to saints and sinners alike. How astounding is the affirmation *"Herein is love, not that we loved God, but that he loved us"* (1 John 4:10)? Christ's message to the Jews of His time is the one the world needs to hear today, *"If God were your Father, ye would love me"* (John 8:42). All who do not love Him, who came as the personification of the love of God, must face the solemn apostolic denunciation, *"If any man love not the Lord Jesus Christ, let him be Anathema* [or cursed] *Maranatha"* (1 Corinthians 16:22).

> O Love of love, flow in!
> This hateful root of sin
> Pluck up, destroy within:
> O Love of love, flow in.[111]

---

111. Horatius Bonar, "O Light of Light, Shine In," 1899.

May grace be ours to *"keep ourselves in the love of God"* (Jude 1:21). So how can we maintain the spirit and attitude of love in the midst of a world filled with controversy and warfare in which we are exhorted to *"contend earnestly for the faith"* (verse 3)? Well, we can *"contend"* without becoming contentious, and strive to defend the truth *in love*. It is our privilege and joy to live and walk continually in the atmosphere of love; therefore, we must not allow the distracting, discouraging things to rob us of our constant communion with the loving Lord. We must cling to the glorious truth that God is love and therefore, cannot act contrary to His nature, even when the shadows gather around us, and trials, sorrows, and separations beset our pilgrimage. Unlike us, God cannot make a mistake or wrong turn because of His perfect love and wisdom.

My God! I love Three;
Not because I hope for heaven thereby,
Nor yet because we love Thee not
May die eternally.

Not with the hope of gaining aught,
Not seeking a reward;
But as Thyself hast loved me
O everlasting Lord![112]

---

112. "My God, I Love Thee"

CHAPTER 53

THREE REALMS OF OMNIPOTENCE

One God and Father of all, who is above all,
and through all, and in you all.
—Ephesians 4:6

Paul gives us a trinity of domains representing God's divine ascendancy—*above, through,* and *in*—what a comforting and assuring verse! In Ephesians, he wrote about *"the church, which is Christ's body,"* and the mystery *"hid in God"* that was revealed to the apostles by the Holy Spirit (Ephesians 3:1–12). He exhorted this believing company *"to live peacefully with all men"* (Romans 12:18) and *"to keep the unity of the Spirit in the bond of peace"* (Ephesians 4:3). The history of the Christian church, however, reveals how difficult it is to live at peace and keep in unity with fellow Christians. Misunderstandings and jealousies have only brought strife and division which dishonors the Head of the church and hinders the spread of Christ's gospel to the world. Paul, however, writes of an ideal church in four impressive trinities that maintains unity amid diversities in race, knowledge, culture, temperament, and position.

1. The trinity of oneness: *"One body, and one spirit...in one hope of your calling"* (Ephesians 4:4).

2. The trinity of headship: *"One Lord, one faith, one baptism"* (verse 5).

3. The trinity of sovereignty: *"One God and Father of all—who is above all, and through all, and in you all"* (verse 6).

4. The trinity of objectives: *"For the perfecting of the saints, for the work of the ministry, and for edifying of the body of Christ"* (verse 12).

Ministers of the Word are not only Christ's ascension gifts to the church, but are channels of His gifts for the benefit of the members of His body. They function in this threefold way, working for the saints, the ministry, and the body of Christ.

There is an important truth we can glean from the third triad. Those who are regenerated by the Spirit are members of *one body*, are led by *one Spirit*, are sharers in *one hope*, have only *one Lord*, are living by *one faith*, and are all sealed by *one baptism*. The ultimate source and inspiration of the inward unity is God, who generates cause in all things and who works everything together in perfect harmony. Paul describes Him as *"One God and Father of all"* (Ephesians 4:6).

So what was Paul's reasoning for using the adjective *all* four times in the verse? It is because he was thinking of persons instead of things (as in the phrase, *"that He might fill all things"* (verse 10), which is evident from *"But unto every one of us is given grace"* (verse 7), and also by the pronoun *"you"* in verse 6. Many ancient manuscripts have *"us"* instead of *"you."* While God is the Father of all His creation—for He speaks of Himself as the *Father* of the rain (see Job 38:28)—the *"all"* here refers especially to the regenerated members of Christ's church, all the *"elect according to the foreknowledge of God the Father"* (1 Peter 1:2).

He is *one* God, Scripture claiming His divine sovereignty and supremacy over all things. He alone is the living and true

God; manufactured gods are only false imitations. He is absolutely sovereign, working to carry out His good pleasure and counsel in achieving His eternal purpose in Christ for the church. (See Ephesians 1:5, 11).

He is *one* Father, the relationship implying birth. It also implies the fatherhood of God, strictly used in connection with those *"predestinated unto the adoption of children by Jesus Christ"* (Ephesians 1:5), which is very prominent in Ephesians. (See Ephesians 1:3, 6–7; 2:18–19; 3:14–21.) The ultimate and infinite glory of all unity is the full realization of the *"one God and Father of all"* (Ephesians 4:6). We certainly hear a great deal these apostate days—about the fatherhood of God and the brotherhood of man—which implies that God is the Father of *all* men, good and bad; and that *all* men, despite their race or degree of personal morality, are brothers. However, not much is said about the Savior Christ, through which God becomes our heavenly Father. Furthermore, it is through Him that fellow-believers become our brothers and sisters. Scripture distinguishes between a child of God and a child of the Devil. Jesus told the Pharisees that the Devil was *their* father. Paul wrote specifically to God's children, who received salvation through faith in Christ.

PREEMINENCE— "WHO IS ABOVE ALL"

Our Father-God is sovereign over all. We read that believers, for His *"pleasure they* [the redeemed] *are and were created"* (Revelation 4:11), and to them, His will is *"law eternal."* Just as *all* means *"all who are His,"* it is a comforting truth to know that He is above all His people— presiding, ruling, and owning. He forever sits on His throne as a King over them. In our days of shallow and corrupt images of God, Scripture encourages our hearts in the truth of His *transcendence*. There is a message of kindred truth in Revelation: the supreme exaltation of Christ from whom all blessings flow. (See Revelation 1:10, 20–23.)

As we read the psalmist's prayer, "*Lead me to the rock that is higher than I*" (Psalm 61:2), we learn that we all need to hide in Him whose ways are higher than ours. (See Isaiah 55:9.) Man is so puny in the sight of our omnipotent God! Solomon said, "*Every official has a higher one set over him, and the highest keeps watch over them*" (Ecclesiastes 5:8 NEB). Indeed, God is high over all. Although we live in a troubled, sinful, and suffering world, He is above all working out His sovereign plan in spite of man's rejection and hell's evil machinations. No one can stay His omnipotent hand. In *Paradise Lost*, John Milton described the deposition and doom of "the infernal serpent,"

> Him the Almighty Power
> Hurled headlong flaming from th' ethereal sky...
> Who durst defy th' omnipotent to arms.

In *Prometheus Unbound*, Percy Shelley wrote of those "defying power, which seems omnipotent." We will always reap tragic results when trifling with the omnipotence of God.

But how blessed we are to rest in Him and know that our Father's kingdom rules over all. Shelley also wrote, "To be omnipotent but friendly is to reign."

Because God is also our Father, His is "the sweet omnipotence of love."[113] He carries out His sovereign works with a friendly, loving, and fatherly heart. He is over us, watching us

---

113. Charles Wesley, "All Things Are Possible to Him."

at all times and under all circumstances wherever we may be; He waits to make us full recipients of His grace. In addition, He cannot fail, for all power in heaven and in earth is His! James reminds us that *"every good gift and every perfect gift is from above, and cometh down from the Father of lights,* [or "who gives light"] *with whom is no variableness* [variation], *neither shadow* [cast by] *of turning"* (James 1:17).

> All good gifts around us,
> Are sent from heaven above.[114]

PROVIDENCE— "WHO IS THROUGH ALL"

Paul also reminds us that the sovereign Lord pervades His people, all through whom He is working out His will— *"In whom…worketh all things after the counsel of His will"* (Ephesians 1:11). As Christ is the Head over *all* things to the church, He is able to exercise providential care over all members of the mystic fabric. Shakespeare said, "There's a special providence in the fall of a sparrow."[115] God does more than just fill us; He seeks to meet all our needs through His beloved Son. He counts the hairs on our head; and He is cognizant of all our spiritually, physically, and materially needs. The mighty One can do exceeding abundantly above *all* that we can ask or think.

> Fear not, but trust in Providence,
> Wherever thou mayst be.[116]

---

114. Matthias Claudius, "All Good Gifts Around Us," 1782.
115. William Shakespeare, *Hamlet*, Act 5, Scene 2.
116. Thomas Haynes Bayly, *The Pilot*.

It was once said that "through all" can mean "operating through all," which through His Spirit, He seeks to do. Ellicott once said "*Through all* is the diffusive power of the forces—physical, moral, and spiritual—by which the world of nature, still more the world of man, most of all the society of Christians, are swayed as wholes."

> Is your life a channel of blessing?
> Is the love of God flowing through you?
> Are you telling the lost of the Savior?
> Are you ready His service to do?[117]

PRESENCE—"WHO IS IN ALL"

How different our lives would be if we lived by the full assurance that the divine truth dwelled inside of us!

In actuality, every child of God is a cabinet of the Trinity— the Father, Son, and the Holy Spirit residing inside them. "*We will come unto him, and make our abode in him*" (John 14:16–23). This is such a deterrent to sin and incentive for holiness this mystery is: "*Christ in you, the hope of glory*" (Colossians 1:27). The heart of the redeemed is His shrine, His home. The dominating factor in the Paul's witness was not only that Christ reigns forevermore, but as he stated, "*Christ liveth in me*" (Galatians 2:20).

Do we not have the same confidence and consciousness that Jesus is with us as our perpetual Comforter? Are we among the number of those who rest in His promise to never leave nor forsake us? Do we believe the truth of divine indwelling "in the individual for creation, sustenance, and regeneration—which

---

117. Harper G. Smyth, "Make Me a Channel of Blessing," 1903.

is the breath of life—both the physical and spiritual life"? Let us not lose sight of His *immanence* as we accept His preeminence. F.W. Faber's lines are most appealing:

> God is never so far off as even to be near:
> He is within! Our spirit is the home He holds most
> dear.
> To think of Him as by our side, is almost as untrue
> As to remove His throne beyond these skies of
> starry blue.
> So all the while I thought myself homeless, forlorn,
> and weary,
> Missing my joy, I walked the earth—myself God's
> Sanctuary.

There are those who have seen in this threefold sentence a reference to the three persons of the blessed Trinity. Although this passage clearly points to God the Father, it may be true that we can trace the manifestation of the Father through the Son and Holy Spirit through the expressions *above all*, *through all*, and *in all*.

God is above all, and because He is our Father, He plans to provide everything for His children. "There is no place where earth's sorrows are more felt than up in heaven."[118]

God the Son, alive forevermore, continually reveal Himself known through all who are redeemed by His blood. He is actively perfecting the church through all of life, including the trials.

God the Spirit, the eternal inhabitant, is a well of water that springs up and flows out of our bodies to refresh the dry, arid wilderness around us.

---

118. Frederick W. Faber, "There's a Wideness in God's Mercy," 1854.

There is another apostolic triad we can link to the one we just considered. It too emphasizes God's supremacy. Paul included this one in his letter to the Romans: *"Of him, and through him, and to him, are all things: to whom be glory for ever"* (Romans 11:36).

God is the beginning, the end, and everything in between. He is the originator, sustainer, and conclusion of all things—*of, through,* and *to.* All that comes *from* Him returns *to* Him. When we think of ourselves—all our faculties and possessions—we must remember that everything comes from the giver life and must return to Him in honor and glory. Whatever we do should be for the glory of God. How much safer we would be if, when confronted by a temptation or decision, we asked ourselves the simple question, "Does this tend to the glory of God in and through me?" The governing principle in all things concerning our personal, public, and religious life should be: *"Do all to the glory of God"* (1 Corinthians 10:31).

> To God be the glory,
> Great things He hath done.[119]

---

119. Fanny Crosby, "To God Be the Glory," 1875.

CHAPTER 54

THREE ORDERED BLESSINGS

Grace, mercy, and peace, from God our Father,
and Jesus Christ our Lord.
—1 Timothy 1:2

Paul's salutations, just like his benedictions, are rich in spiritual significance and suggestiveness. His almost invariable salutation in the opening of his epistles is "grace and peace." These twin blessings were also used by Peter in his epistles, as well as John in 2 John and Revelation 1:4. Furthermore, Jude used a triad of mercy, peace, and love. (See Jude 2). Paul's "grace and peace" somewhat correspond to two ordinary forms of Jewish salutation. The Greek and Romans used the first in a somewhat counterfeit form. The apostle takes these ordinary teens and gives them a heightened and deepened Christian significance. Together we understand that *grace* indicates the favorable way the Father and the Son receive us; and we are filled with *peace* as a result of this favor, which is the proper attitude of every Christian.

"Grace is the peculiar state of favor with God and Christ, into which the believing one is admitted. Peace is the state of mind resulting from the sense of favor."

The joy Thy favor gives,
Let me again obtain.[120]

---

120. Nahum Tate and Nicholas Brady, "Have Mercy, Lord, on Me," 1698.

But in the trinity of virtues, with which Paul opens 1 Timothy, *mercy* is given the central place. Why did the apostle depart from his usual salutation of grace and peace to introduce mercy? Ellicott suggests that...

> The nearness of death, the weakness of old age, the dangers, ever increasing, which crowded around Paul seem to call forth from him deeper expressions of love and tender pity. Jesus Christ, his hope, burned before him, a guiding star, ever brighter and clearer; and the mercy of God, which the old man felt he had obtained, he longed to share with others.

This introduction in the letter is not only a heartfelt salutation, but a prayer and divine *promise* that any saint can claim. The order in which these heavenly blessings come are: (1) grace, (2) mercy, and (3), peace—an irreversible order.

GRACE

This attribute comes first simply because there would be no other blessing from God the Father and Jesus Christ our Lord without it. *Grace* is the source from which all blessings flow. It is divinely "rich" and "free;" it is also self-moving, self-originating, self-vindicating, and "the mysterious spring-head in the everlasting hills." Behind all blessing is God's initiative. The reason Paul couples the Father and the Son in the bestowal of grace is because the mind of God and the mind of Jesus are one and the same. The approach God takes to man and Jesus takes to man are the same. Furthermore, God's grace is mediated through Jesus, who became the incarnate grace of God. Not only was He the channel or expression of divine grace, He *is* God's grace to men. Grace came both *by* Christ Jesus and in Him.

Expositors of the Word give *grace* many different meanings. Grace is generally God's unmerited favor, which is bestowed on man who does not deserve it. The most satisfying explanation of the term is explained by the renowned theologian Joseph Butler, who wrote that *grace* is...

> A most comprehensive word of boundless reach and an infinite depth of significance, signifying unlimited favour to the undeserving, all who by reason of transgression have forfeited every claim to divine favour, and have lost all capacity for meritorious action.

In the Bible concordance, we discover the following: (1) *God* is the God and Giver of all grace freely bestowed on us (see Ephesians 1:6 RV; James 4:6; 1 Peter 5:10); (2) *Jesus Christ* is identified with the Father as the source and the giver of grace—in fact, He personified grace (see John 1:17; Romans 5:15; 1 Timothy 1:14); and (3), the *Holy Spirit* is, as one of His wonderful names indicates, *"the spirit of grace."* (Zechariah 12:10; See Hebrews 10:29.) It is He who transfers blessings over to the repentant sinner.

Scripture is referred to as *"the word of his grace"* (Acts 20:32); this is because without its divine revelation, we would not know of divine favor or have any hope. We are saved and kept saved through God's abundant grace. Might we ever sing, "Amazing grace! How sweet the sound!"[121]

We are debtors to God's matchless grace every moment of every day. We need continuing grace just as bad as converting grace! Paul confessed, *"By the grace of God I continue."* We all

---

121. John Newton, "Amazing Grace," 1779.

need fresh grace every day. It is good news that our Father in heaven is *"the God of all grace"* (1 Peter 5:10)—a reservoir that never dries up. We have a constant need for grace, and thankfully there is grace that never runs dry! G. H. Knight said,

> The same generous love that bore with my rebellions as a prodigal is needed to bear with my infirmities as a child; forgiving grace to pardon me, sanctifying grace to refine me, guiding grace to lead me on, restraining grace to keep me in, vivifying grace to stir my sluggishness to greater zeal.

Annie Johnson Flint assures us,

> His love has no limit,
> His grace has no measure,
> His power no boundary known unto men;
> For out of His infinite riches in Jesus
> He giveth and giveth and giveth again.

MERCY

Out of grace flows a stream of *mercy*. They are actually twin blessings, the one very much like the other. The Revised Version of the Old Testament often uses the word *lovingkindness* for *mercy*, as in Psalm 136. *Mercy* is the outcome of kindness and love, meaning pity and compassion; it consists of forbearance, gentleness, longsuffering, and other similar virtues. Evidently, *mercy* is one of the prominent blessings mentioned in the Bible because while terms like *grace* and *gracious* appear approximately two hundred times, the words *mercy* and *merciful* occur close to three hundred times. The word used for "compassion" is the same as "mercy" in the Greek text. Furthermore, all three persons of the godhead are associated with divine compassion:

God the Father is rich in mercy in His divine character. (See Psalm 103:8; 115:1; Ephesians 2:4; Titus 3:5; 2 Corinthians 1:3.)

Christ came to show mercy to all those in need. He was always moved with compassion for the sick and heavy-laden. (See Mark 5:19; 1 Timothy 1:2; Jude 21.)

The Holy Spirit shares this divine trait with us, helping us grow this virtue within ourselves. (See Galatians 5:22–23.) This essential virtue of the godhead permeates all It does—*"His tender mercies are over all His works"* (Psalm 145:9). In addition, man is required to show mercy toward both other men and creatures that need pity. (See Deuteronomy 25:4; Psalm 37:21; 109:1, 16.) The parable of the unmerciful servant teaches us that a person receiving mercy should respond by showing that mercy to others. (See Matthew 18:21–35.) Shakespeare emphasizes this idea in the question: "How canst thou hope for mercy rendering none?"[122] Alexander Pope expressed a similar thought:

> Teach me to feel another's woe,
> To hide the fault I see!
> That mercy I to others show,
> That mercy show to me![123]

It is somewhat surprising to see how much evangelical truth and spiritual perception can be found in Shakespeare's works. We find another reference to mercy in a different scene of *The Merchant of Venice*:

---

122. William Shakespeare, *The Merchant of Venice*, Act 4, Scene 1.
123. Alexander Pope, "The Universal Prayer."

> The quality of mercy is not strain'd:
> It droppeth as the gentle rain from heaven
> Upon the place beneath. It is twice blest:
> It blesseth him that gives and him that takes.
> 'Tis mightiest in the mightiest; It becomes
> The throned monarch better than his crown:
> His sceptre shows the force of temporal power,
> The attribute to awe and majesty,
> Wherein doth sit the dread and fear of kings;
> But mercy is above this sceptred sway,
> It is enthroned in the hearts of kings,
> It is an attribute of God Himself;
> And earthly power doth then show likest God's
> When mercy seasons justice.
> Therefore, Jew, Though justice be thy plea, consider
> this—
> That in the course of justice, none of us
> Should see salvation: we do pray for mercy;
> And that same prayer, doth teach us all to render
> The deeds of mercy.

Although *grace* and *mercy* are often linked together, there is still a difference between the two. The central point of *grace* is the freedom of God's love, while *mercy* points to our misery, helplessness, and eventual relief. God's free grace is displayed in the forgiveness of sins—extended to men *as* they are in their guilt. Mercy is extended to them because they are wretched and miserable. We are such debtors to His inexhaustible grace and pardoning mercy! Even after crying, "*God be merciful to me a sinner*" (Luke 18:13), and then receiving His saving mercy, we are still in need of constant fresh mercy. Samuel Rutherford used to say, "God has bags of mercy lying by Him, the seals of which have never been broken." As *the Father of mercies* (2 Corinthians 1:3) and thus *rich in mercy* (Ephesians 2:4), He has infinite resources to draw upon.

Mercy is our hourly need and is always at our disposal. As we think of our sinful past, we thank God for His abundant mercy; but in the present—with all its shortcomings, inconsistencies, and sins, along with self-will, self-indulgence, and self-glory—we are still in dire need of mercy. Looking onto our future, we know that we will need mercy up until our very last breath. Are we not grateful, then, that *His mercy endureth for ever* (Psalm 136)? In the hymn "There's a Wideness in God's Mercy," F. W. Faber described the unfailing quantity and quality of God's mercy:

> There's a wideness in God's mercy
> Like the wideness of the sea;
> There's a kindness in His justice,
> Which is more than liberty.

PEACE

Wordsworth enunciated a biblical truth when he wrote, "Peace—the central feeling of all happiness." Man cannot be perfectly happy if he is not at peace with God. *Great peace have they which love thy law: and nothing shall offend them* (Psalm 119:165). Did another poet have the Prince of Peace in mind when he wrote, "His face wore the utter Peace of one whose life is hid in God's own hand"?

Christ not only provided peace through the cross, He personified peace—*He is our peace* (Ephesians 2:14). This blessing, therefore, is not *something* but *someone*. *Peace* is mentioned four hundred times in Scripture, referring to a condition of freedom from disturbance, whether outwardly, as of a nation from war or enemies, or inwardly, within the soul. The Hebrew word *Shalom* has the primary meaning of "soundness," "health," and comes to signify "prosperity," well-being in general, all good in relation to both man and God.

Alexander Cruden said that when Paul combined *peace* with grace and mercy in the apostolic salutation, it was almost like he said,

> I wish that the free, undeserved love and favour of God, and a lively sense thereof in your souls, may be continued to, and increased in, you; and that as a fruit of this, you may enjoy all blessings, both inward and outward, especially peace of conscience, and a secure enjoyment of the love of God.

The reader is encouraged to look at the nature of *peace* described in the previous triad.[124] F. R. Havergal's poem is worthy of repetition:

Peace, peace!
Wrought by the Spirit of might,
In thy deepest sorrow and sorest strife,
In all changes and chances of mortal life,
It is Thine, beloved! Christ's own bequest,
Which vainly the tempter shall strive to wrest;
It is now thy right!

---

124. Alexander Cruden, *A Complete Concordance to the Old and New Testament*, Volume 1, pages 53–57.

CHAPTER 55

THREE GLORIES OF THE GLORIFIED LORD

Jesus Christ...the faithful witness, and the first begotten of the dead, and the prince of the kings of the earth.
—Revelation 1:5

In the first four words of the last book of the Bible, we read *"The Revelation of Jesus Christ"* (Revelation 1:1). The key to understanding this book, along with other apocalyptic books, is to understand the Lord around whom all prophecy revolves. Lovers of the Word will find it profitable to read Revelation carefully, while listing all the names and titles that testify to Him—both actual and symbolic. Among these names are the three wonderful descriptions we will consider in this chapter. These titles together declare that He is sufficient for all our needs, along with the needs of the whole world. They form a threefold cord that is not quickly broken. Yet even these three strong designations are "too mean to speak His worth, too mean to set my Savior forth."[125]

Together, these three titles emphasize distinct attributes of Christ, who has every right to the glories He has earned. First we have His relation to God and the truth—*"the faithful witness."* Then we have His relation to the dead, whether saved or lost—*"the firstborn of the dead."* Third we have His

---

125. Isaac Watts, "Join All the Glorious Names," 1709.

supremacy over the earth's governing authorities—*"the prince of the kings of the earth."*

Clearly, these names, along with all other names in Revelation, reveal that Jesus Christ is a divine person, with all the authority and power associated with Deity. John lived some five hundred years after Ethan the Ezrahite, so it is remarkable how the language Ethan uses to describe the bow in the cloud as a faithful witness resembles John's testimony of Jesus Christ: *"I will make him my firstborn, higher than the kings of the earth...as a faithful witness in heaven"* (Psalm 89:27, 37).

Those who are familiar with Revelation know that this triple title given to Christ corresponds with the three prominent truths of this book: Christ the revealing Prophet, the life-giving High Priest, and the perfect Ruler of mankind.

THE FAITHFUL WITNESS

One of John's favorite terms is *witness* or *testimony*—his signature word. He uses it seventy-two times in both his own writings and his records of Christ's use of the word.

Jesus uses it to describe the purpose of His mission on earth, *"To this end was I born, and for this cause came I into the world, that I should bear witness unto the truth"* (John 18:37). This claim is supported several times in the Apocalypse: *"The faithful witness"* (Revelation 1:5); *"He that is true...openeth, and no man shutteth; and shutteth, and no man openeth"* (Revelation 3:7); *"The faithful and true witness, the beginning of the creation of God"* (verse 14); *"The testimony of...[the] Faithful and True"* (Revelation 19:10–11); *"I testify* [witness] *unto every man"* (Revelation 22:18).

All these explicit passages, along with others of the same thought, testify to Christ's trustworthiness. They testify to the pervasive and universally recognized ascriptions to the Deity found in Revelation. The triple use of the epithet "*faithful*" is in marked contrast to all preceding witnesses for God, many who were not as faithful as they might have been. As Walter Scott put it, "Christ alone passed through earth in His solitary and rugged path of unswerving devotedness to God, without break or flaw and in all holy separateness to God."

The Gospels reveal that His life was one long, faultless witness to God and the truth. "[I] speak," He said, "*that which we* [I] *know, and testify that which we* [I] *have seen*" (John 3:11). Although a man, Christ Jesus did not lie, for He was a faithful witness to God's righteousness, justice, love, and grace; a faithful witness when He spoke about Himself and His work; a faithful witness against all sin, no matter where it was found; a faithful witness to God's pardoning love and power to deliver from sin; a faithful witness in His promises, precepts, and warnings; and a faithful witness who spoke authoritatively about His Father, along with men and the world.

It is because He stands out among men as faithful and true that we can believe His every word, for His witness is authentic as *the Truth*. This fact should end man's tiring search for the truth. He is, indeed, "*a witness to the people*" (Isaiah 55:4).

> Who didst bear witness to the truth,
> Which but stirred up appalling wrath.
> From poor degraded sons of earth,
> Who would not hear the Master's voice
> Calling—repent, believe, rejoice.

Would not receive this great witness
From God, of truth and righteousness,
Through Whom alone we may have peace.

Jesus commended Antipas in His message to the Church at Pergamos, faithful to his death saying, *"My faithful martyr, who was slain among you"* (Revelation 2:13). The English word *martyr* translates into the same Greek word that means "witness" in other instances. Both Jesus and Antipas were martyred for their loyal witness; both sealed their faithful testimony with their blood.

THE FIRSTBORN OF THE DEAD

In *The Lord of Glory*, Benjamin B. Warfield described the words *firstborn* and *heir* in Hebrews 1:

> "Firstborn" and "heir" are little more than specially honorific ways of saying Son. God's Firstborn as such takes rank above all other existing beings: even all of the angels shall do Him reverence. God's Firstborn is also naturally God's Heir, an Heir whose inheritance embraces the universe, and whose tenure stretches to eternity.

We have a specific reference to the Lord's resurrection in this title. Christ Himself told John in the Patmos vision, *"I am He that liveth, and was dead; and, behold, I am alive for evermore, Amen; and have the keys of hell and of death"* (Revelation 1:18). Death could not overcome its prey in the face of Christ's sacrifice. He told His enemies that He had power to lay down His life and take it up again; He even demonstrated this when he rose triumphant over the grave.

The term *first-begotten* or *firstborn* refers to dignity not necessarily associated with birth. (See Psalm 89:27.) The term *firstborn* suggests "supremacy," not the "first in time" or "first in chronological sequence." Christ is referred to as both *"the first-fruit"* and *"the firstborn of the dead"* (Revelation 1:5). The first denotes that He was first in time in the coming harvest of those who sleep, as Paul emphasizes in his exposition on resurrection. (See 1 Corinthians 15.) But the latter title signifies that Jesus is first in rank of all those who will rise from the dead. No matter when, where, or how Christ will enter the world, He will necessarily take first place by virtue of all that He is in Himself as the Lord of glory.

Wonderful as He was in His work as a "faithful witness" among men, Jesus will be even more wonderful in His risen, ascended life. We will have an even closer fellowship with other believers when He is in His position as the triumphant Lord, who conquered death. He says to those who share in His risen life, *"Because I live, ye shall live also"* (John 14:19). Death no longer carries a sting, because our conquering Lord is near. He is our unseen Advocate at the Father's right hand.

> The Firstborn from the dead, the sent,
> Of all Thou art preeminent;
> Bright harbinger of that blest hour,
> When, in Thy resurrection power,
> Thy sleeping ones shall hear Thy voice,
> And, with Thy caught-up ones, rejoice
> To meet Thee in the air, and be
> Forevermore, O Lord, with Thee.

THE PRINCE OF
THE KINGS OF EARTH

The title *prince* is used to describe Jesus in several ways. He is the *"Prince of princes"* (Daniel 8:25), the mighty One we bow before. He is *"Messiah the Prince"* (Daniel 9:25), whom Israel will recognize and own. He is *"the Prince of Peace"* (Isaiah 9:6), the source and author of all peace. He is *"the Prince of life"* (Acts 3:15) who vanquished all His foes. He is *"a Prince and a Savior"* (Acts 5:31) to all who receive Him. And He is *"prince of the kings of the earth"* (Revelation 1:5), exercising universal dominion.

Throughout the years, the world has seen many proud monarchs and haughty dictators; yet God's King is *"higher than the kings of the earth"* (Psalm 89:27). He owns the redemption rights to the kingdoms of this world through His death and resurrection. He will claim these rights when He returns to the earth, revealing Himself as the King of kings and Lord of lords.

Then He will inaugurate His reign of peace and righteousness. When He finally asserts His rights, the enemy will become His footstool and He will establish His own government. We must take special notice of the present tense used in connection with these three titles: *"Who is."* Certainly, Jesus *is* coming as the promised and prophesied Prince, but, as Ellicott reminds in this exposition,

> The message does not come from One who will be, but who is the true ruler of all earthly potentates. The disposition to dwell on the future and more visibly recognized reign of Christ hereafter has tended to

obscure the truth of His present reign. It is instructive to notice that the Revelation, which describes so vividly the manifestations of Christ's Kingdom (see Revelation 11:15; 12:10), claims for Him at the outset the place of the real King of kings. Such was the faith of John.

Professor Plumptre agreed with this fact, saying,

Above all emperors and kings, above all armies and multitudes, John thought of the Crucified as ruling and directing the course of history, and certain in His own due time to manifest His sovereignty.

Reminding us of what real kingship is, Dean Farrar says,

A handful reach the philosophers, myriads die for Christ; they in their popularity could barely found a school; Christ from His Cross rules the world.

The witness of Scripture is that *the Lord God omnipotent reigneth* (Revelation 9:6), and that the world should tremble before this His name.

Then, what is the personal and practical aspect of Christ's kingship? Is it not when I am ready to surrender my life to the Prince of Peace? Has He had His crowning day in my heart, as I look and pray for His kingdom to come? Have I brought forth the royal diadem and crowned Him King over the empire of my heart, mind, and will? Believing as I do that He is my *Savior*, is He also *sovereign* over my life? Did He not die and rise again so that He could be Lord of my life?

> Yes, Prince of all the mighty kings
> Of earth-born sons art Thou;

This name alone true comfort brings
To captives, when brought low
Under the rude oppressor's hand,
For all must yield to Thy command.

There are three marvelous titles for the Lord that strengthen and comfort the church. We see One in heaven who walked the path of faith and obedience (see Hebrews 12:1–2), and the One who will always be the best example of a faithful witness. We rejoice in the One who grappled with death and overcame it and who, as the conquering Lord, can make us more than conquerors. We rest in the One who is Lord and Master over all government, ignorant as they may be of this lordship. No wonder John, after this threefold vision of the marvelous Lord, breaks into a sudden doxology, *"To him be glory and dominion for ever and ever. Amen"* (1 Peter 5:11).

CHAPTER 56

THREE SEQUELS
OF WAITING ON GOD

*They shall mount up on wings like eagles; they shall run, and
not be weary; and they shall walk, and not faint.*
—Isaiah 40:31

The Bible is full of divine promises which are hard to miss as we journey through the Word. Isaiah's great and precious promise of the gifts accruing for us as we wait on the Lord is one of these lofty summits. But in order to fully understand its implication, we must first examine this truth in light of its context. In Isaiah 40:1–30, the prophet graphically contrasted God's greatness with man's weakness. He drew on the conclusion that the Creator and Sustainer of the earth never wearies with exhaustion from the heavy loads He bears.

In a different example, Isaiah speaks of men who try to *"weary God"* (Isaiah 7:13), but because He is the everlasting One, He never falters in His strength; neither does He change. Despite His tasks of attending to His people and controlling the world, he never gets tired. Not only does He never faint, but He gives power to those who do. Thus the paradox, *"To them that have no might he increaseth strength"* (Isaiah 40:29).The preeminent thought throughout the whole narrative is that in order to receive strength, we must realize our weakness. (See Matthew 5:6; Luke 6:21.) God is always ready to help us help ourselves. Those who grow faint and weary and collapse under the burdens of life soon discover the utter folly of trusting in themselves. We have no might in ourselves; but in Christ, there is strength and increasing strength. Discovering our weaknesses assists us in receiving His power. (See 2 Corinthians 12:9.)

No one can search out His understanding on his own. And because of His omnipotence, He knows all the needs of His children. Therefore, we can rest in the confidence of His strength. Although young men are strong, they must not think of themselves as stronger than they really are, robbing them of receiving divine strength. If they do not wait on God, this attitude will fail them in spite of their youthful vigor. Such waiting produces infinite resources outside of the self. Expectant faith accompanies a waiting attitude, and God never fails to respond to this dependence on Him. In fact, such waiting brings a triple reward.

There is another truth we can glean from these three features of waiting on the Lord. *"Mounting up with wings"* can represent the youthful vitality, with all its visions and aspirations. The youth mount up with wings like eagles as they aspire about what they will do in the future and who they will be. They fly on the wings of imagination.

Running can represent the middle-aged, who no longer dream of soaring high and no longer desire the vigorous activity of youth. What once was a *flight* is now a *fight*—a fight to maintain life amid many obligations. Wings can no longer operate when the feet must stay on the ground.

Walking can indicate old age, when neither flying nor running is a possibility, and the pace is considerably slower. When describing the fading, failing years, Solomon says that it is a period when the keepers of the house tremble and strong men bow themselves. (See Ecclesiastes 12:1–3.)

Yet despite the age, we all need God; we can claim His grace and strength through faith no matter what period of life we are in. Experience teaches us that the young are not hard to win for Christ; it is harder to influence those that are halfway through life; it is harder still to reach the old, who are hardened to sin.

> In the freshest prime of morning,
> Or fullest glow of noon,
> The note of heavenly warning
> Can never come too soon.[126]

MOUNT UP WITH WINGS

Furthermore, this trinity has a *descending* climax, *"Mount up...run...walk."* The praying, waiting child of God gathers fresh strength from Him who is our strength. They go from strength to strength. (See Psalm 84:7.) The word translated "renew" actually means "exchange," for the Lord does not renew the old strength of the flesh, but exchanges it for His unfailing strength—what a welcome, beneficial exchange this is! New power replaces old weakness. This change is symbolized in the verse, *"They shall mount up with wings as eagles"* (Isaiah 40:31) or, *"They shall put forth fresh feathers as eagles."* The psalmist says, *"Thy youth is renewed like the eagle's"* (Psalm 103:5)—in reference to the fresh and vigorous appearance of a bird with new plumage.

The eagle does not renew its old feathers; rather, it molts and receives a new covering of feathers. Along with a fresh

126. Sarah G. Stock, "O Master, When Thou Callest," 1888.

plumage, he receives a fresh lease on life. And just like the eagle, we receive new feathers when we wait on God—a new vigor and a quickened life. If God is our arm every morning, then we will desire to soar closer to Him, leaving our sinful lives behind. We learn that the Christian life is indeed flight, but that sometimes we are afraid of heights. We are too earthbound, too lost in the fogs and mists of doubt and despair, too submerged in the world's dirt and dust. Paul was a man who knew what it was to mount up on the wings of an eagle. He found himself caught up to heaven where he received many revelations. (See 2 Corinthians 12:1–7.) Devout affections can be the eagle's wings we need to mount upon to reach heaven. *"Unto thee, do I lift up my soul"* (Psalm 25:1).

God's sustaining and strengthening power reveals itself to us through many ways and at different times. His power enables us to soar above the difficulties, disappointments, trials, and failures of our lives like "an eagle rises, and bathes itself in heaven's blue till its feathers gleam in the sunshine, and cares nothing for the turmoil, the smoke, and the clouds that lie beneath." May we rise on the wings of prayer and faith through His grace, so that we can soar above the earthborn clouds. It is here that we receive a clearer vision of the One who strengthen us with all might!

> Upward where the stars are burning,
> Silent, silent is their turning
> Round the never-changing pole;
> Upward where the sky is brightest,
> Upward where the blue is lightest,
> Lift I now my longing soul.[127]

---

127. Horatius Bonar, "Upward, where the Stars Are Burning," 1866.

RUN AND NOT BE WEARY

Our lives in Christ are not only a *flight*, but a *race* that must be run without weariness. *"So run, that ye may obtain"* (1 Corinthians 9:24). However, we will never win the crown if we are distracted by too much baggage. A runner wearies quickly if he carries clothing or shoes that are too heavy. "The King's business requireth haste." We must be in shape to run His errands! We must have the determination to press forward in the Christian race with alacrity. Although running a track may appear less exciting than mounting on wings, we need to be equally equipped and ready for the race as we are for the flight. A joyful heart should be paired with a springy step.

Or have we become too weary to race—unable to hear His voice? Do our feet drag from too many encumbrances? Paul wrote to the Galatians *"Ye did run well; who did hinder you?"* (Galatians 5:7). The apostle claimed that he had not run in vain, finishing the course in triumph. If God's Word *"runneth very swiftly"* (Psalm 147:15), then we must be prepared to match its speed. If we are lagging behind, then may we ask God to impart His strength in us! Let us pray the prayer of Abraham's servant as he sought a bride for Isaac, *"O Lord God...I pray Thee, send me good speed this day"* (Genesis 24:12).

> Run the straight race through God's good grace,
> Lift up Thine eyes, and seek His face;
> Life with its way before us lies,
> Christ is the path, and Christ the prize.[128]

---

128. John Monsell, Jr., "Fight the Good Fight with All They Might," 1860.

WALK AND NOT FAINT

Because our lives in Christ are *pilgrimages*, we need Him to order our steps aright. Walkers do not exhibit the speed of the runners. Yet as believers we are to *walk*, as well as *run* and *mount up*. Although walking may be of a more humble order, we still need the power to walk steadily on the path of obedience, without fainting or lagging behind. We cannot always run or soar, but at least He strengthens us to walk strongly to the end. Physical weariness may overtake a walker; even Jesus was weary on His journey through Samaria, as He sat by the well to receive a drink of fresh water. But spiritual walking is different: weariness never overcomes Christ's followers. Those who wait on the Lord and seek the sweet air of His presence do not fail; this kind of faith brings no spiritual fatigue. Christ always gives grace to keep pace with Him, and He always walks with us, even when we are surrounded by the valley of the shadow of death.

> When we walk with the Lord,
> In the light of His Word,
> What a glory He sheds on our way;
> While we do His good will,
> He abides with us still,
> And with all who will trust and obey.[129]

---

129. John H. Sammis, "Trust and Obey," 1887.

CHAPTER 57

THREE DOWNWARD STEPS

Blessed is the man that walketh not in the counsel of the ungodly, nor standeth in the way of sinners, nor sitteth in the seat of the scornful.
—Psalm 1:1

As we see, the psalmist binds three triads together in this opening verse of the Psalms. In fact, this brief prologue to the Book of Psalms is built up on a series of triads. For instance, in Psalm 1:1–6, we have a triad of *negatives*: *"walketh not," "standeth not,"* and *"nor sitteth"*; a triad of *positives*: *"in his law doth he meditate," "he shall be like a tree,"* and *"whatsoever he doeth shall prosper"*; and a triad of *ungodly gloom*: *"like the chaff which the wind driveth away," "the ungodly shall not stand in judgment,"* and *"sinners shall not stand in the congregation of the righteous."*

Now let us seek to understand the implication of the first trinity in the first psalm with the Spirit's aid. First of all, the first word of the psalm is very popular in the Bible, recurring with its cognates hundreds of times. The Hebrew word for *blessed* is a plural noun, actually meaning "blessedness." How bountiful God is to reward those who love and obey Him! But what a chasm exists between the first and final words of Psalm 1: *"blessed"* and *"perish."* They suggest the difference between the saved person and the lost person—the gulf between heaven and hell.

It has been said that where the word *blessed* is hung out as a sign, we will surely find a godly man within. This first psalm, then, like the Master's Beatitudes, begins with a benediction. May we share in this benediction! The three opening verses are unique in that they present both positive and negative characteristics of a richly blessed man of the Lord. Verse one describes the things he *will not do*, while verse two and three describe the things he *will do*, along with the rewards for such action. As we can see in the opening verse, the psalmist gives negative characteristics in a series of triads, suggesting that there are three movements or gradations in failure. Men seldom reach the depth of vice all at once. In *Pilgrim's Progress*, John Bunyan talks about traveling *upwards* to the Celestial City; in contrast, here we see the sinner's traveling *downwards* to the pit of destruction. He cites three companies and degrees of sin, with each depth leading only to a deeper depth.

At first there is only "a good-natured curiosity about evil, but that leads to a delighted intimacy; and that again to a complete assimilation. Sinning first without consideration, he goes on to sinning without fear, and ends by sinning without compunction." Danger is not even suspected with such a gradual slope. Spurgeon said that "Going in the way of Cain," is easily succeeded by "running greedily after the error of Balaam" and "perishing in the way of Korah." May the Lord enable us to walk with caution on the King's highway, aware of the perils that loom nearby.

THE UNGODLY

Such a person, although not conspicuously sinful, is still guilty of living his life without God. He is godless, lacking self-control and a victim of his ungoverned passions. (See Isaiah 57:20.) He is not concerned about his own salvation, let alone that of others. The psalmist says that a man who says there is not God is a "fool." Literally translated, Psalm 14:1 says, "*The fool hath said in his heart, there is no God.*" Although a godless person may not be an avowed atheist, he is a practical atheist in that he lives as if there were no God at all.

THE SINNERS

"Sinners" is the general term for wrongdoers in Scripture— those who do not have God in their hearts. We see that those who are indifferent to God become actively sinful against Him. At the heart of this attitude lies the idea of missing the mark, failing to live up to God's standards. A sinner is one who falls short of the glory of God. Each sinner follows his own particular way of transgression, not many sinners commit every vice. Each turns *"his own way"* (Isaiah 53:6). Each sinner has his or her easily besetting sin.

THE SCORNFUL

Those who despise God's control are not far from defying Him, ridiculing and blaspheming Him and His law. This last aspect of the progressive sinful nature is worse than the first. Only fools mock sin and its repercussions. They live in a state of bold and blatant impiety, marking a dreary end of a dreary road. Habitual sin ends in a heart that deliberately prefers those who despise virtue.

Then we have three movements to watch and shun, for the words expressing our *conduct* and *career*, namely *counsel* and *way*, are connected with the words *walk*, *stand*, and *sit*. Here are two triads that are bound together.

WALK NOT IN THE COUNSEL

Companionship is occasionally hinted at in the true children of God, who are instructed not to yoke themselves with unbelievers. Why should any believer follow the counsel of an unbeliever when he can have the wiser counsel of the Lord God? If we allow the Lord to order our steps, then we will not find ourselves following the ungodly in their cunning, wicked ways.

STAND NOT IN THE WAY

If we give a ready ear to the *counsel* of the wicked, then we will start finding delight in their society and imitating their *way*. When a man starts to walk in the wrong direction with the wrong company, he begins to yield to a fixed state. Blood-washed sinners, who profess to have a renewed heart, should be found standing in grace with the congregation of the righteous—*"Let the wicked forsake his way"* (Isaiah 55:7). All those who "stand not" are blessed in that way.

SIT NOT IN THE SEAT

Those who stand with sinners find themselves openly and boldly joining the ranks of those they walked with in the past. A *scat* is taken among them as one who finds a congenial home in their presence. The *ungodly* man has his own self-produced *counsel*; the *sinner* his own self-chosen *way*;

the *scorner* his own *seat*. The seat he occupies may be high, but it lies close to the gate of hell. Bold impiety should be deplored, no Christian should be found inside such a camp. *Sitting down* implies that a scorner has a seared conscience, who is not a confirmed believer in all unbelief. *"Sitting down they watched Him there"* (Matthew 27:36). It is not long before God will laugh the scorner into his derision. (See Psalm 2:4.)

The Gospels give us a fitting illustration of the ungodly saint who is guilty of these three movements away from God. In his threefold denial, Peter followed from far off and eventually found himself lingering, *walking* and listening to the counsel of the ungodly. Peter is pictured *standing* at the door of the high priest's house, surveying the scene. Ultimately, Peter *sat down* with the scorners and warmed himself at their fire. Our only hope for safety is close fellowship with the Creator, who is altogether separate from sinners. *"Blessed is the man"* is somewhat emphatic in the original text, meaning *"that* man"—the true Nazarite who lives to accomplish God's will and finds daily delight in His Law. May we develop a great sensitivity to temptation, lest we stray from God's path and fall into bondage to the fatal influences of this world.

> Blessed is he who will keep in the way
> That will upward and onward lead;
> Walking by faith in His love every day,
> Who supplieth his daily need.[130]

---

130. Ida L. Reed, "Blessed Is He That Is Trusting the Lord."

CHAPTER 58

THREE RECIPES
FOR HEART'S-EASE

*In nothing be anxious; but in everything by prayer and
supplication with thanksgiving let your requests [or anything]
be made known unto God.*
—Philippians 4:6 RV

Surely there has never been a more effective recipe for
a peaceful heart than this beautiful triad of truthfulness,
prayerfulness, and thankfulness. This divine prescription for
a peaceful heart is only for those who fully rely on the Great
Physician. As one writer expressed it,

> It has no application to those sinful cares springing
> from pride, ambition, or self-conceit, but only to the
> worrying anxieties that too often find lodgment in a
> Christian heart, when confronted with new burdens
> and difficulties in life.

Phillips' translation of Paul's exhortation to the saints at
Philippi reads, "*Don't worry over anything whatever; tell God
every detail of your needs in earnest and thankful prayer.*" And
to what result? "*And the peace of God, which passeth all understanding, shall keep your hearts and minds through Christ Jesus*"
(Philippians 4:6).

ANXIOUS FOR NOTHING

The Greek word for *careful* in the phrase *"Be careful for nothing"* suggests anxiety and distraction. F. B. Meyer says that the word *anxiety* comes from the word *anger*, referring to the physical act of choking.

> Worry chokes the life of faith; it does not help us to meet our difficulties; so far from this it unfits us, for our mind is too flurried to think clearly and carefully, our hand trembles too much to perform the delicate operation.

The Lord exhorted the disciples to *"Take no anxious thought."* They were not to be anxious about anything, whether great or trivial. This was because there was nothing out of the sphere of the heavenly Father's tender care. They had a solution to every problem in Him; a cure for every ailment; and a foil for every weapon of the adversary.

> Be still, my heart, these anxious cares
> To thee are burdens, thorns, and snares:
> They cast dishonor on the Lord,
> And contradict His gracious Word.[131]

The axiom says, "When you worry you are not trusting." Yet there are some who seem to worry about everything life brings along their way, unhappy if they are not worrying. They almost seem to say, "Why trust when you can worry?" After sinning, Adam said, *"I was afraid."* Fear may well characterize those who are outside of His will. God's children, however, who are saved by faith in Christ, have no need to worry. Worry is both a sin against God and a sin against themselves. In fact,

---

131. John Newton, "Be Still My Heart, My Anxious Cares."

the Bible forbids worry. Those in a covenant relationship with the Lord can rest in His promised care: *"No good thing will he withhold from them that walk uprightly"* (Psalm 84:11). If the saints do not live in a way that the world can see their heavenly Father through them, then how do they expect to lead sinners to Christ? Anxiety does not empty tomorrow of its sorrow, but robs today of its strength. Doesn't Peter urge God's children to cast *all* their cares upon God, because He cares for them? Why would they unnecessarily burden themselves with painful anxiety and worry? Instead, they should be singing the song of assurance—

> In every hour is perfect peace,
> I'll sing He knows, He knows![132]

Perhaps our greatest difficulty is not *bringing* our cares to God, but failing to *leave* them with Him. We cast our burdens on Him, only to pick them up and carry them again, as if His shoulders were not strong enough to bear our load. In his poem, Bishop Handley Moule embodies this idea of casting all our anxieties on the Lord:

> Cast all thy care, and not a part,
> The great things and the small;
> The Lord's all-loving, mighty heart
> Has room and thought for all.
>
> Yes, He will ponder every care,
> Consider each detail;
> Thyself, thy burthen, let me bear;
> He will not, cannot, fail.[133]

---

132. Mary G. Brainard, "He Knows, He Knows," 1869.
133. Bishop Handley Moule, "Cast Thou Thy Care upon the Lord."

PRAYERFUL ABOUT EVERYTHING

How broad is our invitation—*"In everything by prayer and supplication...let your requests be made known unto God"* (Philippians 4:6).

> Thou art coming to a King,
> Large petitions with thee bring;
> For His grace and power are such
> None can ever ask too much.[134]

Those who trust in God have a large and unrestricted offer of relief from worry and perplexity. The loving Father, who stands beside His care-worn child says, "Now, My redeemed one, tell Me everything; whether your anxieties are great or very small, whether they are connected with the past, or the present, or some future decision you dread, whether your cares are about your soul, or your physical need, or of those dear to you, tell Me everything for My ear is ever open to hear your cry. Nothing that troubles your heart, My child, can be a trifle to the heart of your heavenly Father, so tell it all."

Not only did Paul tell the Philippians to stop worrying, but he also told them *how* to give their burdens to God, who promised to carry them until their traveling days were over. *"What time I am afraid, I will trust in Thee"* (Psalm 56:3). One quote says that "courage is fear that has gone to prayer." But if we do not ask God to lift our loads, we will not experience His relief—*"Ye have not because ye ask not"* (James 4:2). As we humbly admit our need, the Father meets us where we are. *"Ask and it shall be given you"* (Matthew 7:7).

---

134. John Newton, "Thou Art Coming to a King."

The apostle says that "*in everything*" our requests must be made known to God through "*prayer and supplication.*" The difference between these terms is that prayer is more *general*, while supplication is more *specific*. Both terms have the article in the original text: "*the*" prayer and "*the*" supplication. Ellicott suggests that it "probably refer[s] to the recognized worship of the church." Such prayer has a way of changing people. The cares, troubles, and trials of this life do not have authority over us. Thank God there is always a way out! Amid all the trials and burdens that plagued Daniel, his heart remained serene and peaceful. His secret was that His heart always remained open to God.

> What a Friend we have in Jesus,
> All our sins and griefs to bear.
> What a privilege to carry
> Everything to God in prayer.
> Oh, what peace we often forfeit,
> Oh, what needless pain we bear;
> All because we do not carry
> Everything to God in prayer.[135]

THANKFUL FOR ANYTHING

There are some things in life that are hard to be grateful for. But Paul did not say *for* everything be thankful, but "*in everything...with thanksgiving.*" If we cannot bless God *for* the many unwelcome experiences that come our way, the least we could do is bless Him *in* them or as we endure them, confident that He works all things together for the good of those who love and trust Him. God, the master

---

135. Joseph M. Scriven, "What a Friend We Have in Jesus," 1855.

potter, knows how to mold His vessels for His work. When we make a request to God, we must always remember what He has done for us in the past—counting our blessings. This strengthens our faith. We are encouraged to think of how He was mindful of us in the past, knowing that He will be mindful of us again. Therefore, it is right and proper to combine *thanksgiving* with *prayer and supplication,* for praise is the proper flavor of prayer. Thanksgiving implies that we have faith in God and creates a right heart within us to receive His blessings.

A thankful heart does much to lighten our cares and anxieties as we remember God's goodness. He promises to be our sufficiency at all times, which is why the psalmist asks himself, *"Why am I so cast down, O my soul, and why is my heart disquieted within me"* (Psalm 43:5)? One of God's prescriptions for peace is being thankful for anything. The promised cure for those who cast their burdens on the Lord is His peace which passeth all understanding, garrisoning our hearts and minds by Christ Jesus. We discover strength in quietness and confidence.

F. B. Meyers once said that divine peace is "like a pure, strong, beautiful angel will descend to act as sentry to heart and mind—to the *heart,* keeping out unholy affection, and to the *mind,* checking the entrance of rebellious, restless, and distracting thoughts." Paul said that this peace will *keep* our heart and mind—the word *keep* refers to our sentry duty. Paul lived with a soldier who *"kept him"* (Acts 28:16), that is, acted as a guard over him. Meyer said,

> It is as though the peace of God, like some sentinel angel, went to and fro before the portal of our inner life, keeping back all intruders who would break in

upon the purity of our affections, or the integrity of our thoughts.

We do not know whether or not archbishop Trench had this triad in mind when he composed his appealing poem. However, we do know that it draws on the thoughts in Paul's exhortation to be anxious for nothing, prayerful about everything, and thankful for anything:

> Lord, what a change within us one short hour
> Spent in Thy presence will prevail to make;
> What heavy burdens from our bosoms take,
> What parched ground refresh as with a shower!
>
> We kneel, and all around us seems to lower;
> We rise, and all, the distant and the near,
> Stands forth in sunny outline, brave and clear;
> We kneel, how weak; we rise, how full of power.
>
> Why should we ever weak or helpless be,
> Why are we ever overborne with care,
> Anxious or troubled, when with us is prayer,
> And joy, and strength, and courage are with Thee?[136]

136. Richard C. Trench, "Lord, What a Change Within Us," 1865.

CHAPTER 59

THREE PHASES OF THE RISEN CHRIST

They said one to another, Did not our heart burn within us,
while he talked with us by the way, and while he opened to us
the Scriptures?
—Luke 24:32

What a marvelous expository teaching session that must have been to elicit such a response! What an inestimable privilege it must have been to have the Lord of the Scriptures personally unfolding its treasures! That wonderful, privileged day the disciples experienced, seeing Scripture as,

> The golden casket
> Where gems of truth are stored,
> It is the heaven-drawn picture
> Of Christ, the living Word.[137]

We see that there are three phases of the risen Christ in Luke's glowing testimony. He retells one of His experiences with the Lord in this memorable occasion. It is not hard to sense the intimate character in Luke's writing. He was among those who walked and talked with Christ before the crucifixion. Of all the evidence of Christ's victory over the grave, perhaps the strongest is when He conversed with the disciples

---

137. William Walsham "O Word of God Incarnate," 1867.

after He rose from the grave. In this triad, we see the triple glory of Christ's manifestation as the conqueror of death.

THE EVER-PRESENT CHRIST

The glad-hearted disciples once said, *"He talked with us by the way"* (Luke 24:32), or as the Revised Version puts it, *"He spake to us in the way."* One of the most pleasant aspects of the resurrection was that the risen One could accompany the disciples in their walks. Although He appeared as a common traveler, the disciples soon found that He was Lord of *"the way,"* and that He could make those eight miles of country road seem like the shortest walk ever. We know that His fellow travelers were sorely troubled men, heart-broken to lose their best friend and Savior. All the hope they had was buried in the grave with Him. It seemed that their golden days were gone. But remorse changed to rapture when they saw the risen One join them again on the way to Emmaus.

Jesus said of His disciples before the cross, *"Ye are they which have continued with me in my temptations"* (Luke 22:28). And indeed, He valued their companionship as they walked and talked together for almost three years! The disciples probably asked themselves if He would be less accessible than He was in the days of His flesh. But they soon came to see that the resurrection had not changed Him as far as companionship was concerned. He was still the same tender, friendly Jesus they always knew, except with a *presence* that death could no longer break! "Although bedewed with new glory, He comes as close as ever to those His heart approves of and pities."

Since then, Christ proved to be the most faithful companion they ever knew, present throughout the ups and downs of their daily lives; the One who accompanied them through all their trials and triumphs, pain and pleasure—the Friend that *"sticketh closer than a brother"* (Proverbs 18:24). He accompanies His children along the paths of life, flooding the prosaic streets we tread with His matchless glory. I strongly agree with Dr. Dinsdale T. Young teaching on this triad:

> His companionship destroys the monotony of the most monotonous way, and the steepness of the most uphill way, and the peril of the most declivitous way. He causes a vulgar road to be crowded with the angels of God.

How true it is that there are some roads we could never travel without Christ's companionship, who promised never to leave us nor to forsake us! Although darkened ways may lie before us, the light of His countenance will prosper if we rely on His abiding presence. He dwells among His children, accompanying them through their lives with His precious blood. As M. D. Babcock reminds us,

> I need not journey far,
> This dearest Friend to see;
> Companionship is always mine; He makes His
> home with me.
> O glorious Son of God,
> Incarnate Deity,
> I shall forever be with Thee
> Because Thou art with me.[138]

---

138. Maltbie D. Babcock, "No Distant Lord Have I."

THE EXPOSITORY CHRIST

Jesus said to the Jews who rejected Him as the Messiah, *"Search the Scriptures...they are they which testify of me"* (John 5:39). Here we find Him expounding on *all* the Scriptures claim Him to be. We must give attention to the double opening Luke gives: *"He opened to us the Scriptures"* (Luke 24:32) and *"opened He their understanding, that they might understand the Scriptures"* (Luke 24:45).

Because truth is only revealed through revelation, we need to have the eyes of our understanding enlightened by the Holy Spirit. We must not forget the limits of Scriptures Jesus points out in chapter 24: the Law of Moses, the Prophets, and the Psalms. (See Luke 24:44.) The Bible at that time only consisted of the Old Testament; the New Testament was not written till years after that memorable Emmaus experience. Therefore, we have even a richer depository of truth than the disciples. The divine expositor, who saw that all truth revolved around His person and program, reveals Himself to our inquiring minds as we look to Him for guidance.

Dinsdale Young said,

We cannot overstate the significance of the fact that our Lord's primary solicitude when He rose from the dead, was the Bible. Too great attention cannot be called to our Saviour's holy enthusiasm for the Word of God. He lived and died devoted to it with death-less devotion.

Christ was not independent of the part of the Bible He had after the resurrection. On the other hand, He hastened to the holy oracles as soon as He rose from the grave, with all the old affection He used to have for them. Furthermore, He unfolded its treasures to His disciples who also loved them, but who now understood them better than ever before. A fresh glory seemed to gild the sacred page as Jesus *opened* it.

The Bible is a sealed Book until Jesus opens it through His Spirit. We do not seek to understand the Scriptures through learning and developing a trained reasoning faculty, but by the illumination of the Holy Spirit, who inspired holy men to write them. Quoting Dinsdale Young again,

> When we sit alone with our Bible and invoke the companionship of Jesus, how He gives us to understand the wonderful words of life! Even unlettered men who have the divine expositor near see wondrous things in God's law.

The question we should ask ourselves is, do we know what it is to have Christ open *all* His Scriptures to us? Note the recurring *all* in the narrative. (See Luke 24:27.) There are scholars who cannot see Jesus in any of the Old Testament Scriptures. However, Christ can easily go throughout the books of the Bible, beginning with Moses and the five books He wrote, and expound on all the things concerning Himself. If the Old Testament was not a mirror of the Messiah, then His witness was a great error and fraudulent in drawing attention to Himself as the fulfiller of its prophetic and symbolic declarations.

> Oh, send Thy Spirit, Lord, now unto me,
> That He may touch my eyes, and make me see:
> Show me the truth concealed within Thy Word,
> And in Thy Book revealed I see the Lord.[139]

---

139. Mary A. Lathbury, "Break Thou the Bread of Life," 1877.

THE ENKINDLING CHRIST

Jeremiah could say that *"His word was in mine heart as a burning fire shut up in my bones, and I was weary with forbearing, and I could not stay"* (Jeremiah 20:9; See also Job 32:18, 19; Psalm 39:3). The disciples experienced something of this glowing heart as Jesus talked with them about the Scriptures. *"Did not our heart burn within us"* (Luke 24:32)? Yes, their hearts did burn, and they became weary with forbearing, longing for Pentecost so that they could share with others through the exposition of the Scriptures. Before China became a Communist country, a missionary asked a Chinese educationalist what his country's greatest need was, to which he replied, "Men and women with hot hearts to tell the story of Jesus!"

How the divine expositor ignited the hearts of the disciples, kindling a flame that even martyrdom could not extinguish! Tradition claims that Jesus said, "He that is near Me is near the fire." And this is true, for none can be under His tuition and influence without discovering the secret mystery of the burning heart. If only we could experience more of His irradiating exposition of Scripture! John Wesley said that he felt his heart "strangely warmed" as he listened to a teaching on the Word in an Aldersgate meeting; and out of that heart came a great evangelical revival that impacted the world!

The verb tense Luke used to describe the burning heart indicates that this kindling was permanent. The disciples did not experience some momentary enthusiasm or flash of fervor. And the warmth did not cease after the period of Biblical exposition ended. The glow of the fire remained, and became even more intense at Pentecost where the fire of the

Holy Spirit came upon the disciples. Regarding their testimony, Matthew Henry said that the best hearers are those who listen with a burning heart. But unfortunately, there is little hope of kindling hearts if a refrigerator stands at the pulpit! Preachers that are on fire for Christ have the opportunity of restoring the hearts of those who have grown cold. The church has lost the ardor of the apostolic age, and because she lacks a burning heart, she fails in her God-given task of warming a cold world.

The life and ministry of Henry Ward Beecher provides a good example of how to spread the heart-fire. While out walking on a cold winter's day, he came across a half-frozen urchin at a street corner trying to sell a few papers. "How many papers have you left?" Beecher asked the pinched-face lad. "About a dozen, sir!" As the preacher bought the lot, he said to the boy, "You must be very cold standing there so long." Immediately he replied, "I was so cold, sir, till you came along, but I'm warm now." The moral is that it takes a warm heart to set a cold heart afire. We must have hearts and tongues set on fire for Christ!

> Give tongues of fire and hearts of love,
> To preach the reconciling Word;
> Give power and unction from above,
> Where'er the joyful sound is heard.[140]

---

140. Isaac Watts, "Give Tongues of Fire."

BRIEF EXAMPLES
OF VARIOUS FORMS OF
TRIPLICATE TRUTH

After giving many illustrations of how to use the trinities of truth found in Scripture, we provide in this concluding section further ways of developing scriptural triads. The bones are supplied here in the knowledge that the diligent minister of the Word will be able to clothe them with flesh. We have already seen that many Bible verses contain triplets of truth waiting to be explored. There is nothing artificial about these threefold cords. Distinctly expressed, their form arrests our attention and impresses us as being divinely inspired by the Holy Trinity.

In the majority of verses, the three cords of truth are marked off by a comma, semicolon, colon, question mark, or period. When reading the Bible, it is well to have a pencil and paper at hand to jot down the triads you find along the way. While space prevents an exhaustive list of verse-trinities, here are a few examples of triads that would be good to expound. It is essential to look up the marginal references of any verse and discover how others have explained Scripture. Furthermore, the reader will probably find more triplet verses in the Psalms than any other book in the Bible.

Three Stimulating Phrases:

Trust in him at all times; ye people, pour out your heart before him; God is a refuge for us. (Psalm 62:8)

Three Cameos of God:

The LORD God is a sun and shield; the LORD will give grace and glory; no good thing will He withhold from them that walk uprightly. (Psalm 84:11)

Three Beneficial Diet Hints:

Wine that maketh glad the heart of man, and oil to make his face to shine; and bread which strengtheneth man's heart. (Psalm 104:15)

Three Results of Emulating Parental Example:

When thou goest, it shall lead thee; when thou sleepest, it shall keep thee; and when thou awakest, it shall talk with thee. (Proverbs 6:22)

Three Relevant Facts:

The ox knoweth his owner; and the ass his master's crib; but Israel doth not know, my people doth not consider. (Isaiah 1:3)

Three Proposed Tabernacles:

One for thee, and one for Moses, and one for Elijah. (Matthew 17:4 RV)

Three Weightiest Matters (Matthew 23:23):

+ Judgment
+ Mercy
+ Faith

Three Apostolic *I Ams*:

- "*I am debtor...*" (Romans 1:14)
- "*I am ready...*" (Romans 1:15)
- "*I am not ashamed...*" (Romans 1:16)

Three Tributes to God's Law:

The commandment is holy, and just, and good.

(Romans 7:12)

Three Triads Outlining Christian Character:

Let love be without dissimulation. abhor that which is evil; cleave to that which is good.   (Romans 12:9)

Not slothful in business; fervent in spirit; serving the Lord.   (Romans 12:11)

Rejoicing in hope; patient in tribulation; continuing instant in prayer.   (Romans 12:12)

Three Inducements to Peace of Heart:

Let your conversation be without covetousness; and be content with such things as ye have: for he hath said, I will never leave thee, nor forsake thee. (Hebrews 13:5)

Then with the aid of a serviceable Bible concordance, such as *Young's Analytical* or the *Unabridged Cruden's*, trace particular words that are used only three times in Scripture. The word *awe*, for instance, enables the preacher to emphasize an attitude somewhat remote from the phraseology of modern religious life, where *trembling* is substituted for *levity*. Even hymns that minister to fear are being dropped. As J. H. Jowett said,

The words "stand in awe" indicate a severity which is the corollary of the Lord's holiness. It is because these terrors are left out in our religious conceptions and in our preaching that the frivolity of men is gratified and coddled by illegitimate sweetness.

Three Elements of Awesomeness:

- *"Stand in awe, and sin not"* (Psalm 4:4)
- *"Let all the inhabitants of the world stand in awe of Him"* (Psalm 33:8)
- *"My heart standeth in awe of thy word"* (Psalm 119:161)

Furthermore, repetition of certain phrases opens another field for the ministers of the Word. Sometimes these phrases are made up of two or three words, arresting the reader's attention. For instance, *"walk worthy"* or *"worthily"* occurs three times, and represents a divine and perfect claim on our daily walk:

- Of our vocation (Ephesians 4:1)
- Of the Lord (Colossians 1:10)
- Of God (1 Thessalonians 2:12)

Another significant illustration is the phrase, *"before the foundation of the world,"* which speaks of the work of the Deity, flowing through grace:

- *"Thou lovedst me before the foundation of the world"* (John 17:24)
- *"Chosen us in him before the foundation of the world"* (Ephesians 1:4)
- *"The precious blood of Christ...foreordained before the foundation of the world"* (1 Peter 1:19–20)

As pointed out in the introduction to our study, the number *three* is often the number of divine fullness. Thus, the three persons of the Trinity constitute that fullness:

- *"The fullness of God…"* (Ephesians 3:19)
- *"The fullness of Christ…"* (Ephesians 4:13)
- *"The fullness of the Godhead…"* (Colossians 2:9)

It is also interesting to observe the references to groups of three men that occur throughout Scripture. Already we have dealt with the three sons of Noah—Shem, Ham, and Japheth; and the three patriarchs—Abraham, Isaac, and Jacob. And there are other figures linked together such as Noah, Daniel, and Job. (See Ezekiel 14:14, 20.)

Then we have:

- The three mysterious men who appeared to Abraham (Genesis 18:2)
- The three men of each tribe to represent the land of Canaan preparatory to dividing it among the tribes (Joshua 18:4)
- The three friends of Job (Job 2:11)
- The three companions of Daniel (Daniel 3:23, 26)
- The three travelers Saul met, with their three kids and three loaves (1 Samuel 10:3)
- David's three mighty warriors (2 Samuel 23:16–23)

We have further trios in the New Testament:

- The three travelers (Luke 10:36)
- The three loaves (Luke 11:5)
- The three disciples who formed Christ's inner cabinet— Peter, James, and John (Matthew 17:1)
- The three men who sought Peter (Acts 10:19)

Furthermore, examine passages where *three times* and the equivalent term *thrice* might yield unusual applications of spiritual truth. You might also find reference to *three years*.

Occasionally, a series of triads will have a common theme. For instance, look at the fruit of the Spirit given by Paul. (See Galatians 5:22–23.) These nine graces describe the complete character of the Christian and divide themselves into three groups, or sets of triplets:

+ The first triad—love, joy, and peace—suggest condition, or disposition of the soul
+ The second triad—long-suffering, gentleness, and goodness—depict conduct, or external manifestations
+ The third triad—faith, meekness, and temperance—represent character or personal results in life

In the *Expositions*, Alexander Maclaren gives a slightly different organization of these nine graces:

+ The life of the Spirit in its deepest aspects—love, joy, and peace
+ The life of the Spirit in its manifestations to me—longsuffering, gentleness, goodness
+ The life of the Spirit in its relation to the difficulties of the world and ourselves—faith, meekness, temperance

And additional triad referring to the fruits of the Spirit is:

+ The color of the fruit—what the Trinity inspires
+ The flavor of the fruit—what the world admires
+ And the form of the fruit—what the saint requires

Another way of dealing with the threefold cords of Scripture is to trace their usage in the composition of a book. Other numbers, of course, are prominent in certain books of the Bible, such as seven in Revelation. In *A Guide to the*

Gospels, Graham Scroggie points out that among all the numbers, Matthew employs *three* most liberally:

- Three angel messages to Joseph in his dreams (Matthew 1:20; 2:13, 19)
- Three incidents of the childhood of Jesus: the magi's visitation (Matthew 2:1–12); the flight to Egypt (verses 13–15); and the return (verses 19–23)
- Three temptations in the wilderness (Matthew 4:1–11)
- Three descriptions of the Messiah's mission (Matthew 4:23)
- Three instances of "*whosoever*" of judgment (Matthew 5:22)
- Three Beatitude triads: "*blessed*" occurring nine times, making a treble triplet (Matthew 5:3–11)
- Three aspects of Christian witness (Matthew 5:16)
- Three examples of righteousness (Matthew 6:1–18): alms, prayer, and fasting
- Three secrets of spiritual health: a sound heart (Matthew 6:21)—with no disordered action (verse 19); a single eye (verse 22)—with no distorted vision (verse 24); and a serene mind (verse 33)—with no distracted thought (verses 30–31)
- Three prohibitions (Matthew 6:19–7:6): hoard not, judge not, and give not
- Three degrees of prayer earnestness (Matthew 7:7): ask; seek; and knock
- Three commands (Matthew 7:7–20): ask, enter, and beware
- Three pairs of contrasts (Matthew 7:13, 17, 24–27): broad and narrow ways, good and bad trees, and wise and foolish builders
- Three repetitions of "*in thy name*" (Matthew 7:22)

- Three miracles of healing (Matthew 8:1–15): leprosy, palsy, and fever
- Three miracles of power (Matthew 8:23–9:8): storm; demoniacs; and sin
- Three miracles of restoration (Matthew 9:8–34): health, life, and sight
- Three instances of "*fear not*" (Matthew 10:26, 28, 31)
- Three times "*is not worthy of me*" (Matthew 11:7–9)
- Three cities indicted (Matthew 11:20–23): Chorazin, Bethsaida, and Capernaum
- Three times "*at that season*" (Matthew 11:25; 12:1; 14:1)
- Three descriptions of Jewish state (Matthew 12:44): empty, swept, and garnished
- Three times "*verily*" (Matthew 18:3, 13, 18)
- Three classes of eunuchs (Matthew 19:12)
- Three parables of warning (Matthew 21:28–24:15)
- Three questioners (Matthew 22:15, 23, 25): Pharisees, Sadduces, and lawyers
- Three faculties with which God should be loved (Matthew 22:37): heart, soul, and mind

Others are:

- Temple and gold, altar and gift, heaven and throne (Matthew 24:16–22)
- Mint, dill, cummin contrasted with judgment, mercy, truth (Matthew 24:23)
- Prophets, wise men, scribes (Matthew 24:34)
- Blood occurs three times (Matthew 23:35)
- Three parables against negligence: faithful and unfaithful servants (Matthew 24:45–51), the virgins (Matthew 25:1–13), and the talents (verses 14–30)
- Three men entrusted with talents. (Matthew 25:15)
- Three denials of Peter (Matthew 26:69–75)

+ Three questions of Pilate (Matthew 27:17, 21–23)
+ Three mockeries of the Crucified One (Matthew 27:39–44)
+ Three signs to attest the messiahship of the Crucified One: the rending of the veil (Matthew 27:51), the earthquake (verse 51), and the resurrection of Saints (verse 52)
+ Three women specially mentioned at the cross (Matthew 27:56)
+ Three features of Christ's Commission: make disciples (Matthew 28:19), baptize (verse 19), and teach (verse 20)

This same idea of a trinity of truth that can be applied to a whole chapter as well as a whole book is borne out of the following triads in 1 John 5 from my good friend Henry J. Heydt in *Christian Victory* magazine:

Three statements regarding love:

+ To love the Father is to love His children (1 John 5:1)
+ To love and obey God assures us that we will love His children (1 John 5:2)
+ To truly love God is to obey Him (1 John 5:3)
  Three things to believe:
+ That Jesus is the Christ (1 John 5:1)
+ That Jesus is the Son of God (1 John 5:5)
+ The record God gives of His Son. (1 John 5:10)

Three things to do:

+ To love God and His own (1 John 5:1)
+ To keep His commandments (1 John 5:3)
+ To overcome the world. (1 John 5:4.)

Three things to have:

+ Confidence (1 John 5:14)
+ Answered prayer (1 John 5:15)
+ Understanding. (1 John 5:20)

Three witnesses to Christ (1 John 5:8):

+ The Spirit
+ The water
+ The blood

Three aspects of witnessing (1 John 5:9–10):

+ The witness of men
+ The witness of God
+ The witness within

Three aspects of prayer (1 John 5:14–15):

+ Asking
+ Hearing
+ Receiving

Three facts regarding sin (1 John 5:16–18):

+ All unrighteousness is sin
+ There is a sin unto death which is not to be prayed for
+ The child of God does not practice sin

Three facts about what is true (1 John 5:20):

+ We may know Him that is true
+ We are in Him that is true
+ This is the true God and eternal life

One of the smallest books of the Bible, Jude is made up of only twenty-five verses, offering another illustration in the effective use of triads. One of the early church fathers, Origen, said that Jude is, "An epistle of few lines, but one filled full of the strong words of heavenly grace." It is also an epistle built on the principle of triads. In this "Preface to the Apocalypse," as it has been called, we have a whole crop of trinities:

Three descriptions of those to whom Jude wrote (Jude 1):

+ Sanctified by God the Father
+ Preserved in Christ Jesus
+ Called

Three blessings desired for readers (Jude 2):

+ Mercy
+ Peace
+ Love

Three reasons for the epistle (Jude 3–4):

+ Write of the common salvation
+ Earnestly contend for the faith
+ Warn of apostates

Three historical instances of apostasy (Jude 5–7):

+ The unbelieving Israelites;
+ The fallen angels;
+ The cities of the plain.

Three features of apostate teachers (Jude 8). Filthy dreamers who:

+ Defile the flesh
+ Despise dominion
+ Speak evil of dignities

Three persons associated with contention (Jude 9):

+ The archangel Michael
+ The devil
+ Moses

Three indicators of the corrupt character of apostasy (Jude 11):

+ The way of Cain
+ The error of Balaam
+ The gainsaying of Core

The expression *"these are"* occurs three times, setting forth the character of apostates. Altogether, there are five characteristics of the first group and five of the second group. (See Jude 12–18.) For the third set (see verse 19), three signs clearly distinguish those who:

+ Separate themselves
+ Are sensual
+ And have not the Spirit

There are twenty different descriptions of the apostates Jude warned the saints about. One is tempted to linger over these warnings to expound their significance in the light of present-day apostasy. Jude uses the appellation "beloved" three times to describe the saints that are true to their faith. (See Jude 3, 17, 20.) Then he gives them their sevenfold duty as they contend for the faith. (See verses 20–23.) Jude concludes his priceless epistle with one of the greatest benedictions in the Bible formed by a triad:

> Now unto him that is able to keep you from falling; and
> to present you faultless before the presence of His glory
> with exceeding joy; to the only wise God our Saviour, be
> glory and majesty, dominion and power, both now and
> ever. Amen. (Jude 24–25)

Our concluding illustration of triads is found in the last book of the Bible. E. Bullinger said that the first or introductory section of Revelation is specially marked by the divine seal of three.

This Revelation was (Revelation 1:1):

+ Divinely given;
+ Divinely sent;
+ Divinely signified

John bore record of (Revelation 1:2.):

+ The divine truth—*"the Word of God"*
+ The divine witness—*"the testimony of Jesus Christ"*
+ The divine vision—*"all things that he saw"*

The divine blessing was bestowed on (Revelation 1:3):

+ The reader
+ The hearer
+ The keeper of this record

The divine being is presented as the One (Revelation 1:4, 8):

+ Who was
+ Who is
+ Who is to come

The coming Lord is presented as (Revelation 1:5):

+ The divine Prophet—*"the faithful witness"*
+ The divine Priest—*"the first-begotten of the dead"*
+ The divine King—*"the Prince of the kings of the earth"*

His people are (Revelation 1:5–6):

+ Divinely loved
+ Divinely cleansed
+ Divinely crowned

Christ is revealed as:

+ The divinely powerful One—*"the Almighty"*
  (Revelation 1:8)
+ The divinely eternal One—*"the first and the last"*
  (Revelation 1:11)
+ The divinely living One—*"He that liveth, and was dead"*
  (Revelation 1:18)

The content of the divine revelation is made up of (Revelation 1:19):

+ The things which thou hast seen
+ The things which are
+ The things which shall be

Those who look will find trinities of truth through the whole book up to the last chapter with the Master's threefold "Surely, I come quickly," along with the three last heralds of the second advent:

+ The voice of the Savior—"*I come quickly*" (Revelation 22:20)

+ The voice of the Spirit—"*The Spirit and the bride say, Come*" (Revelation 22:17)

+ The voice of the saint—"*Even so, come, Lord Jesus*" (Revelation 22:20)

ABOUT THE AUTHOR

When Dr. Herbert Lockyer (1886–1984) was first deciding on a career, he considered becoming an actor. Tall and well-spoken, he seemed a natural for the theater. But the Lord had something better in mind. Instead of to the stage, God called Herbert to the pulpit, where, as a pastor, Bible teacher, and author of more than fifty books, he touched the hearts and lives of millions of people.

Dr. Lockyer held pastorates in Scotland and England for twenty-five years. As pastor of Leeds Road Baptist Church in Bradford, England, he became a leader in the Keswick Higher Life Movement, which emphasized the significance of living in the fullness of the Holy Spirit. This led to an invitation to speak at the Moody Bible Institute's fiftieth anniversary in 1936. His warm reception at that event led to his ministry in the United States. He received honorary degrees from both the Northwestern Evangelical Seminary and the International Academy in London.

In 1955, he returned to England, where he lived for many years. He then returned to the United States, where he spent the final years of his life in Colorado Springs, Colorado, with his son, the Rev. Herbert Lockyer Jr., a Presbyterian minister who became his editor.